Modern
Artillery

300 Artillery Pieces

Modern
Artillery

300 Artillery Pieces

Ian Hogg

Revised edition published in 2016

Copyright © 2000 Amber Books Ltd.

First published in 2000

Published by
Amber Books Ltd
74–77 White Lion Street
London
N1 9PF
United Kingdom
www.amberbooks.co.uk
Appstore: itunes.com/apps/amberbooksltd
Facebook: www.facebook.com/amberbooks
Twitter: @amberbooks

ISBN: 978-1-78274-327-9

Design: Wilson Design Associates

Printed in China

Picture Credits:
All picture © TRH Pictures

Artwork Credits:
All Aerospace Publishing except the following:
John Batchelor: 14, 15, 18, 19, 22, 23, 29, 43, 44, 46, 47, 48, 49, 50, 51, 52, 54, 58, 59, 60,
61, 69, 73, 74, 80, 86, 90, 91, 104, 116, 118, 134, 135, 140, 146, 150, 154, 155, 156, 157,
165, 246, 300
Bob Garwood: 68, 70, 71, 72, 160, 161, 185, 233, 234, 235, 249, 262, 280, 283, 284, 285,
286, 287, 296

CONTENTS

Introduction 7

Field and heavy artillery 14

Air defence artillery 94

Anti-armour weapons 127

Light support weapons 160

Surface-to-surface missiles 186

Air defence missiles 209

Railway artillery 236

Self-propelled artillery 247

Free-flight rockets 289

Glossary 312

Index 313

Introduction

Future military historians will surely look back upon the 20th century and say 'There was the zenith of artillery'. Artillery will, of course, still retain its pre-eminence on the battlefield, but for sheer diversity of types and multiplicity of designs, for size, for numbers and for tactical influence, the likes of artillery as it stood in 1945 will never be seen again. This book attempts to show a fraction of that diversity, a cross-section of the weapons used by various nations between 1900 and 1999.

Artillery began the century in turmoil. In 1897 the French army had revealed its new weapon, the 75mm gun Mle 97, which later became so well-known as 'the Famous French 75'. This gun introduced the concept of the 'quick-firing gun', a field gun which had on-carriage recoil control, a rapid-acting breech mechanism, a one-piece round of ammunition, and a shield. The one-piece round of ammunition – a metal cartridge case with a percussion cap in the base and a charge of smokeless powder inside it, with

The crew of an 8in (203mm) Mark V Howitzer pose for a photograph during the Battle of Albert in July 1916. Note how well the gun has been dug in and camouflaged.

A 15cm (5.9in) Hummel self-propelled gun of the German Hohenstaufen Division is carefully loaded onto a railway bogey for transportation to the front.

the shell firmly fixed in the case mouth – allowed rapid loading in one movement. The quick-acting breech added to the speed of loading. The recoil system ensured that the gun carriage stayed in the same place when the gun was fired, so the gun detachment could gather closely around the gun, protected from enemy fire by a shield, thereby allowing fast supply of ammunition and loading. A detachment could therefore load and fire upwards of 20 accurate rounds a minute.

This was phenomenal. It made every other artillery piece in the world obsolete overnight. It is interesting to recall that the French had done the same thing with small arms a decade before with their 1886 Lebel rifle, which had significantly outperformed their those of their rivals. With both weapons, they clung to them long after they had become obsolescent and allowed other nations to forge ahead with better designs. But in 1900 all the other artilleries of the world were pestering their gunmakers for 'quick-firing' guns. By 1914 all the belligerent armies had QF guns as their first-line artillery, though the reserves were usually equipped with makeshift conversions of obsolete guns; but accelerated wartime production soon provided a profusion of modern equipment.

The war also introduced some weapons which had been in gestation during the 1900s. It should be remembered that at the turn of the century the governing factor in gun design was weight – the amount of weight a six- or eight-horse team could be expected to pull all day. In the case of field artillery, the British laid down a gun weight of 30 cwt (1525kg or 1.5 tons). Medium (or 'siege' as they were still known) guns might go higher but would probably divide into two loads to fall within the limits. But the 1900s also saw the arrival of the motor tractor, and several armies conducted trials; the Italians, for example, tried a combination using a motor tractor on the road, and horse teams for cross-country work. The petrol engine was a capricious and unreliable device, whereas the horse was fully understood, so the motor was largely ignored. But there were two new fields which were far more revolutionary: the anti-balloon gun and the heavy howitzer.

REVOLUTIONARY NEW WEAPONS

In 1909 there was a large aviation exhibition in Germany, and gunmakers appeared with their solution to the air menace: quick-firing guns on motor trucks. Not only could they go where the threat was but they could even pursue the flying machine – in theory, anyway. Most armies were quite certain that the aeroplane would be a useful scouting instrument, but little beyond that; nevertheless, enemy scouts were unwelcome, so anti-balloon guns received limited support.

In Germany, Herr Krupp had developed some large coastal defence howitzers in the 1890s and now re-designed one of these in a more portable form, proposing to move it into position by rail. The Army, reasonably enough, pointed out that railways did not always go where the guns might be wanted, and asked if Herr Krupp could use the new Daimler-Benz tractors. Krupp came back with a 42cm (16.5in) howitzer which could be transported behind tractors in pieces, assembled on site with a motor crane, and used to bombard fortresses which had only been designed to withstand attack from a 24cm (9.5in) gun, as that had been the largest calibre weapon which could be taken into the field by horses. Herr Krupp was given the go-ahead by the army, who christened the gun Big Bertha after his daughter.

The years 1914–18 proved the wisdom of the men who had thought of anti-balloon guns and Big Bertha, and other new ideas appeared: trench mortars which threw bombs high in the air to fall vertically into narrow trenches. Smoke shells to conceal the movement of troops. Star shells to illuminate the battlefield, and coloured stars for signalling. Shells filled with gas. As the war grew more involved so the guns became bigger, so that each antagonist could reach further into the opponent's territory and shell railway junctions, store dumps, headquarters and rest areas. The railway gun allowed the heaviest possible guns up behind the line, guns which could fire half-ton shells for 20 miles or so. The ultimate came with the Paris Gun, shelling the French capital from almost 70 miles away.

Between the wars the armies of the democracies were starved of money, manpower and equipment, until re-armament began in the late 1930s. During the fallow years design staffs were busy, drawing designs and refining them so that in 1939, once again, the belligerent armies had modern designs in their first line, though, as before, their reserves were making do with left-overs from 1918. Only the British were fully mechanised; Germany and Russia had horse-drawn field artillery until 1945, while the US Army was still deploying cavalry for reconnaissance in 1940.

RAPID DEVELOPMENT DURING WORLD WAR II

Fundamentally speaking, the guns of World War II were not much better than those of World War I; the difference lay in the more general adoption of motor traction for big guns, pneumatic tyres, the wide use of split-trail carriages, more efficient ammunition, and metallurgical advances in gun manufacture. The anti-balloon gun became the anti-aircraft gun and, accompanied by the infant radar and finally the magical proximity fuze, it became more effective than had ever been imagined. The increased use of tanks had led to the development of a completely new class of gun, the anti-tank gun; but as the tank gained thicker armour, so the anti-tank gun had to grow in step in order to overcome it, and in the last months of the war it became apparent that the anti-tank gun had become too big to be used. By definition, an anti-tank gun had to be handy, easily concealed, and quick to manoeuvre; but the last guns of this group which appeared in 1945 weighed 10 tons or more and were no longer viable.

What saved the day was another invention which had barely been thought of in 1918; the recoilless gun. This vented most of the propellant gas backwards so as to balance the recoil force exerted by the shell going forward. No recoil meant no recoil mechanism, and no need for a massive carriage to withstand the firing shock, but also low velocities and the need to develop a better method of defeating armour than simply throwing

A MRLS rocket launcher spectacularly fires one of its rockets on a testing range. It was first used in anger in the Gulf War to bombard Iraqi positions.

something very hard very fast. The timely development of the shaped charge and later the squash-head (or HE Plastic) shell enabled explosive to be used to defeat armour instead of simple brute force.

World War II also saw the rise of the self-propelled gun. Lack of money had stifled its development, but the need for artillery to keep pace with the fast-moving armoured formations which the war produced soon put artillery on tracks. This also led to the assault gun, modified tanks with heavy guns which accompanied the leading infantry for immediate gun support when they ran into opposition. Finally, of course, World War II saw the birth of the guided missile and the perfection of the rocket as a self-contained projectile weapon.

The late 1940s were years of military confusion as the armies came to terms with the nuclear age and the guided missile. Coastal artillery was dismantled in many countries; there was no point if a missile could fly straight over the top of your guns. All the money and design effort was poured into guided nuclear weapons and air defence missiles, jet aircraft and aerial weapons. The British and American artillery regiments in Korea in the 1950s used World War II weapons and techniques; indeed, between 1945 and 1960, 15 years after World War II ended, the only new piece of equipment received by the British field artillery was a thermometer.

THE SEARCH FOR GREATER ACCURACY AND LETHALITY

Once the engineers and scientists had exhausted nuclear weapon development, they tried their skills on artillery. There was no fundamental change in the principles: guns were still tubes closed at one end in which a charge of powder was burned to blow a projectile out of the other end. What changed were the ancillaries; computers were introduced to do ballistic calculations which had been done by pencil, paper and logarithms, which meant that they could be done to a far higher level of accuracy and far more quickly. Fuzes used electronic chips to perform timing and switching functions previously done by coarse mechanical methods. Gyro-compasses, infrared, lasers and radar could be used, together with satellites, to fix the position of the gun accurately. Pilotless aircraft carrying infrared or television cameras and other sophisticated methods of surveillance could provide information for the guns to a greater distance inside enemy lines than a observer with binoculars could hope to see. All of which gave the guns far more data than ever before, leading to more accurate fire and faster response times.

A loader's eye view of breech of the towed FH-70 155mm (6in) gun, seen here in British service.

Engineers and scientists now turned to guns themselves. During the war a great deal of basic research into gun manufacture, shell design and propellant chemistry had taken place; much of it unfinished and abandoned when the war ended. New technology now provided answers which had not been apparent in 1945. Gun design improved, producing stronger and lighter guns; shell design improvements brought projectiles with stub wings and hollow tails, reducing drag and increasing range. Since faster response by 'our' artillery probably meant faster retaliation by 'their' artillery, the self-propelled gun took on new importance, while the standard towed gun was now endowed with 'auxiliary propulsion' so that it could 'shoot and scoot' under its own power to some hiding place before retaliatory fire arrived and without having to wait for its tractor.

By this time artillery had embraced the missile; by the early 1960s heavy anti-aircraft artillery was almost entirely replaced by missiles, while monster long-range guns were a thing of the past, the intercontinental ballistic missile which could span half the globe or the 'tactical' missile which had a range of a mere few hundred miles taking their place. Air defence against low-flying ground attackers remained largely the business of light automatic guns, given a new lease of life by electro-optical sights allied to electronic computers, combinations which could measure a target's speed and course and predict with superlative accuracy where it would be when the shell got there.

However, science and engineering ingenuity work both ways; as well as producing new and better guns, they can produce new and more difficult targets and counter-measures, The helicopter may seem to be an easy target, but it is far more difficult to hit than it looks, and some clever technology has had to be called upon to counter it. A supersonic missile flying a few feet above the ground is a lethal threat: how can you stop it? How do you camouflage your gun so that infra-red sensors cannot detect it?

In the course of a century, then, we have come from black powder and non-recoil carriages, controlled by a man sitting on a horse and using a pair of field-glasses and a wet finger, to guns which can fire 20 or 30 miles and hit targets they cannot see with shells that can steer themselves to the target. From rockets which were no more than glorified fireworks to missiles which fly 5000 miles and then spew out independent warheads which fly off each to its own particular target. From anti-balloon cannons to automatic Gatling guns which throw up to 6000 20mm shells into the air in a minute. The question we now ask is not 'What will they think of next?' but 'What can they think of next?' for we seem to have arrived at a point where it is difficult to imagine anything which has not already been achieved. No doubt the 21st century will hold a few surprises for us.

65mm Mountain Gun

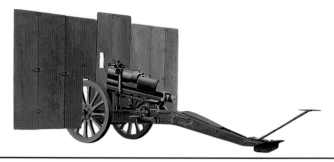

Introduced for the Italian mountain artillery arm in 1913, the 65mm (2.55in) Mountain Gun could be rapidly dismantled into six pack loads for carriage by mule or, in extreme circumstances, by men. It could also be horse- or vehicle-drawn where conditions allowed. Like all mountain guns, it had no unnecessary frills nor a single ounce of excess weight, as it was expected that the gun would be used in difficult territory and in severe weather conditions, such as ice and snow. It was replaced in mountain artillery use during the 1920s and subsequently passed to the Italian infantry for whom it was ideally suited due to its lightweight nature, and who retained it as their close support gun until the 1940s.

Country of origin:	Italy
Calibre:	65mm (2.55in)
Weight in action:	556kg (1225lb)
Gun length:	17 calibre: 1.105m (43.5in)
Elevation:	-10° to +20°
Traverse:	8°
Shell type & weight:	shrapnel; 4.30kg (9.47lb)
Muzzle velocity:	345m/sec (1132ft/sec)
Maximum range:	6800m (7435yds)

2.75in Mountain Gun

Used by the Indian Mountain Artillery, the 70mm (2.75in) Mountain Gun was essentially a 'Screw-Gun' in which the barrel consisted of two parts, connected by a screw joint. This feature permitted a substantial barrel but allowed it to split so that each part was within the limits of weight for mule carriage, an important consideration for guns designed to be used where either vehicles or horse teams could not go. The gun broke into six mule-loads and could be assembled and brought into action in less than two minutes. It was principally used on the North West Frontier of India, although some went to Mesopotamia (now Iraq) during World War I.

Country of origin:	United Kingdom
Calibre:	70mm (2.75in)
Weight in action:	586kg (1252lb)
Gun length:	27.8 calibre: 1.96m (75.6in)
Elevation:	-15° to +22°
Traverse:	8°
Shell type & weight:	shrapnel; 5.67kg (12.5lb)
Muzzle velocity:	393m/sec (1290ft/sec)
Maximum range:	5400m (5905yds)

Canone de 75 Mle 1897

The Canone de 75 Mle 1897, widely known as the 'Famous French 75', introduced the 'quick-firing' concept (on-carriage recoil system, one-piece round of ammunition, shield, quick-action breech) and made every other gun obsolete overnight. It, too, became obsolete in its turn but the French kept on using it until 1940, by which time it was hopelessly outclassed. Many were captured by the Germans after the fall of France, and they were adapted for use as a stopgap anti-tank gun to counter the T-34 tank in 1941. It was adopted by the US Army in 1917 and used by them until 1945, even being used as an anti-ship gun mounted on B-25 bombers. It was also used by several other armies, including those of Poland, Portugal, Greece, Romania, Ireland and the Baltic states.

Country of origin:	France
Calibre:	75mm (2.95in)
Weight in action:	1160kg (2557lb)
Gun length:	36 calibre: 2.70m (106.3in)
Elevation:	-11° to +18°
Traverse:	6°
Shell type & weight:	shrapnel; 7.24kg (15.9lb)
Muzzle velocity:	529m/sec (1735ft/sec)
Maximum range:	8500m (9295yds)

Canonne da 75/27

Another pioneering design, the Canonne da 75/27 introduced the split trail into artillery for the first time in 1912. Designed by Colonel Deport of France, the guns were built under licence in Italy in large numbers. The gun also introduced another very unusual feature: the dual recoil system. This allowed the gun barrel to recoil inside a short tubular cradle; this, in turn, recoiled across the usual sort of rectangular cradle. However, the gun elevated independently of the second cradle so that the heat of the barrel did not transmit itself to the recoil system. It worked, but it has never been repeated. The gun barrel could be elevated to 65°, so that it could be used in mountainous terrain. Some modernised examples were used by the German occupying forces in Italy in 1943–5.

Country of origin:	Italy
Calibre:	75mm (2.95in)
Weight in action:	1076kg (2372lb)
Gun length:	27 calibre; 2.13m (83.85in)
Elevation:	-15° to +65°
Traverse:	54°
Shell type & weight:	HE; 6.50kg (14.32lb)
Muzzle velocity:	510m/sec (1673ft/sec)
Maximum range:	7600m (8310yds)

Krupp 75mm Field Gun M1903

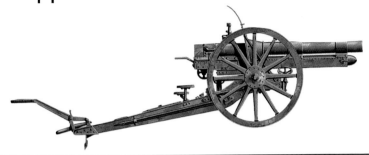

This 1903 model was one of the German manufacturer Krupp's stock lines, a basic model which could be given minor modifications to suit the wishes of the customer. In addition to any commissioned designs that might be required, every gun designer would have a number of stock guns in different calibres which could be quickly supplied to a customer. In this case the customer was Romania, who bought 360 of the 75mm (2.95in) M1903 field gun between 1903 and 1908, and continued to use them until 1942, although by that time the guns were obsolete. They used a hydro-spring recoil system and the usual Krupp horizontal sliding block breech.

Country of origin:	Germany
Calibre:	75mm (2.95in)
Weight in action:	1070kg (2358lb)
Gun length:	30 calibre: 2.25m (86.58in)
Elevation:	-8° to +16°
Traverse:	4°
Shell type & weight:	shrapnel; 6.547kg (14.42lb)
Muzzle velocity:	500m/sec (1640ft/sec)
Maximum range:	8000m (8748yds)

Skoda 75mm Mountain Gun M1915

Between 1899 and 1915 the Austro-Hungarian Army went through four different designs of mountain gun before getting it right with the Skoda 75mm (2.95in) Mountain Gun M1915; it subsequently remained in use by the Austrian, Hungarian and Czech armies until the early years of World War II. It was also exported to several other countries between the wars. Like all mountain guns, it could be quickly broken down for mule carriage, in this case into six loads, and could be elevated to a high angle. The very large shield required additional bracing, and the slightly curved trail gave good ground clearance and could be folded in half and fitted with shafts for animal draught.

Country of origin:	Austria-Hungary
Calibre:	75mm (2.95in)
Weight in action:	620kg (1387lb)
Gun length:	15 calibre: 1.12m (44in)
Elevation:	-9° to +50°
Traverse:	7°
Shell type & weight:	shrapnel; 6.50kg (14.32lb)
Muzzle velocity:	350m/sec (1148 ft/sec)
Maximum range:	7000m (7655 yds)

Obice de 75/18 Mod 35

The Obice de 75/18 Mod 35 was introduced for use by fast horse-drawn batteries, and could be split into two parts for faster movement. Designed by the Italian manufacturer Ansaldo, ballistically it was the same as the 1934 Mountain Howitzer and was sometimes used as such, although it could not be broken down into pack loads. A split trail gun, it is easily recognised by the large rubber-tyred wheels and the peculiar frame-type cradle around the gun barrel. It remained in use throughout World War II, and was a modern and very handy field piece, in contrast to many other Italian artillery pieces in service at that time. A number were sold to Portugal in 1940 to obtain foreign currency, and others went to South American states in return for raw materials.

Country of origin:	Italy
Calibre:	75mm (2.95in)
Weight in action:	1100kg (3435lb)
Gun length:	18.3 calibre: 1.572m (61.88in)
Elevation:	-10° to +45°
Traverse:	50°
Shell type & weight:	HE; 6.30kg (13.88lb)
Muzzle velocity:	400m/sec (1312ft/sec)
Maximum range:	9400m (10,280yds)

Type 35/75mm Gun

The Type 35/75mm (2.95in), the most modern gun in Japan's armoury when World War II began, had been developed as a result of experience in Manchuria. A split trail design, it was probably the last field gun ever made with seats for the gunners on the shield. These guns were intended to replace the 1908 field gun in horse batteries, but production never caught up with demand and the 1908 subsequently stayed in service. Throughout its service life the gun was never adapted for vehicle traction, so horse or mule teams were used right up to 1945. The inability of the gun to be moved quickly caused a number of them to be lost due to counter-battery fire or their being abandoned.

Country of origin:	Japan
Calibre:	75mm (2.95in)
Weight in action:	1007kg (2220lb)
Gun length:	31 calibre: 2.325m (91.37in)
Elevation:	-8° to +43°
Traverse:	50°
Shell type & weight:	HE; 5.70kg (12.56lb)
Muzzle velocity:	520m/sec (1700ft/sec)
Maximum range:	10,700m (11,700yds)

7.5cm Infantry Gun IG18

The 7.5cm (2.95in) Infantry Gun IG18 was issued to German infantry battalions after World War I for their own close support, entirely separate from the organic divisional artillery. It was a useful little gun with an odd 'shotgun' breech mechanism. The barrel lay in a square trough, the rear end of which was the breech block; opening the breech merely raised the rear end of the barrel clear of the 'block', and as the cartridge was loaded, so the barrel dropped back into place and the breech was closed. Two versions of the gun were developed that could be broken down into loads: one for mountain infantry use, and the other for paratroops, although only six of the latter were built, as the recoilless gun proved more suitable.

Country of origin:	Germany
Calibre:	75mm (2.95in)
Weight in action:	400kg (882lb)
Gun length:	11.2 calibre; 884mm (32.80in)
Elevation:	-10° to +75°
Traverse:	12°
Shell type & weight:	HE; 6.00kg (13.22lb)
Muzzle velocity:	210m/sec (688ft/sec)
Maximum range:	3375m (3690yds)

75mm Mountain Gun Geb. G. 36

This unusual-looking weapon is actually a quite conventional 75mm (2.95in) howitzer, and if it had wheels it would look quite normal. However, since a mountain gun is often used in snow, the unusual undercarriage of this version is designed for easy towing over snow by a team of skiers, and also to give extra flotation so that the gun can be fired off deep snow without digging itself too far in. Note how the cradle is trunnioned at its rear end in order to allow the breech to recoil without hitting the ground at high elevations, and also note the proliferation of handles, grips and catches to allow the whole thing to be rapidly broken into eight mule loads. Due to the lightness of this equipment it was not to be fired at elevations below 15°, otherwise it jumped violently and became unstable.

Country of origin:	Germany
Calibre:	75mm (2.95in)
Weight in action:	750kg (1654lb)
Gun length:	1.45m (57.09in)
Elevation:	-2° to +70°
Traverse:	40°
Shell type & weight:	HE; 5.75kg (12.68lb)
Muzzle velocity:	476m/sec (1558ft/sec)
Maximum range:	9150m (10,000yds)

10cm Skoda Light Howitzer vz 14/19

When the Czech army was formed in 1919 after the treaty of Versailles, it was handed a collection of old Skoda-designed Austrian and German artillery, which it gave back to Skoda for modernisation. The 10cm (3.93in) Skoda Light Howitzer vz 14/19 was derived from the Austrian M1914 Howitzer and modernised by being given a longer barrel and trail, improved recoil system, improved sights and a coat of paint. It was a sound design and remained in service until the German annexation of 1939, whereupon it was scrapped and replaced by the German leFH18. Examples were sold to Greece, Hungary, Poland and Yugoslavia, and thousands were in service in Central Europe by 1939.

Country of origin:	Czechoslovakia
Calibre:	100mm (3.93in)
Weight in action:	1548kg (3412lb)
Gun length:	24 calibre: 2.40m (94.5in)
Elevation:	-7.5° to 50°
Traverse:	6°
Shell type & weight:	HE; 16.0kg (35.27lb)
Muzzle velocity:	395m/sec (1295ft/sec)
Maximum range:	9800m (10,715yds)

Ordnance QF 13pdr

Developed in 1904 as a result of British experience in South Africa during the Boer War, the Ordnance QF 13pdr (76.2mm/3in) became the Royal Horse Artillery gun for supporting cavalry. Some were sent to India, but most were based in the United Kingdom and were ready to move to France in 1914. Once World War I moved into the trench lines, it had too short a range to be useful and was withdrawn from service. Most were converted into very serviceable anti-aircraft guns and were widely used by the field armies. Following the end of World War I, some were re-converted into their original field gun shape and are still in use today for ceremonial and display purposes.

Country of origin:	United Kingdom
Calibre:	76.2mm (3.0in)
Weight in action:	1014kg (2235lb)
Gun length:	24 calibre: 1.86m (73.23in)
Elevation:	-5° to +16°
Traverse:	8°
Shell type & weight:	shrapnel; 5.67kg (12.5lb)
Muzzle velocity:	510m/sec (2673ft/sec)
Maximum range:	5395m (5900yds)

15pdr BLC Field Gun

This field gun takes its odd title of BLC (Breech Loading, Converted) from the fact that it had originally been issued without any form of recoil control as the 15pdr BL Gun in 1896. After the 13pdr and 18pdr guns had entered service, it was decided to upgrade the 15pdr gun to bring it as close to a modern QF gun as possible, by fitting the barrel with a more modern breech mechanism, removing the trunnions, fitting the carriage with a cradle and a hydro-spring recoil system, and then fitting the gun into the cradle. They were issued to the Territorial Army in 1907, and several TA units took them to France in 1914 for use in combat. However, their range was not sufficient for the new type of warfare and they were replaced by 18pdr guns and returned to Britain for use as training weapons until worn out.

Country of origin:	United Kingdom
Calibre:	76mm (3in)
Weight in action:	1158kg (2553lb)
Gun length:	28 calibre: 2.54m (84in)
Elevation:	-10° to +20°
Traverse:	8°
Shell type & weight:	shrapnel; 6.35kg (14.0lb)
Muzzle velocity:	484 m/sec (1590ft/sec)
Maximum range:	5260m (5750yds)

QF 15pdr Gun Mk 1

During the South African War, the Boers, with their Krupp guns, were outranging the British artillery, and as a quick solution 108 76.2mm (3in) guns were bought from Ehrhardt of Germany in 1901 in the greatest secrecy. They were introduced into British service as the QF 15pdr Gun Mark 1, and were the first British field guns to have on-carriage recoil systems. It had an interrupted screw breech and pole trail, and the wheels were replaced by British service items. The gun was still used by Territorial Army batteries in 1914, and went to France with their units until removed from service in 1916. A few batteries of these guns were sent to Egypt, but they saw little, if any, action.

Country of origin:	United Kingdom
Calibre:	76.2mm (3.0in)
Weight in action:	980kg (2180lb)
Gun length:	30 calibre: 2.28m (89.75in)
Elevation:	-5° to +16°
Traverse:	6°
Shell type & weight:	shrapnel; 6.35kg (14.0lb)
Muzzle velocity:	511m/sec (1676ft/sec)
Maximum range:	5850m (6400yds)

76.2mm Field Gun M1942

Experience after the German invasion of 1941 convinced the Russians that what they needed was a combination field and anti-tank gun, and they therefore designed this M1942 weapon as their standard field piece. It has a low, tubular split trail carriage and a long barrel so as to provide the necessary velocity for firing anti-tank shot. Like most Russian designs it was light for its power and could out-perform most other 76.2mm (3in) guns, despite its relative simplicity. It was produced in greater numbers than any other artillery piece of World War II, and the gun remained in service in the Communist bloc for many years after the end of the war in 1945.

Country of origin:	USSR
Calibre:	76.2mm (3.0in)
Weight in action:	1116kg (2460lb)
Gun length:	42.6 calibre: 3.24m (127.55in)
Elevation:	-5° to +37°
Traverse:	54°
Shell type & weight:	HE; 6.20kg (13.67lb)
Muzzle velocity:	680m/sec (2230ft/sec)
Maximum range:	13,300m (14,545yds)

76.2mm Field Gun M1939

After several years of patching up and refurbishing Tsarist guns, the Soviets began developing their own designs in the early 1930s, and their new standard field gun was the 76.2mm (3in) Model 1936. Several thousand were built, and after some experience had been obtained, it was re-designed and some improvements made. The barrel was shortened. the recoil system was split above and below the barrel instead of all being in a single block underneath the barrel, and the carriage was made somewhat lighter. The end result was this 76.2mm Model 1939, an excellent weapon which the Germans captured in such numbers that, together with the Model 1936, they were adopted in German service as anti-tank guns and German ammunition was made for them.

Country of origin:	USSR
Calibre:	76.2mm (3.0in)
Weight in action:	1570kg (3461lb)
Gun length:	42 calibre: 3.20m (126 in)
Elevation:	-6° to +45°
Traverse:	57°
Shell type & weight:	HE; 6.40kg (14.11lb)
Muzzle velocity:	680m/sec (2230ft/sec)
Maximum range:	13,300m (14,545yds)

Field and Heavy Artillery

77mm FK16

The 77mm (3.03in) FK16 was little more than a slightly improved version of the German 77mm/96 field gun, most of the improvement being in matters of construction and a quicker wartime manufacture. Approximately 3500 were built during World War I and they remained the standard gun used throughout the 1920s, being one of the few weapons allowed to the German army after the treaty of Versailles, although some were given to countries such as Belgium and the Netherlands as war reparations. In the 1920s many were re-barrelled into 75mm (2.95in) calibre and served continuously until 1945. The box trail, wooden spoked wheels and seats on the shield all proclaim the era from which this design originated.

Country of origin:	Germany
Calibre:	77mm (3.03in)
Weight in action:	1325kg (2921lb)
Gun length:	35 calibre: 2.695m (106.10in)
Elevation:	-10° to +40°
Traverse:	4°
Shell type & weight:	HE; 7.20kg (15.87lb)
Muzzle velocity:	540m/sec (1770ft/sec)
Maximum range:	9100m (9950yds)

77mm Field Gun M96nA

The Model 96 New Type was the principal German field gun at the outbreak of World War I, and was also standard in the Bulgarian and Turkish armies. A robust Krupp design, with hydro-spring recoil system and the Krupp sliding block breech, it remained in production throughout the war and over 5000 were still in service towards the end. Many were taken by the Polish, Estonian, Lithuanian and Latvian armies which were being formed in 1919 and served with them until they were replaced by more modern designs in the 1930s. The calibre was chosen because other nations' guns of 75mm (2.95in) or 76.2mm (3in) could be bored out to accept German ammunition, but they could not do the same to captured German weapons.

Country of origin:	Germany
Calibre:	77mm (3.03in)
Weight in action:	925kg (2039lb)
Gun length:	27.3 calibre: 2.102m (82.67in)
Elevation:	-13° to +15°
Traverse:	8°
Shell type & weight:	shrapnel; 6.85kg (15.1lb)
Muzzle velocity:	465m/sec (1525ft/sec)
Maximum range:	7800m (8530yds)

Ordnance QF 18pdr Gun

Like the 13pdr (76.2mm/3in) gun, with which it is almost identical but for size, the British Ordnance QF 18pdr (83.8mm/3.3in) gun appeared in 1904 as a result of lessons learned in the wars in South Africa against the Boers. It used a pole trail, hydro-spring recoil system, an interrupted-screw breech firing a fixed round of ammunition, and had a shield to protect the gun detachment. By 1914 it was the standard field gun of the British and Commonwealth armies. Some examples were even manufactured in India. In subsequent years it acquired a box trail, then a split trail, and the wooden wheels were changed for pneumatic tyres. Many of the final versions were re-barrelled to become the 25-pounder (87.6mm/3.45in) Mark 1.

Country of origin:	United Kingdom
Calibre:	83.8mm (3.3in)
Weight in action:	1284kg (2831lb)
Gun length:	29.4 calibre: 2.46m (96.85in)
Elevation:	-5° to +16°
Traverse:	8°
Shell type & weight:	shrapnel; 8.40kg (18.5lb)
Muzzle velocity:	492m/sec (1614ft/sec)
Maximum range:	8700m (9515yds)

Ordnance QF 4.5in Howitzer

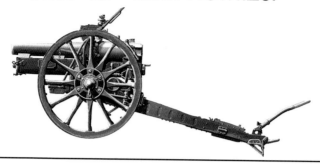

Designed by the Coventry Ordnance Works, the British Ordnance QF 4.5in (114mm) Howitzer appeared in 1910 and went on to become one of the most efficient medium howitzers of World War I. At a time when few field guns could elevate beyond 20°, it became a valuable support to the field artillery, since it could drop shells into trenches and field defences which the flat-trajectory guns could not harm. Several thousand were produced and the gun was sold widely to several countries in post-war years and, modernised with pneumatic tyres, it served throughout World War II as well, when the Germans captured a number of examples that had originally been supplied to Tsarist Russia in 1916.

Country of origin:	United Kingdom
Calibre:	114mm (4.5in)
Weight in action:	1370kg (3020lb)
Gun length:	14.3 calibre: 1.63m (64.17in)
Elevation:	-5° to +45°
Traverse:	6°
Shell type & weight:	HE; 15.90kg (35.0lb)
Muzzle velocity:	313m/sec (1026ft/sec)
Maximum range:	6400m (7000yds)

Ordnance BL 60pdr Mk 1

The Ordnance BL 60pdr (127mm/5in) Mk 1 was another design which stemmed from the South African War, when the British had nothing to compare with the Boer's 155mm (6.1in) 'Long Tom' guns. Introduced in 1905, it used a box trail and was built so that the gun could be pulled back in its cradle and locked there for transport, so equalising the weight between the gun wheels and the limber wheels. A simplified wartime design did away with this feature and put all the weight on the wheels, adapted from those used for traction engines, thus demanding mechanical traction by the Holt tractor, so a third design restored the gun shift yet still lightened the weapon. It remained in service until the middle of World War II.

Country of origin:	United Kingdom
Calibre:	127mm (5.0in)
Weight in action:	4470kg (9655lb)
Gun length:	33.6 calibre: 4.288m (14.06ft)
Elevation:	-5° to +21.5°
Traverse:	8°
Shell type & weight:	shrapnel; 27.22kg (60lb)
Muzzle velocity:	634m/sec (2080ft/sec)
Maximum range:	11,245m (12,300yds)

149mm Skoda Model 14 Howitzer

A conventional design of a medium field howitzer, similar to many contemporaries from other makers, the 149mm (5.86in) Skoda Model 14 Howitzer was at least a durable design, since it was employed after World War I by the Austrians, Czechs, Hungarians and Italians, who captured many examples, well into the 1940s. It was one of the standard Austro-Hungarian Army howitzers of World War I. It used a box trail, and for long distance haulage, the gun and cradle could be lifted from the trail and carried on to a separate wagon, lightening the load on the horse teams. A Model 14/16 was developed with a new barrel and ammunition, which improved the overall range of the gun.

Country of origin:	Austria/Hungary
Calibre:	149mm (5.86in)
Weight in action:	2765kg (6095lb)
Gun length:	14 calibre: 2.08m (81.88in)
Elevation:	-5° to +70°
Traverse:	8°
Shell type & weight:	HE; 42.0kg (92.6lb)
Muzzle velocity:	350m/sec (1148ft/sec)
Maximum range:	8000m (8750yds)

Field and Heavy Artillery

10cm M1917 Gun

Along range medium gun was something the German Army had not thought about before 1914, but as the stalemate in the trenches seemed set to continue, demand for artillery pieces that could inflict serious damage on enemy trench systems was high. and after some hasty improvisations with borrowed naval guns, the 10cm (4.14in) M1917 design was produced by Krupp. As a result, just under 200 were in use by the end of World War I. The long barrel and cradle were removed and placed on a 'cannon wagon' for transport, since it was too heavy to be moved in one load by a horse team. It was also taken into use by Romania and Sweden after the war.

Country of origin:	Germany
Calibre:	105.2mm (4.14in)
Weight in action:	3200kg (7055lb)
Gun length:	45 calibre: 4.735m (15.53ft)
Elevation:	-2° to +45°
Traverse:	6°
Shell type & weight:	HE; 18.75kg (41.33lb)
Muzzle velocity:	650m/sec (2133ft/sec)
Maximum range:	14,100m (15,420yds)

Canon de 105mm Schneider Mle 1913

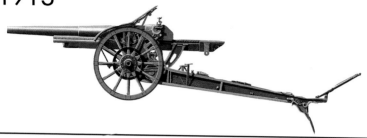

One of the best designs ever to come from Schneider, the Canon de 105mm (4.13in) was ordered by the French in 1913 and over 1300 were in use by 1918. It introduced several novel features, including a screw breech that could swing as it opened instead of having to be withdrawn before opening, a quick-release latch which allowed the gun to be pulled back in the cradle for travelling or removed entirely to a transport wagon, and a new type of hydro-pneumatic recoil system in which the buffer and recuperator were entirely independent of each other. It was widely adopted after the war by Belgium, Czechoslovakia, Estonia, Poland and Yugoslavia, all of whom were rebuilding their armies. It formed the principal gun strength of the French army in 1940.

Country of origin:	France
Calibre:	105mm (4.13in)
Weight in action:	2300kg (5070lb)
Gun length:	28.4 calibre: 2.98m (117.3in)
Elevation:	0° to +37°
Traverse:	6°
Shell type & weight:	HE; 16.0kg (35.27lb)
Muzzle velocity:	550m/sec (1805ft/sec)
Maximum range:	12,700m (13,890yds)

OTO-Melara 105mm Mod 56

The OTO-Melara 105mm (4.13in) Mod 56 was developed in the 1950s to meet a demand from many countries for a 105mm howitzer capable of firing the standard US M1 family of ammunition and yet light enough to be lifted by the helicopters of the time. This weapon is a pack howitzer, capable of being dismantled into 12 pack loads, and the suspension system allows the weapon to be set high, leaving room for the breech to recoil at high angles of elevation, or low for flat-trajectory firing against tanks and similar targets. As such it was a highly flexible gun and was widely adopted throughout NATO in the 1950s. Many examples are still in service.

Country of origin:	Italy
Calibre:	105mm (4.13in)
Weight in action:	1273kg (2806lb)
Gun length:	14 calibre: 1.47m (57.9in)
Elevation:	-7° to +65°
Traverse:	56°
Shell type & weight:	HE; 14.97kg (33.0lb)
Muzzle velocity:	416m/sec (1345ft/sec)
Maximum range:	11,100m (12,140yds)

105mm Light Gun L118

The British used the Italian 105mm (4.13in) Mod 56 for some years, but required something air-portable yet more powerful, and which, in addition, could fire the ammunition which had been developed for the Abbot SP gun. The 105mm Light Gun L118 was the result, a lightweight gun using a tubular box trail and capable of firing in the howitzer role as well. It is provided with a second barrel, chambered for American 105mm ammunition, so that if that ammunition is readily available in some distant theatre, then the gun is changed to suit, rather than requiring small quantities of Abbot ammunition to be hauled over long distances. It is helicopter-portable and is used by Australia, New Zealand, India, the USA and several Middle Eastern countries.

Country of origin:	United Kingdom
Calibre:	105mm (3.0in)
Weight in action:	1860kg (4100lb)
Gun length:	37 calibre: 3.88m (12.72ft)
Elevation:	-5.5° to +70°
Traverse:	11°
Shell type & weight:	HE; 16.05kg (35.38lb)
Muzzle velocity:	617m/sec (2024ft/sec)
Maximum range:	15,070m (16,480yds)

105mm Howitzer M2A1

The 105mm (4.13in) Howitzer M2A1 was the standard divisional field-piece used throughout World War II by the US Army and was distributed around the world thereafter. It is still in wide use and the ammunition has become a virtual standard to which other howitzers have been built. This weapon was developed during the 1920s, perfected in the 1930s, and went into production in 1941. It uses a split trail, hydro-pneumatic recoil system and horizontal sliding breech, and fires semi-fixed ammunition. It is now known as the M101, although there is no significant difference between it and the M2A1, and has been in use in 67 countries. Apart from World War II, it has seen action in many conflicts including Korea, Vietnam and Grenada amongst others.

Country of origin:	USA
Calibre:	105mm (3.0in)
Weight in action:	2030kg (4475lb)
Gun length:	22 calibre: 2.31m (90.94in)
Elevation:	-5° to +66°
Traverse:	46°
Shell type & weight:	HE; 14.97kg (33.0lb)
Muzzle velocity:	472m/sec (1548ft/sec)
Maximum range:	11,200m (12,248yds)

105mm leFH 18

The 105mm (4.13in) leFH 18 was the standard German divisional field-piece used throughout World War II; it was designed by Rheinmetall in 1929/30 and went into service in 1935. A good, sound, orthodox design, it used a split trail with folding spades and a hydro-pneumatic recoil system split above and below the barrel, but retained wooden or pressed-steel wheels and was mostly horse-drawn for all its life. However it was so solidly put together that it was rather heavy, and unable to be as mobile as the army would have liked. Although augmented by improved models in 1939–45, it remained in use and was kept in service by several European armies for some years after the war ended.

Country of origin:	Germany
Calibre:	105mm (4.13in)
Weight in action:	1985kg (4376lb)
Gun length:	24.8 calibre: 2.61m (102.75in)
Elevation:	-6.5° to +40.5°
Traverse:	56°
Shell type & weight:	HE; 14.81kg (32.65lb)
Muzzle velocity:	470m/sec (1542ft/sec)
Maximum range:	10,675m (11,675yds)

105mm leFH18(M)

This weapon was derived from the 105mm (4.13in) leFH 18, but with the gun barrel fitted with a muzzle brake to enable it to fire more powerful ammunition and thus achieve a greater range, but without placing excessive stress on the recoil system and carriage. However, it was found necessary to replace the valves in the recoil buffer and increase the air pressure in the recuperator in order to absorb the extra energy, and the first design of muzzle brake, with single baffles, had to have extra baffles welded on to get the balance between performance and recoil which was demanded. A special long-range shell and cartridge were provided, and the original leFH 18 ammunition could still be fired.

Country of origin:	Germany
Calibre:	105mm (4.13in)
Weight in action:	1985kg (4376lb)
Gun length:	24.8 calibre: 2.61m (102.75in)
Elevation:	-6.5° to +40.5°
Traverse:	56°
Shell type & weight:	HE; 14.25kg (31.41lb)
Muzzle velocity:	540m/sec (1771ft/sec)
Maximum range:	12,325m (13,480yds)

105mm Howitzer M3

In 1941, the US Army requested a new 105mm (4.13in) howitzer, capable of being air-lifted, not more than 1134kg (2500lb) in weight and capable of a range of at least 6401m (7000yds), with which to equip their future airborne divisions. The desired result was reached by cutting down the existing M2A1 Howitzer by 686mm (27in) to make the Howitzer T7, and then fabricating a carriage by taking the existing carriage of the 75mm (2.95in) Howitzer M3A1 and the much modified recoil system of the 75mm Pack Howitzer M8. This was standardised as the Howitzer M3 on Carriage M3 in February 1945, and over 2500 were built. They were used in North Africa by Infantry Cannon Companies, but this tactical notion was short-lived, and for the remainder of the war they armed airborne units only.

Country of origin:	USA
Calibre:	105mm (4.13in)
Weight in action:	1132kg (,495lb)
Gun length:	16.5 calibre: 1.88m (74.35in)
Elevation:	-9° to +69°
Traverse:	45°
Shell type & weight:	HE; 14.96kg (33lb)
Muzzle velocity:	311m/sec (1020ft/sec)
Maximum range:	7585m (8295 yds)

120mm Krupp Howitzer M1905

When Turkey threw in its lot with Germany during World War I it needed to upgrade its forces with some modern weapons, and a number of these Krupp Howitzers were presented to them. The 120mm (4.72in) Howitzer was a popular stock model with most continental gunmakers before 1914, and this particular model had been sold to Japan and one or two other smaller countries, but Krupp apparently had a few on the shelf and enough components to make several more. It was a very conventional design for the period, the only unusual feature being the lack of a shield for its crew, although once the war drove artillery into concealed positions, this was less of a liability.

Country of origin:	Germany
Calibre:	120mm (4.72in)
Weight in action:	1125kg (2480lb)
Gun length:	12 calibre: 1.445m (56.67in)
Elevation:	0° to +42°
Traverse:	5°
Shell type & weight:	HE; 20 kg (44lb)
Muzzle velocity:	275m/sec (902ft/sec)
Maximum range:	5800m (6349yds)

122mm D-30

This all-round traverse howitzer was introduced into Russian service in the early 1960s, and it is reasonable to assume that the designers took a close look at the Skoda leFH43 105mm (4.13in) gun designed for the German army during World War II, since the D-30 employs a very similar system to obtain the desired 360° traverse. The trail of the gun splits into three legs which are then equi-spaced to provide a firm platform, above which the gun carriage can revolve. The folded legs lie beneath the barrel for travelling, and the gun muzzle has the towing connector attached to it, so that the length of the towed equipment is merely the length of the barrel. The D-30 has been adopted by numerous armies around the world.

Country of origin:	USSR
Calibre:	122mm (4.80in)
Weight in action:	3150kg (6945lb)
Gun length:	40 calibre: 4.875m (16ft)
Elevation:	-7° to +70°
Traverse:	360°
Shell type & weight:	HE; 21.761kg (47.97lb)
Muzzle velocity:	690m/sec (2264ft/sec)
Maximum range:	15,400m (16,840yds)

Field and Heavy Artillery

Ordnance BL 5in Howitzer Mk I

The Ordnance BL 5in (127mm) Howitzer Mk I, the first breech-loading field howitzer in the British army, first saw action in the Nile campaign of 1897. A simple structure of steel trail and wooden wheels supported a cradle through which the gun barrel passed and which carried four large recoil springs. These allowed the barrel to recoil about six inches (15.2cm), after which the carriage itself began to roll backwards. It was an improvement on previous recoil systems, and it stayed in service until 1919, although most of its World War I service was as a training weapon. Sixty were given to Tsarist Russia in 1916, and one is tempted to wonder what they made of them.

Country of origin:	United Kingdom
Calibre:	127mm (5.0in)
Weight in action:	1212kg (2672lb)
Gun length:	8.4 calibre: 1.06m (41.73in)
Elevation:	-5° to +45°
Traverse:	nil
Shell type & weight:	HE; 22.68kg (50lb)
Muzzle velocity:	240m/sec (787ft/sec)
Maximum range:	4390m (4800yds)

4.7in Field Gun M1906

The 120mm (4.7in) Field Gun was designed by the US Army Ordnance Department and issued in 1906. By April 1917, when America entered World War I, a total of 60 had been made and issued. A plain and orthodox design, it used a box trail and a hydro-spring recoil system. Once the US were involved in the war they came under a great deal of pressure from the French to adopt their artillery systems, and, as a result, the 4.7 inch gun was re-designed to chamber the French 120mm ammunition, thus simplifying the ammunition supply and reducing the American supply lines. This decision upset manufacturing plans for the gun, however, and eventually only about 16 new guns were made before the end of the war.

Country of origin:	USA
Calibre:	120mm (4.7in)
Weight in action:	3983kg (8780lb)
Gun length:	27.5 calibre: 3.30m (10.82ft)
Elevation:	-5° to +15°
Traverse:	8°
Shell type & weight:	shrapnel; 27.22kg (60lb)
Muzzle velocity:	518m/sec (1700ft/sec)
Maximum range:	7270m (7950yds)

Ordnance BL 5.5in Gun Mk 2

The Ordnance BL 5.5in Gun Mk 2 was designed to replace the British 60pdr gun, and 5.5 inches (140mm) was chosen because this gave a better ballistic shape to the shell. It was originally designed to have hydro-pneumatic balancing cylinders to support the barrel weight, but these caused problems and simple springs were used instead, giving the characteristic 'horns' alongside the barrel. First issued in May 1942, it remained in British service until the early 1980s, and is still is use in Pakistan, New Zealand and South Africa. Originally using a 45.36kg (100lb) shell, it was later provided with a 37kg (82lb) shell which increased the range to 16,550m (18,099yds).

Country of origin:	United Kingdom
Calibre:	140mm (5.5in)
Weight in action:	6190kg (6.09 tons)
Gun length:	31 calibre: 4.358m (14.3ft)
Elevation:	-5° to +45°
Traverse:	60°
Shell type & weight:	HE; 45.36kg (100lb)
Muzzle velocity:	510m/sec (1673ft/sec)
Maximum range:	14,813m (16,200yds)

13.5cm FK 1909

The 13.5cm (5.31in) FK 1909 was introduced into German service in 1909 but it seemed to be a very large gun for not much shell, and by 1914 only 16 had been built by Krupp. War accelerated production, but in 1915 it was decided to withdraw them and replace them with a weapon capable of higher angles of elevation and thus more range. Later in the war, as shortages were felt due to the Allied blockade of Germany, the gun was brought back into service. As a concession to the need for mobility it was fitted with a sprung axle so as to facilitate towing by tractors, and about 200 were in use when the war ended. It is not generally regarded as one of Krupp's better efforts.

Country of origin:	Germany
Calibre:	135mm (5.31in)
Weight in action:	6,730kg (6.62 tons)
Gun length:	35 calibre: 3.97m (13.02ft)
Elevation:	-5° to +26°
Traverse:	4°
Shell type & weight:	HE; 31.7kg (79.88lb)
Muzzle velocity:	695m/sec (2m 280ft)
Maximum range:	16,500m (18,045yds)

149mm Siege Gun, Model of 1877

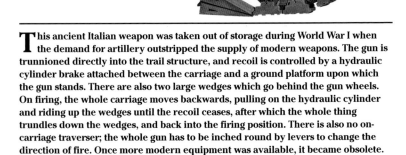

This ancient Italian weapon was taken out of storage during World War I when the demand for artillery outstripped the supply of modern weapons. The gun is trunnioned directly into the trail structure, and recoil is controlled by a hydraulic cylinder brake attached between the carriage and a ground platform upon which the gun stands. There are also two large wedges which go behind the gun wheels. On firing, the whole carriage moves backwards, pulling on the hydraulic cylinder and riding up the wedges until the recoil ceases, after which the whole thing trundles down the wedges, and back into the firing position. There is also no on-carriage traverser; the whole gun has to be inched round by levers to change the direction of fire. Once more modern equipment was available, it became obsolete.

Country of origin:	Italy
Calibre:	149.1mm (5.87in)
Weight in action:	5180kg (5.09 tons)
Gun length:	23 calibres: 3.42m (134.2in)
Elevation:	-10° to +33°
Traverse:	nil
Shell type & weight:	HE; 30.4kg (67lb)
Muzzle velocity:	520m/sec (1706ft/sec)
Maximum range:	9000m (9840yds)

15cm L/40 Feldkanone i.R.

The 15cm (5.87in) L/40 Feldkanone i.R. is one of a number of naval and coastal defence guns which were hurriedly withdrawn from fortifications and naval stores by the German army in 1915 and placed on whatever field carriages could be made to fit, in order to alleviate the desperate shortage of heavy artillery during World War I. The result was a very powerful gun but a very heavy one, and it was placed on a special ground platform which allowed it to traverse bodily, since there was no traverse on the carriage. The naval cradle was dropped into the trunnion bearings of the carriage, and the carriage was anchored to the firing platform as the naval recoil system did not absorb all of the recoil force.

Country of origin:	Germany
Calibre:	149mm (5.87in)
Weight in action:	11,820kg (11.6 tons)
Gun length:	40 calibre: 5.96m (19.55ft)
Elevation:	-5° to +20°
Traverse:	60°
Shell type & weight:	HE; 44.20kg (97.44lb)
Muzzle velocity:	750m/sec (2460ft/sec)
Maximum range:	18,700m (20,450yds)

15cm Field Howitzer FH17

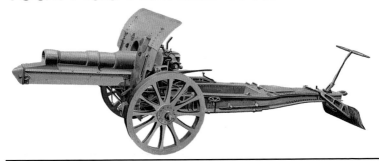

The 15cm (5.87in) Field Howitzer FH17 was a conventional design which Krupp originally produced for the German army in 1913. By the middle of World War I the pre-war stocks had diminished and Krupp was asked to make more – the FH17 was the result. It differed from the 1913 version by being lighter, the result of various wartime manufacturing short-cuts and economies, but the ballistic performance was exactly the same and they are almost impossible to tell apart unless you see the model number stamped on the breech. Quite a few survived long enough in German service to be used as training weapons by the German army during the first years of World War II.

Country of origin:	Germany
Calibre:	149mm (5.87in)
Weight in action:	2200kg (4850lb)
Gun length:	14 calibre: 2.085m (82.1in)
Elevation:	-11° to +43°
Traverse:	1°
Shell type & weight:	HE; 42.0kg (92.6lb)
Muzzle velocity:	365m/sec (1197ft/sec)
Maximum range:	8500m (9295yds)

sFH18

The backbone of the German medium artillery strength during World War II, the sFH 18 was developed in 1926–30, the howitzer being from Rheinmetall and the carriage from Krupp. For movement, the split trail ends were lifted on to a two-wheeled limber and the gun disconnected from the recoil system, pulled back in its cradle, and locked to the trails, so as to distribute the weight evenly. It has the distinction of being the first gun ever to be issued with a rocket-assisted shell, in 1941, which gave it a maximum range of 19,000m (20,778yds). However, it was not very accurate and wore out the gun rather rapidly. After the war, numbers of these howitzers were used by the Albanian, Bulgarian, Czech and Portuguese armies for several years.

Country of origin:	Germany
Calibre:	150mm (5.91in)
Weight in action:	5512kg (12,150lb)
Gun length:	27.5 calibre: 4.125m (13.53ft)
Elevation:	-3° to +45°
Traverse:	64°
Shell type & weight:	HE; 43.50kg (95.9lb)
Muzzle velocity:	495m/sec (1624ft/sec)
Maximum range:	13,250m (14,490yds)

15cm Gun M1877

This antediluvian equipment was probably the oldest model of gun to take part in World War I, many of them being dragged out of Russian fortresses and sent to the front. They were originally designed as siege guns, and were to be used with a wooden ground platform and a stout ground anchor to which a hydraulic cylinder was attached. The piston rod was attached to the gun carriage and as the gun trundled backwards on firing, so it dragged the piston through the cylinder of oil and braked the recoil movement. Without this mechanism, the gun was almost uncontrollable. It was moved in one piece, the trail end being carried on a two-wheeled limber, and most of them were lost during the hasty to-and-fro movement of the Eastern Front in 1915–16.

Country of origin:	USSR
Calibre:	152.4mm (6.0in)
Weight in action:	4880kg (10,758lb), plus 6660kg (14,882lb) for the ground platform and recoil brake
Gun length:	22 calibre: 3.60m (11.8ft)
Elevation:	-16° to +38°
Traverse:	nil
Shell type & weight:	HE; 32.901kg (72.5lb)
Muzzle velocity:	463m/sec (1520ft/sec)
Maximum range:	7800m (8530yds)

152mm Gun-Howitzer M1937 (ML-20)

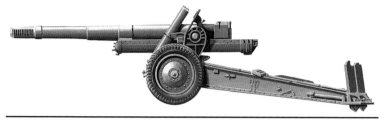

The 152mm (6in) Gun-Howitzer M1937 (ML-20) was developed in the mid-1930s to replace a collection of World War I-era 152mm (6in) guns which had been refurbished in 1933, and was among the first weapons to be classed as a 'gun-howitzer'; in other words, it could fire at high velocity and flat trajectory like a gun, or at low velocity and on a high, looping trajectory like a howitzer, as the task demanded. A split trail weapon, with spring balancing 'horns' alongside the barrel, it was the workhorse of Russian medium artillery throughout World War II and was used by several armies for many years afterwards. The German army was very impressed by them and many captured examples were used against their former owners.

Country of origin:	USSR
Calibre:	152.4mm (6.0in)
Weight in action:	7128kg (7 tons)
Gun length:	29 calibre: 4.42m (14.5ft)
Elevation:	-2° to +65°
Traverse:	58°
Shell type & weight:	HE; 43.56kg (96lb)
Muzzle velocity:	655m/sec (2150ft/sec)
Maximum range:	17,265m (18,880yds)

Field and Heavy Artillery

152mm Howitzer M1943 (D-1)

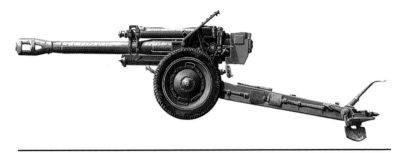

During World War II, in order to speed up production, the Russians frequently 'married' existing guns and carriages to produce new equipment, and the 152mm (6in) Howitzer M1943 (D-1) is a good example. It is the result of taking the existing carriage of the 122mm (4.8in) Howitzer M1938 and grafting on to it the barrel of the existing 152mm Howitzer M1938. In order to achieve this, it was necessary to fit a large muzzle brake on the howitzer to reduce the recoil force to something the smaller carriage could manage, but the result was a sound weapon which was half a ton lighter than the M1938 152mm howitzer it replaced. It remained in service until the late 1980s, and was widely distributed to Communist-inclined countries.

Country of origin:	USSR
Calibre:	152.4mm (6.0in)
Weight in action:	3600kg (7937lb)
Gun length:	24.6 calibre: 4.201m (13.76ft)
Elevation:	-3° to +63.5°
Traverse:	35°
Shell type & weight:	HE; 40.0kg (88.2lb)
Muzzle velocity:	508m/sec (1666ft/sec)
Maximum range:	12,400m (13,560yds)

BL 6in 26-cwt Howitzer Mk 1

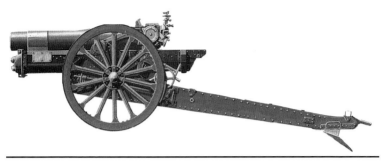

The gun weight, 26 cwt (1320kg/2912lb), in this weapon's title distinguishes it from two other British 6 inch howitzers which were simultaneously in service. It was developed in 1915, to replace the earlier 25cwt and 30cwt models, and became the standard British medium howitzer, over 3600 being manufactured before the war ended. Although many were supplied to other European armies, enough remained in British service to be fitted with pneumatic tyres and used in World War II until the Eritrean campaign of 1941. It was a simple design using a box trail, hydro-pneumatic recoil system, screw breech and bagged charged. It was originally designed around a 45kg (100lb) shrapnel shell, but this gave insufficient range and a 39kg (86lb) shell gradually replaced it. A high explosive shell was also introduced.

Country of origin:	United Kingdom
Calibre:	152mm (6in)
Weight in action:	3693 kg (3.63 tons)
Gun length:	13.3 calibre: 2.218m (87.35in)
Elevation:	0° to +45°
Traverse:	8°
Shell type & weight:	shrapnel or HE; 39kg (86lb)
Muzzle velocity:	427m/sec (1400ft/sec)
Maximum range:	10,425m (11,400yds)

Field and Heavy Artillery

152mm Howitzer M09/30

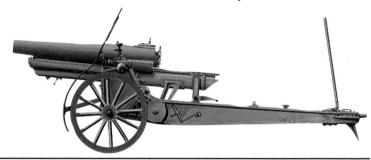

The 09/30 in this weapon's title indicates that this was originally built for the Tsar's Russian army. survived the war, and in 1930 was refurbished and modernised to serve until a newer weapon could be designed and produced. The modernisation was largely confined to the ammunition, producing a lighter shell and more powerful charge, but the carriage was also modified in order to make it suitable for towing behind a motor truck as well as retaining the ability to be horse-drawn. The appearance changed little; it is easily recognisable by the large shield which curved over the wheels and, which in all probability, directed all the mud and dirt straight into the mechanisms of the carriage.

Country of origin:	USSR
Calibre:	152.4mm (6.0in)
Weight in action:	2725kg (6007lb)
Gun length:	14.2 calibre: 2.164m (85.2in)
Elevation:	0° to +41°
Traverse:	6°
Shell type & weight:	HE; 40.0kg (88.2lb)
Muzzle velocity:	391m/sec (1283ft/sec)
Maximum range:	9,850m (10,770yds)

155mm Gun M2

The US Army adopted a 155mm (6.1in) gun from the French in 1917; they liked the calibre and in the 1930s developed a modern version, producing one of the finest guns of the war years. The 155mm M2, which inevitably became known as 'Long Tom', was on a split trail carriage with eight wheels under the gun and a two-wheeled limber for towing. To go into action, the limber was removed, the trails opened, and the wheels lifted off the ground, giving a solid platform which paid off in accuracy. The long barrel was balanced by two hydro-pneumatic cylinders attached to horns above the breech; the recoil system adjusted the length of stroke as the gun was elevated; and the gun could be uncoupled from the recoil system and pulled back across the trail for travelling, to equalise the weight.

Country of origin:	USA
Calibre:	155mm (6.10in)
Weight in action:	13,880kg (13.66 tons)
Gun length:	45 calibre: 6.97m (22.86ft)
Elevation:	-1°40' to +63°20'
Traverse:	60°
Shell type & weight:	HE; 42.96kg (94.7lb)
Muzzle velocity:	853m/sec (2800ft/sec)
Maximum range:	23,220m (25,395yds)

Field and Heavy Artillery

155mm Rimailho Howitzer Model 1904TR

TR means 'Tir Rapide' and Colonel Rimailho's aim was to produce a medium gun capable of the rate of fire of the French 75mm (2.95in) Mle 1897. He achieved this at the price of great mechanical complication. To simplify the action: at the end of the recoil movement, the breech opens and is held back while the gun runs back into battery. As it goes forward, a loading tray slides from beneath it and a cartridge and shell are dropped on to it. The firing lever is then pulled; the loading tray and breech-block run up to the gun breech, ramming the shell and loading the cartridge. The breech closes and locks and the gun fires. A well-trained detachment could reach a rate of 15 shots a minute – no mean feat for a gun of this size. By 1916 the tactical picture had changed and the gun no longer had sufficient range.

Country of origin:	France
Calibre:	155mm (6.10in)
Weight in action:	3200kg (3.14 tons)
Gun length:	15.5 calibre: 2.40m (94in)
Elevation:	0° to + 41°
Traverse:	6°
Shell type & weight:	HE; 42.9kg (92.5lb)
Muzzle velocity:	320m/sec (1050ft/sec)
Maximum range:	6000m (6560yds)

BL 6in 30cwt Howitzer

Introduced in 1896, the BL 6in (152mm) 30cwt Howitzer was the first BL medium howitzer to be adopted by the British Army, although similar but lighter models had been built for the Indian Army in the previous year. It used a hydro-spring recoil system, the gun recoiling in a ring cradle. The carriage was a simple design, with no traverse capability and limited to 35°of elevation. However, the gun could be lifted off, and a 'carriage top' added to the trail. The wheels were then removed and the carriage was laid on to a wooden platform and the gun replaced. It could not reach to 70° for siege bombardment and so the maximum range was increased to 6400m (7000 yds). About 120 were made and they were used in almost every theatre of war in 1914–18, but were gradually replaced by the 6in 26cwt howitzer.

Country of origin:	United Kingdom
Calibre:	152mm (6.0 in)
Weight in action:	3507kg (7733lb)
Gun length:	14 calibre: 2.38m (94.0 in)
Elevation:	-10° to +35°
Traverse:	nil
Shell type & weight:	shrapnel; 53.75kg (118.5lb)
Muzzle velocity:	237m/sec (777ft/sec)
Maximum range:	4755m (5200 yds)

155mm Model 77 Howitzer

The Argentine 155mm (6.10in) Model 77 Howitzer is an interesting development because it is simply the barrel, recoil system and top carriage of the French 155mm SP gun F3 removed from its tracked mounting and placed on to a split-trail field carriage. Argentina bought a quantity of this French equipment, but soon found that it required a field carriage more suited to operating in rough country, such as that found in Patagonia. The carriage is two-wheeled and has a firing pedestal between the wheels so that it can be lowered and the wheels lifted to give a solid platform. The long barrel is balanced by two pneumatic cylinders fitted between the top carriage and the cradle.

Country of origin:	Argentina
Calibre:	155mm (6.10in)
Weight in action:	8000kg (7.87 tons)
Gun length:	32 calibre: 5.15m (16.9ft)
Elevation:	-10° to +67°
Traverse:	70°
Shell type & weight:	HE; 43.00kg (94.8lb)
Muzzle velocity:	765m/sec (2510ft/sec)
Maximum range:	22,000m (24,060yds)

Soltam M68 Gun

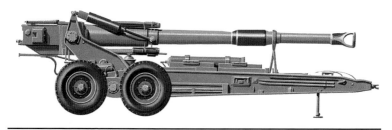

A development of a Finnish design, the Israeli M68 is a split-trail gun-howitzer of reasonable weight and good performance. The carriage has two wheels at the forward end of each trail leg, so that they move with the legs as they are opened. There are loose spades which are driven into the ground and then have the trail locked to them by wedges. The gun had an efficient muzzle brake and a fume extractor, indicating the use of the same gun in a self-propelled carriage. For movement, the top carriage revolves until the barrel is above the folded trail legs, where it is then locked, and the trail ends are hoisted up and hooked to the towing truck. An unusual feature is the use of a sliding block breech with bag charges, the breech block having a sealing ring inset in its front face.

Country of origin:	Israel
Calibre:	155mm (6.10in)
Weight in action:	9500kg (9.35 tons)
Gun length:	32 calibre: 5.18m (17ft)
Elevation:	-10° to +52°
Traverse:	90°
Shell type & weight:	HE; 43.700kg (96.34lb)
Muzzle velocity:	820m/sec (2690ft/sec)
Maximum range:	23,500m (25,700yds)

155mm Howitzer FH-70

The 155mm (6.10in) Howitzer FH-70 was a co-operative development between Britain, Germany and Italy in 1968–74, one of the few such efforts which worked. The result was an advanced design, using an auxiliary power unit to provide self-propulsion for short distances, capable of firing a wide range of modern projectiles. It uses a split-trail carriage, the gun being swung over the trail legs for travelling, and provided with steerable wheels on the trail for self-movement. An efficient muzzle brake cuts down the recoil, and the vertical sliding block breech is used with combustible charges. In addition to the three original partners, the gun is also used by Japan, Saudi Arabia and Malaysia. A self-propelled version, however, proved to be a technical disaster and was abandoned in 1986.

Country of origin:	International (United Kingdom, Germany and Italy)
Calibre:	155mm (6.10in)
Weight in action:	9300kg (9.15 tons)
Gun length:	38 calibre: 6.02m (19.75ft)
Elevation:	-4.5° to +70°
Traverse:	56°
Shell type & weight:	HE; 43.5kg (95.90lb)
Muzzle velocity:	827m/sec (2713ft/sec)
Maximum range:	24,700m (27,010yds)

155mm Gun G-5

Unveiled at an exhibition in Athens in 1982, the 155mm (6.10in) Gun G-5 astonished the rest of the world with its technical advances. It was, to some extent, based on the theories of Dr. Gerald Bull and adopted a special 'extended range' projectile with stub wings. The remainder of the gun was fairly conventional, although it had auxiliary propulsion while most other people were still thinking about it. Using a split trail with four-wheeled bogie, the gun has a muzzle brake and a semi-automatic screw breech similar to that on the US M109 howitzer. The barrel swings over the trail for travelling, and a steerable wheel can be lowered from the train when the auxiliary motor is in use.

Country of origin:	South Africa
Calibre:	155mm (6.10in)
Weight in action:	13,750kg (13.56 tons)
Gun length:	45 calibre: 6.975m (22.88ft)
Elevation:	-3° to +75°
Traverse:	82°
Shell type & weight:	HE; 45.50kg (100lb)
Muzzle velocity:	897m/sec (2942ft/sec)
Maximum range:	30,000m (32,810yds)

155mm Howitzer FH-77A

The design of the Swedish 155mm (6.10in) Howitzer FH-77A, started in 1985, was the first of the 'modern' 155mm howitzers, using an auxiliary engine system to drive the gun wheels for short movements and also provide hydraulic power for elevating the gun, lowering the trail wheels, loading and ramming. When being towed across rough country, the driving wheels of the howitzer can be switched on by the tractor driver so as to give additional power. The lavish use of power assistance means that the number of men needed to operate this weapon is no more than six. In the event of engine failure, hand pumps can supply the necessary hydraulic pressure.

Country of origin:	Sweden
Calibre:	155mm (6.10in)
Weight in action:	11,500kg (11.32 tons)
Gun length:	38 calibre: 5.89m (19.32ft)
Elevation:	-3° to +50°
Traverse:	60°
Shell type & weight:	HE; 42.40kg (93.47lb)
Muzzle velocity:	774m/sec (2540ft/sec)
Maximum range:	22,000m (24,050yds)

155mm Howitzer M198

The American 155mm (6.10in) Howitzer M198 was developed in the late 1960s as a lightweight replacement for the existing M114 howitzer, capable of being air-lifted and with a greater range. Production began in 1978 and in addition to US service it has been adopted by several other armies. The design is quite conventional – a split trail two-wheel carriage, the wheels of which can be lifted off the ground when firing, and a gun with muzzle brake and screw breech with pad obturation for firing bagged charge. There are two hydro-pneumatic balancing cylinders attached to the cradle to take the weight of the gun. An auxiliary propulsion unit was designed for this gun, but not adopted.

Country of origin:	USA
Calibre:	155mm (6.10in)
Weight in action:	7163kg (7.05 tons)
Gun length:	39 calibre: 6.09m (19.98ft)
Elevation:	-5° to +72°
Traverse:	45°
Shell type & weight:	HE; 42.91kg (95.6lb)
Muzzle velocity:	684m/sec (2244ft/sec)
Maximum range:	18,100m (19,795yds)

155mm Gun Model TR

The 155mm (6.10in) Gun Model TR entered service with the French Army in 1989 and replaced the earlier Model 50 gun. It is a modern design, comparable with the FH-70 or -77 types in using a split trail carriage with an auxiliary propulsion unit which also provides power for the operation of the loading system, elevating and traversing the gun and raising and lowering the wheels and trail legs when emplacing the gun. It is normally operated by eight men, although the power assistance means that in emergencies three men can successfully bring the gun into or out of action. The powered loading and ramming system also means that the gun can be loaded at any angle of elevation and does not need to be brought down to a loading angle.

Country of origin:	France
Calibre:	155mm (6.10in)
Weight in action:	10,750kg (10.58 tons)
Gun length:	40 calibre: 6.20m (20.34ft)
Elevation:	-6° to +66°
Traverse:	65°
Shell type & weight:	HE; 43.25kg (95.35lb)
Muzzle velocity:	830m/sec (2723ft/sec)
Maximum range:	24,000m (25,245yds)

15cm Howitzer M1915

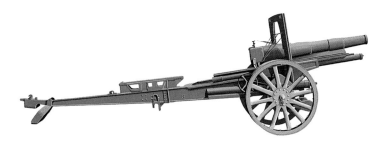

Japanese designs of the early part of the twentieth century were generally near-copies of European guns, and this 15cm (5.87in) Howitzer M1915 looks as if the designers had been studying the French Schneider designs closely, as it clearly resembles the French artillery pieces of the time. It was a quite conventional box-trail design, although like all Japanese artillery, it had a lower safety factor than most others and therefore was lighter, for its relative size and power, than you might expect. It remained in use after World War I, and saw a great deal of action in China and Manchuria in the 1930s after the Japanese invasions, before being replaced by a more modern design in 1936.

Country of origin:	Japan
Calibre:	149.2mm (5.87in)
Weight in action:	2790kg (6150lb)
Gun length:	11 calibre: 1.64m (64.6in)
Elevation:	-5° to +45°
Traverse:	6°
Shell type & weight:	HE; 36.0kg (79.4lb)
Muzzle velocity:	345m/sec (1132ft/sec)
Maximum range:	7600m (8310yds)

155mm ODE FH-88 Gun-howitzer

A design by Ordnance Development & Engineering (ODE) of Singapore, the 155mm (6.10in) ODE FH-88 Gun-howitzer went into service in 1989 with the Singapore army. It has the now common pattern of split trail carriage with four-wheel suspension and an auxiliary propulsion unit ahead of the wheels. The gun is revolved for travelling so that it lies over the trail legs, and two caster wheels can be lowered to support the trail legs when the auxiliary propulsion feature is in use. Power is also provided for loading, elevating, opening and closing the trail legs and lowering the caster wheels. The gun has a double-baffle muzzle brake and a semi-automatic screw breech which opens during the run-out movement of the barrel. The internal dimensions are such that all NATO-standard ammunition can be fired.

Country of origin:	Singapore
Calibre:	155mm (6.10in)
Weight in action:	12,800kg (12.59 tons)
Gun length:	40 calibre: 6.10m (20ft)
Elevation:	-3° to +70°
Traverse:	60°
Shell type & weight:	HE; 43.00kg (98.8lb)
Muzzle velocity:	765m/sec (2510ft/sec)
Maximum range:	19,000m (20,780yds)

155mm Santa Barbara SB-155/39 Howitzer

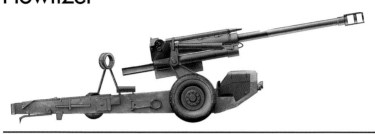

As the title suggests, this is a 39-calibre weapon developed by the Empresa Nacional Santa Barbara, the Spanish government armaments factory. It is very similar to others of the same period – the 1980s – in being a split-trail howitzer with muzzle brake, which lies along the top of the trails when travelling. The wheels are lifted from the ground when firing, the carriage resting on a firing pedestal. The trail legs have small wheels which can be lowered to assist in opening and closing. Loading is aided by a power rammer assembly behind the breech. The standard weapon has no other assistance, but an auxiliary-propelled design is also in existence which uses the more usual type of light diesel engine to drive hydraulic motors in the gun wheels.

Country of origin:	Spain
Calibre:	155mm (6.10in)
Weight in action:	9500kg (9.35 tons)
Gun length:	39 calibre: 6.045m (19.83ft)
Elevation:	-3° to +70°
Traverse:	60°
Shell type & weight:	HE; 43.50kg (95.9lb)
Muzzle velocity:	800m/sec (2625ft/sec)
Maximum range:	24,700m (27,010yds)

155mm Royal Ordnance Light Towed Howitzer

The 155mm (6.10in) Royal Ordnance Light Towed Howitzer has been developed primarily to fill a US Army demand for a lightweight 155mm howitzer which can be helicopter-lifted without any loss of ballistic performance compared to the standard M114 model. The Royal Ordnance LTH began development in 1986, prototypes were fired in 1991, and it was accepted as a US service weapon in 1998. The design uses titanium, carbon fibre and similar modern lightweight materials in order to save weight and the result is some 58 percent lighter than a conventional howitzer with no sacrifice of stability or power. Design studies have been completed on five variant models, with barrels ranging from 23 to 51 calibres long, but the accepted standard is a 39-calibre weapon.

Country of origin:	United Kingdom
Calibre:	155mm (6.10in)
Weight in action:	3810kg (8400lb)
Gun length:	39 calibre: 6.045m (19.83ft)
Elevation:	-5° to +70°
Traverse:	45°
Shell type & weight:	HE; 42.91kg (94.6lb)
Muzzle velocity:	not disclosed
Maximum range:	24,000m (26,685yds)

155mm Howitzer Mle 1950

The 155mm (6.10in) French Howitzer Mle 1950 was developed in the late 1940s and was one of the first post-war artillery designs to appear. It was also adopted by Sweden, Israel , Syria, the Lebanon and Switzerland at various times and remained in service in some of these countries well into the 1990s. It was a conventional weapon on a split trail carriage with a four-wheeled bogie beneath the gun, and a firing pedestal beneath the axles which is lowered to provide three-point support with the two trail ends. The barrel has a slotted muzzle brake and is supported by two hydro-pneumatic balancing presses attached to the cradle. The recoil system is split into individual cylinders and arranged around the barrel for maximum cooling effect.

Country of origin:	France
Calibre:	155mm (6.10in)
Weight in action:	8100kg (7.97 tons)
Gun length:	22 calibre: 3.41m (11.18ft)
Elevation:	-4° to +69°
Traverse:	80°
Shell type & weight:	HE; 43.0kg (94.8lb)
Muzzle velocity:	650m/sec (2133ft)
Maximum range:	18,000m (19,685yds)

Field and Heavy Artillery

22.5cm Heavy Trench Mortar

The 22.5cm (8.86in) Heavy Trench Mortar was an early and fairly primitive pattern of smooth-bore trench mortar developed by Austria, using a fixed baseplate with two elevating screws. The picture above shows the equipment loaded on to its transporting trailer, from which it slid into its firing emplacement quite easily. There was no form of recoil control, the tube driving down on to the baseplate, which could easily become embedded, and there was no traverse of the barrel on its mounting, the whole thing being shifted by means of levers. The projectile was simply a cylinder of gas or high explosive, with no driving band or tail unit, and used a time fuse.

Country of origin:	Austria
Calibre:	225mm (8.86 in)
Weight in action:	432kg (952lb)
Gun length:	6 calibre: 1.35m (53.1in)
Elevation:	+25° to +75° degrees
Traverse:	nil
Shell type & weight:	HE and gas; 48.01kg (105.8lb)
Muzzle velocity:	170m/sec (557ft/sec)
Maximum range:	1555m (1700yds)

7.2in Howitzers Marks 1 to 4

Between the wars, the Royal Air Force had claimed that their bombing ability rendered long range artillery superfluous, and consequently the design of heavy guns had been neglected. When war came the RAF did not have the equipment or ability to assist the field army, so heavy guns had to be hurriedly assembled. These four models of a 182.9mm (7.2in) howitzer were actually World War I 203mm (8in) weapons, re-barrelled to fire a more modern shell further; the difference between the Marks 1,2,3 and 4 being simply a matter of which Mark of howitzer had been converted. They all had identical barrels and performances. Although somewhat primitive in design, and with a recoil system which was not up to its work, they served until a better model could be developed.

Country of origin:	United Kingdom
Calibre:	182.9mm (7.20in)
Weight in action:	10,323kg (10.18 tons)
Gun length:	22.4 calibre: 4.09m (13.41ft)
Elevation:	-10° to +45°
Traverse:	8°
Shell type &weight:	HE; 90.72kg (200lb)
Muzzle velocity:	518m/sec (1700ft/sec)
Maximum range:	15,450m (16,900yds)

Field and Heavy Artillery

194mm Gun GPF

GPF stands for 'Grand Puissance, Filloux', or 'gun of great power'. This one was designed by Colonel Filloux, and is one of a number of heavy guns he designed for the French Army during World War I. Developed in 1917, this was simply a heavier barrel fitted to the carriage of the existing 155mm (6.1in) GPF which Filloux had designed. In broad terms, the 194mm (7.63in) weapon had about twice the shell-power of the 155mm gun, when weight of shell, explosive content and range were all taken into consideration. Transportation was in two units, the barrel being removed from the carriage and placed on a special transport wagon. The towing tractor was provided with a winch which was used to transfer the barrel from the wagon and on to the carriage, or vice versa. They remained in service until 1940.

Country of origin:	France
Calibre:	194mm (7.63in)
Weight in action:	15,600kg (15.35 tons)
Gun length:	42.2 calibre: 6.57m (21.55ft)
Elevation:	0° to 35°
Traverse:	55°
Shell type &weight:	HE; 80.86kg (178.2lb)
Muzzle velocity:	640m/sec (2100ft/sec
Maximum range:	18,300m (20,010yds)

BL 8in Howitzer Mark 7

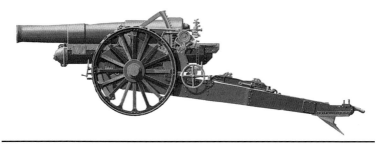

Britain entered World War I with just a handful of heavy guns, and provision of more was a priority. Since machinery for making 203mm (8in) guns existed, manufacture of the guns was quickly organised and basic carriages designed. These were heavy, had box trails and large wheels, and as the recoil systems were not perfect, huge ramps were placed behind the wheels. On firing, the whole weapon ran back and up the ramps, absorbing much of the recoil force, and then ran back down ready to reload and fire again. If the ramps were not exactly positioned, it ran up and jumped over the end. The Mark 7 was a perfected design developed in 1916; it had greater range and better recoil system, but it still used ramps. Many were converted into 182.9mm (7.2in) models in World War II.

Country of origin:	United Kingdom
Calibre:	203mm (8.0in)
Weight in action:	8890kg (8.75 tons)
Gun length:	18.5 calibre: 3.76m (12.33ft)
Elevation:	0° to +45°
Traverse:	8°
Shell type &weight:	HE; 90.72kg (200lb)
Muzzle velocity:	457m/sec (2460ft/sec)
Maximum range:	11,250m (12,305yds)

8in Howitzer M1

During World War I the US Army had no heavy artillery and so acquired numbers of British 203mm (8in) howitzers. Between the wars they developed this design which could fit on the same carriage as the 155mm (6.1in) Gun M22. It was a split-trail carriage with an eight-wheel bogie under the gun, the wheels being raised from the ground to settle the carriage down for firing. Changing barrels also meant adjusting the traversing mechanism, the recoil system and the balancing presses, and was not something done in the field, but it made great economic sense to have one design shared by two pieces. It had a reputation for accuracy, and was in service after 1945, largely because it had a nuclear shell. Although now given up by the US Army, it is still used by many other nations, but without the nuclear shell.

Country of origin:	USA
Calibre:	203mm (8.0in)
Weight in action:	14,380kg (14.15 tons)
Gun length:	25 calibre: 5.08m (16.66ft)
Elevation:	-2° to +65°
Traverse:	60°
Shell type &weight:	HE; 90.72kg (200lb)
Muzzle velocity:	595m/sec (1952ft/sec)
Maximum range:	16,925m (18,510yds)

203mm Howitzer M1931 (L/25)

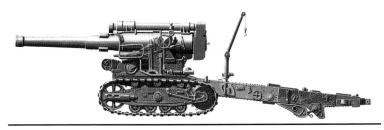

During World War II the Russians did not waste any time in the manufacture of super-heavy artillery; they had an effective ground attack aircraft, the Stormovik, which was directly under army control just as the Stuka dive-bomber was in the German Army, and this acted as the heavy artillery. The heaviest gun put into the field was this 203mm (8in) Howitzer M1931 (L/25), and one suspects that had it not already existed, it would not have been built during the war. There were a number of versions of this weapon, but the most common was this model on the tracked carriage. When inspected closely, it can be seen that this carriage has been derived directly from an agricultural tractor design, and was ideal for floating such a heavy gun across the snow and mud of the Russian winter and spring.

Country of origin:	USSR
Calibre:	203mm (8.0in)
Weight in action:	17,700kg (17.42 tons)
Gun length:	25 calibre: 5.07m (16.63ft)
Elevation:	0° to +60°
Traverse:	8°
Shell type &weight:	HE; 100kg (220lb)
Muzzle velocity:	607m/sec (1990ft/sec)
Maximum range:	18,025m (19,710yds)

Field and Heavy Artillery

21cm Howitzer

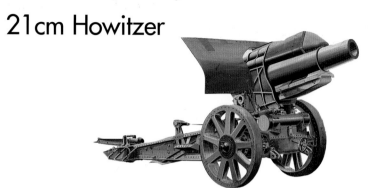

A Krupp design introduced in 1916, this weapon was known as the 'Long 21cm Mortar' and survived to serve again during World War II. In its original form, it was moved in two loads by two horse teams and assembled on the firing site. It was later modified so that it could be towed in a single unit by a tractor; this involved removing the steel wheels and replacing them with rubber-tyred disc wheels, and making a two-wheeled limber to carry the trail end. It originally had a shield, but this was removed from the modified version. Having been designed as siege artillery, it was provided with a special concrete-piercing shell as well as the usual high explosive shell.

Country of origin:	Germany
Calibre:	211mm (8.31in)
Weight in action:	6680kg (6.57 tons)
Gun length:	11 calibre: 2296m (7.53ft)
Elevation:	-6° to +70°
Traverse:	4°
Shell type &weight:	HE; 113.0kg (245lb)
Muzzle velocity:	393m/sec (1290ft/sec)
Maximum range:	11,100m (12,140yds)

Obice da 210/22

The Obice da 210/22 was a modern design accepted for service with the Italian Army in 1938. A total of 346 were ordered, but no more than about 20 had been made by 1942, and after Italy surrendered, those guns which could be seized were taken by the Germans. The factory in northern Italy then continued to make them for the rest of the war for German service, where they were known as the 21cm (8.31in) Haubitze 520(i). The carriage was a split trail with four wheels, raised from the ground for firing, and the gun was trunnioned close under the breech in order to allow the maximum length of recoil at maximum elevation without fear of striking the ground.

Country of origin:	Italy
Calibre:	210mm (8.31in)
Weight in action:	15,885kg (15.63 tons)
Gun length:	23.8 calibre: 5m (16.4ft)
Elevation:	0° to +70°
Traverse:	775°
Shell type &weight:	HE; 101.0kg (222.6lb)
Muzzle velocity:	560m/sec (1837ft/sec)
Maximum range:	15,400m (16,840yds)

Field and Heavy Artillery

21cm Mrs 18

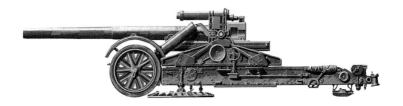

Designed by Krupp to replace the Long 21cm Mortar, and issued in 1936, this proved to be a vast improvement. This shared the same carriage with the 17cm (6.79in) gun 18 but was moved in two pieces, the barrel on a special trailer and the carriage on its own wheels with a limber. The equipment introduced the idea of the dual recoil system; the barrel recoiled in a cradle on the top carriage in the usual manner, but the top carriage also recoiled along the main carriage, sliding back and controlled by hydro-pneumatic cylinders. As a result, the gun was very steady in firing and very accurate. In addition to the conventional high explosive shell, this howitzer had a rocket-assisted shell and a concrete-piercing shell provided for special tasks.

Country of origin:	Germany
Calibre:	210mm (8.31in)
Weight in action:	16,700kg (16.43 tons)
Gun length:	29 calibre: 6.07m (19.91ft)
Elevation:	0° to +70°
Traverse:	16°
Shell type & weight:	HE; 113.0kg (250lb)
Muzzle velocity:	565m/sec (1854ft/sec)
Maximum range:	16,700m (18,265yds)

The Paris Gun

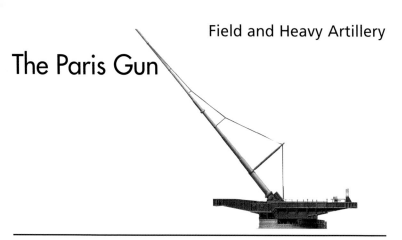

Properly called the 'Kaiser Wilhelm Geschutz', this was a 21cm (8.26in) calibre gun developed by Krupp to bombard Paris from a position within the German lines; it eventually fired from a distance of 75 miles. The gun was based on a 38cm (14.9in) railway gun mounting, with a long liner inserted into the barrel and a smoothbore extension on the end, all anchored to a concrete platform. The propelling charge weighed 150kg (330lb), and the shell went into the stratosphere, reaching a height of 40 km (43,744yds) before returning to earth. The barrel lasted for 65 shots, increasing in calibre with every shot; the shells were made in varying sizes from 21cm (8.31in) to 23cm (9.05in) in calibre and had to be fired in the correct order. A total of 320 shots were fired, of which 180 landed on Paris.

Country of origin:	Germany
Calibre:	210mm (8.26in)
Weight in action:	750,000kg (738 tons)
Gun length:	176 calibre: 37.0m (121.4ft)
Elevation:	0° to +55°
Traverse:	360°
Shell type &weight:	HE; 119.70kg (264lb)
Muzzle velocity:	2000m/sec (6560ft/sec)
Maximum range:	122,000m (75.8 miles)

240mm Howitzer M1

The US Army ordered a 240mm (9.45in) howitzer from a French designer in 1918, but it turned out to be an expensive mistake and eventually it was decided to scrap it and start afresh. Lack of money prevented any action until 1923, whereupon this M1 design was drawn up. The carriage was a massive split trail which was taken into action on a special transport trailer. The barrel also travelled on its own trailer, and a 20-ton Lorain mobile crane was attached to each gun battery to dig the gunpit and assemble the gun. If the crane defaulted, the pit could be dug by hand and the gun assembled by the winches on the tractors. It remained in service with the US and British armies until the wartime ammunition supply ran out in the 1960s.

Country of origin:	USA
Calibre:	240mm (9.45in)
Weight in action:	23,030kg (22.66 tons)
Gun length:	35 calibre: 8.407m (27.58ft)
Elevation:	+15° to +65°
Traverse:	45°
Shell type &weight:	HE; 163.3kg (360lb)
Muzzle velocity:	700m/sec (2286ft/sec)
Maximum range:	23,065m (25,225yds)

Canon de 240 L Model 1884

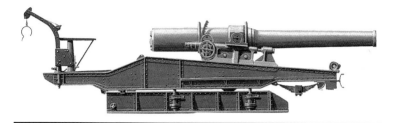

This French weapon originated as a coastal defence gun, but in late 1914 when heavy artillery was desperately needed, many were withdrawn from fortresses and the St Chamond company built a suitable field carriage which allowed the gun and carriage to be towed by tractors in two loads and assembled by winches. The conversion was so successful that St Chamond were then ordered to build another 60 new weapons, plus 60 spare barrels. It was considered to be the most powerful field artillery piece which could be deployed without the need for railway lines. Numbers of these guns survived the war and, as the Canon de 240 Mle 84/17, were deployed in 1939. Few saw action during the 1940 campaign, and they were all taken over by the Germans as the Kanone 564(f) and used for coastal defence.

Country of origin:	France
Calibre:	240mm (9.45in)
Weight in action:	31,000kg (30.5 tons)
Gun length:	26 calibre: 6.70m (21.96ft)
Elevation:	0° to +38°
Traverse:	10°
Shell type &weight:	HE; 140 kg (308lb)
Muzzle velocity:	575m/sec (1886ft/sec)
Maximum range:	17,300m (18,920yds)

24.5cm Heavy Trench Mortar

The Austrian 24.5cm (9.64in) Heavy Trench Mortar generally resembles the German 17cm (6.79in) 'Minenwerfer' trench mortar in being a somewhat elegant design with a hydro-spring recoil system. It was muzzle-loaded, the cartridge, in a cotton bag, being inserted first, then the shell, with pre-engraved driving band, was inserted so that the band engaged with the grooves. A friction primer was inserted into the breech end and the weapon elevated and fired. The interaction between the pre-cut driving band and the rifling grooves gave the shell spin, though at very high angles there was a high probability it would fail to turn over and would descend tail first.

Country of origin:	Austria
Calibre:	245mm (9.64in)
Weight in action:	6187 kg (1362lb)
Gun length:	5 calibre: 1.224m (48.20in)
Elevation:	+30° to +85°
Traverse:	nil
Shell type & weight:	HE or gas; 61.0kg (134.5lb)
Muzzle velocity:	152m/sec (500ft/sec)
Maximum range:	878m (960yds)

St Chamond Mortier de 280 sur Chenilles

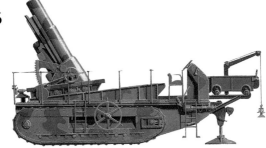

The French considered the tank to be nothing but a gun carrier, and thus began looking at ways of mounting even heavier guns on tracks. This design was quite revolutionary – the gun carriage had electric motors driving the two tracks. The current was supplied from another vehicle, similar to the gun carriage but without a gun, and was provided with a petrol engine driving an electric generator. This hooked on to the gun carriage, a cable was plugged in, and the tractor fed electric current to its own tracks and to those of the gun carriage. All the driver of the gun carriage had to do was steer. A number of these guns were made and used in 1918, though reports of their activities are scarce. A number also carried the 194mm (7.6in) GPF gun; they were last seen being used by the Germans in Russia in 1943.

Country of origin:	France
Calibre:	279.4mm (11.0in)
Weight in action:	28 tonnes (27.5 tons) with tractor
Gun length:	12 calibre: 3.353m (11ft)
Elevation:	0° to + 60°
Traverse:	20°
Shell type & weight:	HE; 203kg (447.5lb)
Muzzle velocity:	315m/sec (1033ft/sec)
Maximum range:	10,900m (11,920 yds)

Field and Heavy Artillery

28cm Kustenhaubitze

This was developed by Germany in the 1890s, when the use of howitzers for coastal defence was popular. The gun could lob a piercing shell high into the air and drop it on to the thinner deck of a warship instead of having to batter its way through the much thicker side armour. The drawback was the lack of accuracy compared with direct fire, but by massing howitzers in groups of eight or more and firing them all at once, the chances of a hit were improved. However, they went out of favour as warships began using longer-ranging guns and could stay out of reach of the howitzers and shell the shore with impunity. Some howitzer batteries were retained into the 1940s, for use where an enemy was constrained by natural features – an estuary or channel – to sail close to land, before finally being scrapped.

Country of origin:	Germany
Calibre:	280mm (11.02in)
Weight in action:	37,000kg (36.4tons)
Gun length:	12 calibre: 3.396m (11.14ft)
Elevation:	0° to +70°
Traverse:	360°
Shell type &weight:	HE; 350 kg (772lb)
Muzzle velocity:	379m/sec (1243ft/sec)
Maximum range:	11,400m (12,465yds)

Skoda 305mm Howitzer

If the 42cm (16.53in) Krupp howitzer of 1914 was 'Big Bertha', then this Skoda howitzer. also used in 1914, was 'Schlanke (slender) Emma'. Very similar in concept, it moved in three loads towed behind a motor tractor. Two went to Germany in 1914 to assist in demolishing the Liege forts in Belgium, but they soon went back east and spent most of the war battering various Russian fortresses and defending positions. Skoda had approached the problem from a different direction to Krupp, and had begun by making a useful 28cm (11in) howitzer which the army called 'Gretel'. This was then scaled-up by degrees until the optimum size was found at 30.5cm (12in) calibre. A slightly more portable model was developed in 1916 and used against Italy, as it was able to lob shells across the mountainous terrain.

Country of origin:	Austro-Hungary
Calibre:	305mm (12.0in)
Weight in action:	20,000kg (19.68 tons)
Gun length:	14 calibre: 4.26m (13.97ft)
Elevation:	+40° to +70°
Traverse:	120°
Shell type &weight:	HE; 380kg (838lb)
Muzzle velocity:	340m/sec (1115ft/sec)
Maximum range:	12,000m (13,125yds)

305mm Howitzer 305/17 Mod 17

This Italian heavy gun was originally a coastal defence weapon, but with some changes in the mounting to allow it to be moved in pieces and assembled on site by winches and ramps, it was converted into a super-heavy field piece and used to bombard Austrian defences in the Alps. It was moved in sections – gun, recoil system and cradle, top carriage, platform – and took a day to assemble. The base was a heavy steel ground platform; on to this went the top carriage, with a system of adjustable pivots and stops which allowed a traverse of 360°. The ring cradle, carrying the hydro-pneumatic recoil cylinders, was fitted to the carriage, and the gun tube slid into the cradle and bolted to the recoil pistons. Dismantling took the same time, so once the war entered a more mobile phase, this gun was left behind.

Country of origin:	Italy
Calibre:	305mm (12.0in)
Weight in action:	33,770kg (33.23 tons)
Gun length:	17 calibre: 5.181m (17ft)
Elevation:	-20° to + 65°
Traverse:	360°
Shell type & weight:	HE; 442kg (975lb)
Muzzle velocity:	540m/sec (1772ft/sec)
Maximum range:	17,600m (19,245 yds)

16in M1919 Coast Gun

As part of their wartime plans, the US Navy began the manufacture of 406.4mm (16in) guns for the battleships they intended to build. The Washington Conference on Naval Limitation of 1921 put an end to these plans, leaving the sailors with a number of surplus guns. They were offered to the US Army as coastal defence guns and were readily accepted; unfortunately they had little money for the manufacture of mountings, and installing these guns was a slow business, though by 1939 they were commanding the approaches to Pearl Harbor, San Francisco and New York. More were erected during the war, covering such places as Boston, San Diego and New Orleans. All coastal defences were scrapped in the late 1940s, and only one of these guns now exists, at Aberdeen Proving Ground near Baltimore.

Country of origin:	USA
Calibre:	406.4mm (16.0in)
Weight in action:	491,768kg (484 tons)
Gun length:	50 calibre: 20.32m (66.66ft)
Elevation:	-7° to +65°
Traverse:	360°
Shell type &weight:	HE; 1,061kg (2340lb)
Muzzle velocity:	822m/sec (2700ft/sec)
Maximum range:	44,935m (27.9 miles)

Big Bertha

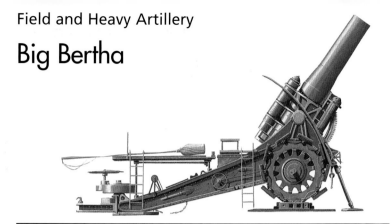

In 1906 Krupp built a 42cm (16.53in) howitzer for coastal defence; he then built a portable version and offered it to the Army. They were impressed, but it was too heavy; if it was lighter, they would be interested. Krupp re-designed the weapon, made it lighter, and made it transportable in five sections, each pulled by a Daimler-Benz tractor. These weapons saw their first action against the fortress of Liege in August 1914, and in four days the fortress surrendered. They went on to bombard other fortifications in Belgium and France, then to the Eastern Front to attack Przemysl and Brest-Litovsk. They had their last outing in the battle of Verdun in 1916, which finally wore them out. By that time their range was too short for them to be worth putting back into production, and they were scrapped.

Country of origin:	Germany
Calibre:	420mm (16.53in)
Weight in action:	43,285kg (42.6 tons)
Gun length:	14 calibre: 5.88m (19.3ft)
Elevation:	+40° to +75°
Traverse:	4°
Shell type &weight:	HE; 820kg (1807lb)
Muzzle velocity:	425 m/sec (1394ft/sec)
Maximum range:	9375m (10,252yds)

914mm Mortar 'Little David'

Testing aerial bombs for penetration is best done by firing them out of a specially built gun, so that you know where the bomb is going to go; dropping them is a chancy business. The US Army had such a gun for bomb-testing during World War II and it occurred to somebody that it would make an excellent siege mortar for hammering the Japanese defences expected when Japan was invaded. 'Little David' was the result, a muzzle loading mortar firing a huge demolition bomb. The mounting was no more than a big steel box dug into the ground, and the barrel was lowered, the cartridge put in, the shell fitted into the rifling, and the barrel then elevated so that they slipped down into place. The war ended before it could be perfected, and no more than the one trial model was ever built.

Country of origin:	USA
Calibre:	914mm (36.0in)
Weight in action:	82,808kg (81.5 tons)
Gun length:	32 calibre: 5.18m (17ft)
Elevation:	+45° to +65°
Traverse:	26°
Shell type &weight:	HE; 1678.0 kg (3700lb)
Muzzle velocity:	not known
Maximum range:	8700m (9515yds)

TCM-20

Broadly speaking, the TCM-20 is simply a modern version of the American wartime trailer-mounted two 12.7mm (0.5in) Browning machine gun equipment, updated by fitting two 20mm (0.78in) Hispano-Suiza HS404 cannons in place of the machine guns and overhauling the construction of the mounting. It has proved to be a very versatile and efficient weapon, with a record of success in various Middle Eastern conflicts, and has been widely sold on the export market as well as equipping the Israeli Defence Force. The two guns are mounted on a pedestal, with an armour shield. Elevation and traverse are powered by electric motors, driven by batteries which are kept charged by a built-in power unit.

Country of origin:	Israel
Calibre:	20mm (0.78in)
Weight in action:	1350kg (2976lb)
Gun length:	1.702m (67in)
Elevation:	-10° to + 90°
Traverse:	360°
Shell type & weight:	HE/I; 122g (4.30oz)
Muzzle velocity:	844m/sec (2770ft/sec)
Effective ceiling:	2000m (6560ft)

20mm Tarasque

One of a large number of designs adopted by the French Army, the 20mm (0.78in) Tarasque is a single gun power-driven unit mounting the F1 20mm cannon; although primarily intended for air defence, it can also be used successfully for ground firing roles. Towed on a two-wheeled trailer, it can be brought into action within 20 seconds. Elevation and traverse are powered by hydraulic motors, the pressure being produced by an auxiliary power unit driving a pump. The gun can, of course, be operated manually should the power supply fail. Other features include optical sights for aerial firing and also a telescope sight for direct shooting in the ground role.

Country of origin:	France
Calibre:	20mm (0.78in)
Weight in action:	650kg (1433lb)
Gun length:	2.065m (81.25in)
Elevation:	-8° to + 83°
Traverse:	360°
Shell type & weight:	HE/I; 125g (4.40oz)
Muzzle velocity:	1050m/sec (3445ft/sec)
Effective ceiling:	2000m (6560ft)

Air Defence Artillery

M167 Vulcan

The M167 Vulcan, a low-level air defence system, was developed in the early 1960s and remained in continuous service until the mid-1990s. It consisted of a 20mm (0.78in) six-barrel M168 Gatling-type cannon, capable of firing at 1000 or 3000 rounds per minute, mounted on a trailer which had three stabilising legs which could be lowered and the gun brought into action very rapidly. The unit is completely autonomous, having its own radar, fire control computer and sights, although it could also receive data from outside radars and predictors. In addition to the towed version, a self-propelled version mounted on a M113 armoured personnel carrier was also produced in significant numbers.

Country of origin:	USA
Calibre:	20mm (0.78in)
Weight in action:	1569kg (3458lb)
Gun length:	1.524m (60.0in)
Elevation:	-5° to + 80°
Traverse:	360°
Shell type & weight:	HE/I; 103g (3.63oz)
Muzzle velocity:	1030m/sec (3380ft/sec)
Effective ceiling:	1200m (3935ft)

Rheinmetall Rh202

This standard German Army air defence weapon consists of two Rheinmetall Rh202 20mm (0.78in) automatic cannons positioned on to a power-driven mounting which is carried on a two-wheeled trailer. The mounting can be removed from the trailer and then sits on three outrigger legs, providing a very stable platform. There is an NSU-Wankel engine which produces the necessary electrical power for elevation, traverse and the fire control computing sight. The Rh202 was also bought by Portugal, Greece, Indonesia and Argentina, who used it to defend Port Stanley airfield in the Falklands war. The cannon is the standard weapon of its class in German service – it also equips the Marder, Luchs and Wiesel AFVs.

Country of origin:	Germany
Calibre:	20mm (0.78in)
Weight in action:	1650kg (3637lb)
Gun length:	2.61m (102.75in)
Elevation:	-5.5° to + 83.5°
Traverse:	360°
Shell type & weight:	HE/L; 120g (4.23oz)
Muzzle velocity:	1050m/sec (3445ft/sec)
Effective ceiling:	2000m (6560ft)

Air Defence Artillery

Oerlikon GAI-B01

The GAI-B01 is a simple single-gun air defence weapon which mounts an Oerlikon KAB 20mm (0.78in) cannon on to a mounting rotating above a three-legged platform. There is no power assistance; elevation is created by means of a handwheel and traverse is simply achieved by the action of the gunner pushing on the ground with his feet. The gun and cradle are counter-balanced so that elevation is made relatively easy, and there is a mechanical computing sight for aerial firing and a telescope for direct ground firing. The entire unit is multi-functional as it can be carried on a trailer, or loaded into a truck, or it can be bolted down into the cargo bed to provide a simple SP equipment. The Oerlikon GAI-B01 is in wide use throughout the world.

Country of origin:	Switzerland
Calibre:	20mm (0.78in)
Weight in action:	405kg (892lb)
Gun length:	2.40m (94.48in)
Elevation:	-5° to + 85°
Traverse:	360°
Shell type & weight:	HE/I; 125g (4.40 oz)
Muzzle velocity:	1100m/sec (3608ft/sec)
Effective ceiling:	1500m (4920ft)

20mm Flak 30

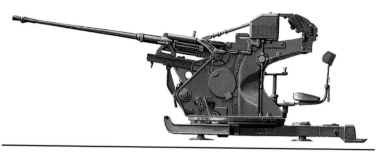

The 20mm (0.78in) Flak 30 was designed by Rheinmetall and went into production for the German Navy in 1934; it was then given a wheeled trailer and adopted by the German Army. The gun was recoil operated and magazine fed. The trailer had a horse-shoe frame with two wheels, into which the mounting fitted, held by two lugs and a locking pin. It only took a few seconds to withdraw the pin and tip the trailer so that the lugs were freed, and the mounting then slid to the ground. The sight was a mechanical computing sight of high quality and great accuracy. The 20mm Flak 30 remained in use throughout World War II, even though more modern equipment was subsequently adopted.

Country of origin:	Germany
Calibre:	20mm (0.78in)
Weight in action:	450kg (992lb)
Gun length:	2.30m (90.55in)
Elevation:	-12° to +90°
Traverse:	360°
Shell type & weight:	HE/I; 120g (4.2oz)
Muzzle velocity:	900m/sec (2952ft/sec)
Effective ceiling:	2000m (6560ft)

20mm Flakvierling 38

After using the 20mm (0.78in) Flak 30 in Spain, the Germans felt that a greater rate of fire would be a distinct advantage, as it would ensure more shells in the sky during the brief course of an engagement. Mauser were asked to improve the gun, which they did effectively, boosting the rate of fire from 280 to 420 rounds per minute. After that success, it seemed a good idea to try two guns, and finally a four-gun mounting, capable of putting 1680 shells into the air per minute, was adopted. A trailer was used to transport the gun, and in an emergency it could be fired from the trailer, but a firm platform on the ground was preferred for accuracy. An electric computing sight was originally used, but this was generally replaced by a simpler sight during the war.

Country of origin:	Germany
Calibre:	20mm (0.78in)
Weight in action:	1520kg (3352lb)
Gun length:	2.252m (88.6in)
Elevation:	-10° to +90°
Traverse:	360°
Shell type & weight:	HE/I; 120g (4.20oz)
Muzzle velocity:	900m/sec (2952ft/sec)
Effective ceiling:	2000m (6560ft)

20mm Breda Model 35

The Italian Army adopted the 20mm (0.78in) Breda Model 35 in 1935 as a dual-function weapon, capable of aerial or ground firing. The gun was, in fact, simply a Breda machine gun enlarged to take a 20mm cartridge. However, it retained one of the unique features of Breda guns – the ammunition was fed into the side on a metal strip and, after firing, the gun carefully replaced the empty case in the strip as it came out of the other side. The mounting was also somewhat complicated, being a three-legged platform carried on a two-wheeled trailer but with a counter-balance system and parallelogram sights to allow the gunner to stand behind the mounting instead of crouching down.

Country of origin:	Italy
Calibre:	20mm (0.78in)
Weight in action:	307kg (676lb)
Gun length:	1.30m (51.2in)
Elevation:	-10° to +80°
Traverse:	360°
Shell type & weight:	HE; 135g (4.7oz)
Muzzle velocity:	840m/sec (2755ft/sec)
Effective ceiling:	2500m (8200ft)

Oerlikon 20mm

The Oerlikon cannon originated in Germany in 1917 and was known as the Becker cannon; after the war, however, the patents were bought by the SEMAG company of Switzerland. In the early 1920s, the company went into liquidation and the Oerlikon Machine Tool company bought what equipment was left, including the gun design. They then improved upon the design by developing suitable mountings, and then began selling their gun all over the world. The weapon pictured is the wartime version, used by almost every combatant except Russia. It was a simple blow-back weapon which could be mounted in aircraft, tanks or on a ground mounting and fired at about 450 rounds per minute.

Country of origin:	Switzerland
Calibre:	20mm (0.78in)
Weight of gun:	66.75kg (147.15lb)
Gun length:	2.21m (87.0in)
Elevation:	-10° to +75°
Traverse:	360°
Shell type & weight:	HE; 120g (4.23oz)
Muzzle velocity:	830m/sec (2690ft/sec)
Effective ceiling:	1100m (3600ft)

Polsten 20mm

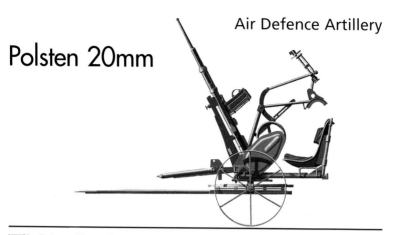

The Polsten 20mm (0.78in) originated in Poland as an attempt by Polish engineers to simplify the Oerlikon design by making it quicker, easier and cheaper to produce. They had just managed successfully to produce a prototype when the Germans invaded Poland in 1939. The prototype and drawings were smuggled out of the country and eventually ended up in Britain, together with some of the design team. They completed the work there and the gun went into production in Britain as an air defence weapon. It was easier to produce than the Oerlikon, only consisting of 119 components rather than the 250 of the original, and cheaper too, but no less effective. It was usually mounted on a three-gun trailer mount, although single gun mounts were also used.

Country of origin:	United Kingdom
Calibre:	20mm (0.78in)
Weight of gun:	54.9kg (121lb)
Gun length:	2.178m (86.75in)
Elevation:	0° to 90°
Traverse:	360°
Shell type & weight:	HE; 119g (4.19oz)
Muzzle velocity:	831m/sec (2725ft/sec)
Effective ceiling:	2200m (7200ft)

Air Defence Artillery

23mm ZU-23

Introduced into Russian service in the 1960s, the 23mm (0.9in) ZU-23 replaced the 14.5mm (0.57in) machine gun as their standard light air defence weapon, and entered service with many Soviet satellite states. The two-gun assembly is usually carried on a wheeled mount, the wheels of which can be folded to enable the platform to be powered to the ground in seconds, (as shown above). The guns are fed by belts from boxes on the outside of the mount, and sighting systems of different types, varying in complexity, can be found on production examples. In addition to this standard mount, the 23mm ZU-23 can be fitted into APCs or on to cargo trucks, and there is also a four-barrel version which fits on to a tank chassis.

Country of origin:	USSR
Calibre:	23mm (0.90in)
Weight in action:	950kg (2094lb)
Gun length:	2.01m (79.13in)
Elevation:	-10° to + 90°
Traverse:	360°
Shell type & weight:	HE/I; 190g (6.7oz)
Muzzle velocity:	970m/sec (3182ft/sec)
Effective ceiling:	2000m (6560ft)

Oerlikon GDF-001 35mm

The Oerlikon GDF-001 35mm (1.37in) is a medium air defence gun, among the best of its kind, and is in wide use throughout the world. The twin-gun assembly sits on a wheeled cruciform platform which can be brought into action within seconds, the wheels folding in order to release the platform. The gun is fed from an automatic loading system, kept topped up with clips of seven rounds by the crew. The sights are of the electronic computing type and the gun's muzzle velocity is constantly checked and correction applied to the computer as the gun wears. The gun can be provided with its own power generator or it can be cabled up to a central power supply. When deployed in company with the Sparrow missile, it forms the 'Skyguard' air defence system.

Country of origin:	Switzerland
Calibre:	35mm (1.37in)
Weight in action:	6400kg (6.30 tons)
Gun length:	3.15m (124in)
Elevation:	-5° to + 92°
Traverse:	360°
Shell type & weight:	HE/I; 550g (19.4oz)
Muzzle velocity:	1175m/sec (3855ft/sec)
Effective ceiling:	4000m (13,125ft)

Air Defence Artillery

37mm M1A2

The 37mm (1.45in) M1A2 was developed in the early 1920s by John M.Browning and the Colt company, Browning himself demonstrating the first gun in 1924. The gun was formally adopted by the US Army in 1927, but it was not until 1938 that the carriage was perfected and the whole equipment put into production, over 7200 eventually being made, seeing service in most theatres of war. It was fed by slips of ten rounds and fired at a rate of 120 rounds per minute. The mounting was a simple four-legged platform carried on four wheels, and the gun could be fired from the wheels if necessary. Although overshadowed by the later 40mm (1.57in) Bofors gun, the 37mm continued to be used throughout the war.

Country of origin:	USA
Calibre:	37mm (1.45in)
Weight in action:	2777kg (6124lb)
Gun length:	1.988m (78.3in)
Elevation:	-5° to +90°
Traverse:	360°
Shell type & weight:	HE; 595g (21oz)
Muzzle velocity:	792m/sec (2600ft/sec)
Effective ceiling:	3200m (10,500ft)

37mm Flak 37

The first 37mm (1.45in) Flak gun adopted by the German Army used a complicated and expensive four-wheeled carriage, and after some experience with it the Army demanded something simpler. The solution was a two-wheeled trailer unit similar to that used with the Flak 30, and this weapon entered service in 1936 as the 3.7cm Flak 36. It was provided with the Flakvisier 36 sight, a simple device, but then the Flakvisier 40 appeared, a clockwork-driven computing sight which worked out the necessary aim-off and displaced the crosswires in the sight automatically. This was a complex device and the mounting had to be altered in order to fit. Guns with this type of sight became known as the Flak 37. Relatively few were made because the gun was replaced by an improved model during the war.

Country of origin:	Germany
Calibre:	37mm (1.45in)
Weight in action:	1544kg (3404lb)
Gun length:	3.626m (142.76in)
Elevation:	-8° to +85°
Traverse:	360°
Shell type & weight:	HE; 635g (22.4oz)
Muzzle velocity:	820m/sec (2690ft/sec)
Effective ceiling:	2000m (6562ft)

37mm Flak 43

The German 37mm (1.45in) Flak 43 was the gun which eventually replaced the Flak 37. It had the body of the Flak 37 gun but with the addition of the gas-actuated mechanism from an aerial cannon, the MK103, instead of the original recoil-actuated mechanism. This device almost doubled the rate of fire. The mounting was also simplified, which subsequently brought the weight down. The clockwork sight was fitted, but in due course it was discovered that this could not cope with the increased speed of aircraft and a new, simpler sight had to be adopted. The gun was also used in a twin configuration, but mounted one above the other, not the usual side-by-side system.

Country of origin:	Germany
Calibre:	37mm (1.45in)
Weight in action:	1248kg (2752lb)
Gun length:	3.30m (129.9in)
Elevation:	-7.5° to +90°
Traverse:	360°
Shell type & weight:	HE; 635g (22.4oz)
Muzzle velocity:	820m/sec (2690ft/sec)
Effective ceiling:	4200m (13,780ft)

40mm Bofors L/60

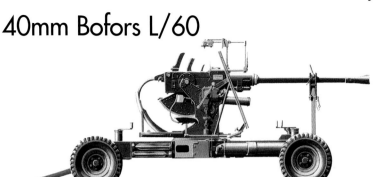

One of the most famous guns in history, the 40mm (1.57in) Bofors L/60 first appeared in 1929, but was slow to take off. However, sales began to pick up in the mid-1930s and by 1939 almost every country in Europe possessed some. The US adopted the gun in 1941 and it remained in production until the 1950s, when Bofors replaced it with the L/70 (described on page 110). The clip-loading and automatic fire were quite unique in a weapon of this size when it was introduced, but it soon built up a reputation for reliability and accuracy which it has never subsequently lost. As well as the field mounting pictured, it was also used on SP mountings and as a ship-board gun.

Country of origin:	Sweden
Calibre:	40mm (1.57in)
Weight in action:	1981kg (4568lb)
Gun length:	2.989m (117.7in)
Elevation:	-5° to +90°
Traverse:	360°
Shell type & weight:	HE; 907g (2.0lb)
Muzzle velocity:	823m/sec (2700ft/sec)
Effective ceiling:	1525m (5000ft)

Air Defence Artillery

40mm Bofors L/70

This weapon is the improved Bofors gun, introduced in the 1950s and rapidly adopted throughout the world. The main difference between this version and the original lies in the barrel – 70 calibres long instead of 60 calibres – and in the mechanism, which has been modified in order to double the rate of fire. It is chambered for a new round of ammunition with a bigger cartridge case and more powerful propelling charge, and the shells and fuses have also been improved. However, the gun is still fed by four-round clips. The carriage is similar to the earlier Bofors gun, but it is stronger and it carries a power unit to provide electro-hydraulic elevating and traversing for the gun, controlled by a joystick control column. There is also provision for handwheel operation should the power fail.

Country of origin:	Sweden
Calibre:	40mm (1.57in)
Weight in action:	5150kg (5.06 tons)
Gun length:	2.80m (110.2in)
Elevation:	-4° to + 90°
Traverse:	360°
Shell type & weight:	HE; 960g (2.11lb)
Muzzle velocity:	1005m/sec (3300ft/sec)
Effective ceiling:	3500m (11,500ft)

40mm Breda 40/L/70

This weapon is essentially the Bofors 40mm (1.57in) L/70 gun, but contained in a special mounting developed in Italy. This fully-shielded unit carries two guns and was first developed for the Italian Navy to counter both aircraft and surface-skimming missiles. It was then placed on a four-wheeled platform as a field weapon, the first customer being the Venezuelan Army. The platform has six stabilising outriggers, and the guns have been modified to accept ammunition from two magazines which are fed by four-round clips. The mounting is accompanied by a generator unit which provides electrical power, via a cable, for elevation and traverse and for the ammunition feed system.

Country of origin:	Italy
Calibre:	40mm (1.57in)
Weight in action:	10,400kg (10.2 tons)
Gun length:	2.80m (110.2in)
Elevation:	-5° to _90°
Traverse:	360°
Shell type & weight:	HE; 960g (2.11lb)
Muzzle velocity:	1005m/sec (3300ft/sec)
Effective ceiling:	3500m (11,500ft)

Air Defence Artillery

5cm Flak 41

In 1935 the Germans realised that there was a gap in the sky between the lowest engagement range of their 88mm (3.46in) guns and the highest range of the 37mm (1.45in) gun, and they asked Rheinmetall to plug it with this 50mm (1.98in) weapon. This design went into production in late 1940, but only 200 were built. The gun was a gas-operated automatic weapon, clip-fed like the Bofors gun, and the mounting was a four-wheeled cruciform. Although the design looked good, it proved to have several faults: it was too high and therefore difficult to conceal, it vibrated badly when firing and so was inaccurate, and the sight was complicated and a source of further errors. These factors were probably why only 200 were made.

Country of origin:	Germany
Calibre:	50mm (1.98in)
Weight in action:	3100kg (6838lb)
Gun length:	4.686m (184.49in)
Elevation:	-10° to +90°
Traverse:	360°
Shell type & weight:	HE; 2.25kg (4.85lb)
Muzzle velocity:	840m/sec (3756ft/sec)
Effective ceiling:	5600m (18,375ft)

75mm Bofors Model 29

Everybody knows the 40mm (1.57in) Bofors gun; not so many people know of the many other designs which Bofors produced, among them this conventional 75mm (2.96in) weapon which appeared at the same time as the 40mm gun. It achieved a good performance for its day and was bought by countries as far apart as Argentina and China. The gun is carried on a pedestal, which sits on a cruciform platform which was transported by attaching a two-wheeled limber to each end. An interesting footnote to history is that this weapon was designed when a number of Krupp engineers were working for Bofors, and several features of this gun appeared on the more famous German 88mm (3.46in) Flak 18 a few years later.

Country of origin:	Sweden
Calibre:	75mm (2.96in)
Weight in action:	4000kg (3.93 tons)
Gun length:	3.90m (12.75ft)
Elevation:	-5° to +85°
Traverse:	360°
Shell type & weight:	HE; 6.30kg (13.9lb)
Muzzle velocity:	840m/sec (2755ft/sec)
Effective ceiling:	8565m (28,000ft)

Air Defence Artillery

75mm Type 88

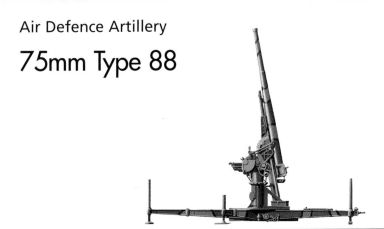

The 75mm (2.96in) Type 88 dates from 1928 and became the most widely-used Japanese air defence gun, both in the defence of Japan itself and with the field armies throughout the Pacific. It was an entirely conventional design of gun, mounted on a pedestal fixed to a five-legged platform, and its performance was no more than average for its class. Movement was created by attaching two wheels beneath the pedestal and folding the outriggers in order to make two extensions from the wheels, one acting as a towing connection and the other anchoring the rear end of the gun, which was elevated and pulled back in its cradle. From 1943 onwards the Type 88s were gradually concentrated on the home islands as the Allied aerial threat grew.

Country of origin:	Japan
Calibre:	75mm (2.96in)
Weight in action:	2442kg (5383lb)
Gun length:	3.315m (10.87ft)
Elevation:	0° to 85°
Traverse:	360°
Shell type & weight:	HE; 6.58kg (14.5lb)
Muzzle velocity:	720m/sec (2360ft/sec)
Effective ceiling:	7160m (23,500ft)

Ordnance QF 3in 20cwt

T he Ordnance QF 3in (76mm) 20cwt was the first British purpose-built anti-
aircraft gun, designed for naval service and introduced early in 1914. Its
peculiar title refers to the weight of the gun itself (20 hundredweight or one ton) as
a means of distinguishing it from the many other 76mm (3in) guns which equipped
the British Army and Navy in those days. The mounting was a rotating pedestal with
a base unit which could be bolted down on a ship's deck or a concrete
emplacement. When the need for mobile guns became apparent it was easily bolted
into a motor truck cargo bed, after which a four-outrigger platform was devised. It
remained in service during World War II, since it was lighter and more mobile than
the later 94mm (3.7in) gun, even though its performance was not as good.

Country of origin:	United Kingdom
Calibre:	76mm (3.0in)
Weight in action:	2721kg (6000lb)
Gun length:	3.556m (140.0in)
Elevation:	-10° to +90°
Traverse:	360°
Shell type & weight:	HE; 7.25kg (16.5lb)
Muzzle velocity:	610m/sec (2000ft/sec)
Effective ceiling:	4785m (15,700ft)

13pdr 9cwt AA Gun

One of the very first British field AA guns to be developed was the 13-pounder (76mm/3in) horse artillery gun on a high-angle mounting. When more power was subsequently required, the same mounting was tried with an 18-pdr (83.8mm/ 3.3in) horse artillery gun, but for various ballistic reasons it proved to be a failure. The correct solution, it appeared, was to re-line the 18pdr gun to 76mm (3in) calibre and fire the 13-pdr shell with the 18-pdr cartridge. This 13pdr 9cwt AA Gun was highly successful and thus became the most common British field AA gun of World War I. It was almost always mounted upon a motor truck, although ground platform carriages began to appear towards the end of the war. It remained in service for several years after the war in both Britain and Canada.

Country of origin:	United Kingdom
Calibre:	76mm (3.0in)
Weight in action:	7620kg (7.5 tons)
Gun length:	2.462m (96.96in)
Elevation:	0° to +80°
Traverse:	360°
Shell type & weight:	shrapnel; 5.89kg (13lb)
Muzzle velocity:	655m/sec (2150ft/sec)
Effective ceiling:	5790m (19,000ft)

3in M3

The 76mm (3in) M3 design was standardised in 1928, the gun having been originally a coastal defence weapon which then underwent considerable modernisation before finally being accepted. The mounting took even more time to create and was not approved until the early 1930s. The mount was always called the 'Spider Mount' because of the very long outrigger legs which folded up into three sections to rest on the carriage during travelling. The performance was average for its day, and after 1940 it was gradually replaced by the 90mm (3.54in) M1 gun. However, there were several still in service in the Pacific area in 1931 and they were put to use in the attack on Pearl Harbor. Thereafter, they were largely confined to use as training and practice guns.

Country of origin:	USA
Calibre:	76mm (3in)
Weight in action:	5534kg (12,200lb)
Gun length:	4.019m (158.23in)
Elevation:	-1° to +80°
Traverse:	360°
Shell type & weight:	HE; 5.84kg (12.87lb)
Muzzle velocity:	853m/sec (2800ft/sec)
Effective ceiling:	8500m (27,900ft)

77mm German 1914

In 1914, 77mm (3.03in) was the standard German field gun calibre and it therefore made sense to adopt it for their air defence gun. Germany had actually been the first country to build such guns, demonstrating several at an aviation show in 1909, and the '7.7cm Ballonkanone' was based upon those early designs. In addition to the specialist weapons, there were a number of improvised designs using the barrel and cradle of the 77mm field gun c/96 and various methods of reaching the necessary elevation. For their day, the performance of the 77mm German 1914 guns was quite good, but by the middle years of the war they were being replaced by more specialised weapons with much improved performance.

Country of origin:	Germany
Calibre:	77mm (3.03in)
Weight in action:	2500kg (5510lb)
Gun length:	2.075m (81.70in)
Elevation:	-5° to + 70°
Traverse:	360°
Shell type & weight:	shrapnel; 7.85kg (17.30lb)
Muzzle velocity:	485m/sec (1591ft/sec)
Effective ceiling:	3050m (10,000ft)

85mm M39

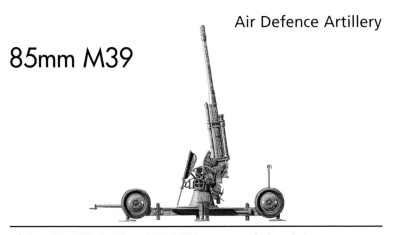

Adopted in 1939, the 85mm (3.34in) M39 was among the best designs ever to come out of Russia, and many were still in use into the 1970s. It was a very 'clean' design, with few excess frills, although this feature began to change when radar and power control began to appear in the 1940s. Like all Russian guns, it was provided with anti-tank ammunition, just in case a tank should appear within range, and this factor was of infinite value when the time came to find a better gun for the famous T-34 tank. The 85mm M39 was also successfully used in the SU-85 assault gun. Virtually every country in the Communist sphere of influence received this gun for their air defences during the 1950s.

Country of origin:	USSR
Calibre:	85mm (3.34in)
Weight in action:	3057kg (3.0 tons)
Gun length:	4.693m (15.35ft)
Elevation:	-2° to + 82°
Traverse:	360°
Shell type & weight:	HE; 9.2kg (20lb)
Muzzle velocity:	800m/sec (2625ft/sec)
Effective ceiling:	7620m (25,000ft)

Air Defence Artillery

88mm Flak 18

One of the most celebrated guns of World War II, the German 'eighty-eight' was adopted in 1933, having been designed by Krupp engineers working in the Bofors factory in Sweden. Its reputation stems from its use as an anti-tank gun; as an anti-aircraft gun it was average. Its superiority over Allied guns lay in numbers, not in performance. It appeared originally as the Flak 18 gun, a single-tube barrel on a pedestal, carried on a four-legged platform supported by two two-wheeled limbers for transport. A new three-piece barrel was introduced so that the worn section near the chamber could be easily replaced, and this became the Flak 36. An improved data transmission system from the predictor to the gun was adopted, and this became the Flak 37. The carriage and performance did not change between the three models.

Country of origin:	Germany
Calibre:	88mm (3.46in)
Weight in action:	4983kg (4.90 tons)
Gun length:	4.93m (16.17ft)
Elevation:	-3° to +85°
Traverse:	360°
Shell type & weight:	HE; 9.40kg (20.72lb)
Muzzle velocity:	820m/sec (2690ft/sec)
Effective ceiling:	8000m (26,245ft)

88mm Flak 41

The performance of the Flak 37, designed in the early 1930s, was falling behind the improving speed and height of other aircraft, and in 1939 the Luftwaffe (who were responsible for German air defences) issued a specification for a new gun. Accepted by Rheinmetall-Borsig, the Flak 41 was the result. Only the calibre remained; the gun, ammunition and mounting were all new. The gun was longer, with the barrel in sections; the cartridge case was larger and held a more powerful charge; and the carriage was new, using a turntable-mounted chassis to which the gun was attached behind the breech, so that the breech stayed the same height whatever elevation was applied to the gun. The turntable was on a four-legged platform. The result was a low-set gun which could be easily concealed, but it was rarely used in the anti-tank role.

Country of origin:	Germany
Calibre:	88mm (3.46in)
Weight in action:	7800kg (7.67 tons)
Gun length:	6.545m (21.47ft)
Elevation:	-3° to + 90°
Traverse:	360°
Shell type & weight:	HE; 9.40kg (20.73lb)
Muzzle velocity:	1000m/sec (3280ft/sec)
Effective ceiling:	10,675m (35,025ft)

Air Defence Artillery

90mm M1

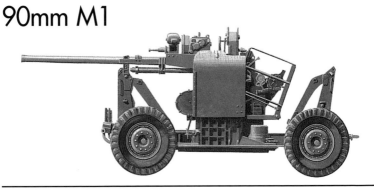

In 1938, the US Artillery Board realised that the 76mm (3in) M3 was falling behind, and requested a heavier gun firing a shell of at least 9.5kg (21lb) in weight. Calculations suggested that a 90mm (3.54in) gun firing a 10.9kg (24lb) shell would be suitable, and development was approved in June 1938. The gun and mounting were standardised as the M1 in March 1940. The trunnions were set behind the breech to give easier loading, and set on a two-wheeled cruciform carriage. In May 1941, the Mount M1A1 was standardised; it had remote power control – enabling electrical signals from the predictor to drive the gun in traverse and elevation – and also had a spring rammer fitted behind the breech to improve the rate of fire. Unfortunately the rammer was a failure and was usually removed by the gunners.

Country of origin:	USA
Calibre:	90mm (3.54in)
Weight in action:	8618kg (8.48 tons)
Gun length:	4.728m (15.51ft)
Elevation:	-0° +80°
Traverse:	360°
Shell type & weight:	HE; 10.61kg (23.4lb)
Muzzle velocity:	823m/sec (2700ft/sec)
Effective ceiling:	10,300m (33,800ft)

3.7in QF Gun Mk 1

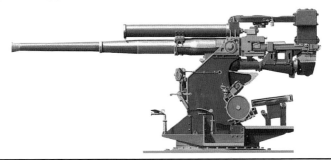

The standard British medium AA gun throughout World War II, this was designed by Vickers in the early 1930s and went into production in 1937. It was a very advanced weapon, with a complicated carriage which was designed at the outset for remote control and data transmission and was not originally provided with sights. (It was this factor which prevented it from being adopted for anti-tank shooting.) It was originally hand-loaded, but in 1943 the 'Machine Fuse Setting No 11' was introduced which took a round of ammunition, set the fuse, loaded and fired it, so boosting the rate of fire to 25 rounds per minute. Mobile and static mountings were built, the static having a large counterweight arm above the breech. By the end of the war, most guns had remote power control and all the gunners had to do was load it and clean it.

Country of origin:	United Kingdom
Calibre:	94mm (3.7in)
Weight in action:	9316kg (9.17 tons)
Gun length:	4.956m (16.26ft)
Elevation:	-5° to +80°
Traverse:	360°
Shell type & weight:	HE; 12.70kg (28.0lb)
Muzzle velocity:	792m/sec (2600ft/sec)
Effective ceiling:	9755m (32,000ft)

Air Defence Artillery

105mm Flak 38

E ven as the 88mm (3.46in) gun was being approved in 1933, the German Army realised that something heavier would be useful for the defence of Germany, and they issued a specification for a 105mm (4.13in) gun capable of reaching to a greater ceiling than the 88mm weapon. The result, after development and trials, was the 105mm Flak 38 from Rheinmetall, which entered service in 1937. It had electro-hydraulic remote power control, power loading and a compact four-legged platform. In 1939, the electric motors were built for alternating current instead of direct, so that they could be driven from the ordinary power supply, and with other changes this became the Flak 39. They were widely used in the defence of Germany; by 1944 there were 1025 mobile, 827 fixed and 116 railway-mounted guns in use.

Country of origin:	Germany
Calibre:	105mm (4.13in)
Weight in action:	10,224kg (10.06 tons)
Gun length:	6.648m (21.81ft)
Elevation:	-3° to +85°
Traverse:	360°
Shell type & weight:	HE; 14.80kg (32.63lb)
Muzzle velocity:	881m/sec (2891ft/sec)
Effective ceiling:	9450m (31,000ft)

Ordnance QF 4.5in Gun

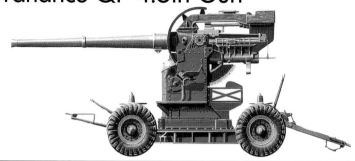

All through the 1920s and early 1930s, the British Army was asking for a heavy AA gun of 120mm (4.7in) calibre. However, once the Treasury had found the money for the 94mm (3.7in) gun, there seemed no possible chance of obtaining another one. Fortunately, the Royal Navy suggested that the Army might like to use one of their 114mm (4.5in) guns, because, as they pointed out, the principal place for these guns was around naval bases and dockyards so that ammunition supply from the Navy would be no problem. The deal was completed and the 4.5 inch went into Army service as a static mounted gun. As forecast, they were never seen outside naval areas or large cities, but the powerful shell and long reach were influential in defending those areas.

Country of origin:	United Kingdom
Calibre:	114mm (4.5in)
Weight in action:	14,965kg (14.73 tons)
Gun length:	5.086m (16.68ft)
Elevation:	0° to +80°
Traverse:	360°
Shell type & weight:	HE; 24.69kg (54.44lb)
Muzzle velocity:	732m/sec (2400ft/sec)
Effective ceiling:	10,521m (34,500ft)

12.8cm Flak 40

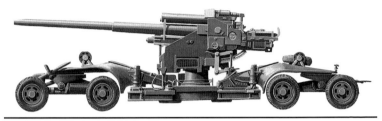

The largest gun used in World War II was this powerful weapon, first fired in 1937. There was nothing unconventional about the gun, it was more or less the Flak 38 enlarged. But transporting it posed problems; it was moved in two pieces, carriage and gun, but the Luftwaffe pointed out that anti-aircraft guns should be quick response weapons, and having to assemble the gun before firing it defeated the object. The Meiller company, trailer experts, devised a platform which could have wheels attached, so it could be towed in one piece. The result was cumbersome, but few were built anyway as the gun was principally used in static positions. It was also placed on a two-barrel mounting on flak towers in major German cities, and some were put on railway trucks for rapid movement in response to threats.

Country of origin:	Germany
Calibre:	128mm (5.03in)
Weight in action:	13,000kg (12.80 tons)
Gun length:	7.835m (25.7ft)
Elevation:	-3° to +88°
Traverse:	360°
Shell type & weight:	HE; 26.02kg (57.36lb)
Muzzle velocity:	880m/sec (2887ft/sec)
Effective ceiling:	10,675m (35,025ft)

7.92mm Panzerbuchse 39

Like several other anti-tank rifles of the period, this is of the same nominal calibre as the service rifle but the actual cartridge used a large case which had been developed for a 13mm (0.51in) weapon, so that there was plenty of powder to provide the desired velocity. The PzB39 was a single-shot weapon using a vertical sliding breech block which was opened by pressing forward and down on the pistol grip. A 'quick-loader' clip of five rounds could be attached to the right side of the action for rapid re-loading. The bullet contained a hardened steel core and a tiny capsule of tear gas; the intention was that the bullet would enter the tank and the tear gas would then disperse and force the occupants to leave. It didn't work; the core penetrated but the capsule was almost always left on the outside of the plate.

Country of origin:	Germany
Calibre:	7.92mm (0.311in)
Length:	1.58m (62.25in)
Weight:	12.36kg (27.25lb)
Barrel:	1.085m (42.75in) long; 4 grooves; right-hand twist
Muzzle velocity:	1212 m/sec (3975ft/sec)
Penetration:	25/300/60° (See glossary for explanation)

Granatbuchse 39

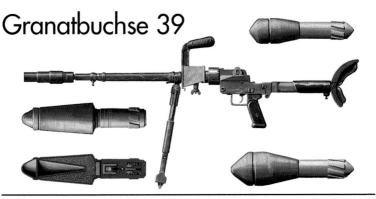

When the PzB39 anti-tank rifle (see page 127) was finally retired, somebody obviously thought that they were too good to scrap out of hand and, in late 1941, a conversion was carried out on a number of rifles. The barrel was shortened and the muzzle threaded to accept the standard pattern of rifle grenade discharger cup (the *Schiessbecher*), and special blank cartridges with wooden bullets were produced, thus turning the old anti-tank rifles into new grenade launchers. This saved wear and tear on the rest of the squad's rifles and gave German infantrymen a dedicated grenade-launcher which had a much better performance than firing the same grenades off the rifle.

Country of origin:	Germany
Calibre:	7.92mm (0.311in)
Length:	1.232m (48.50in)
Weight:	10.43kg (23lb)
Barrel:	612mm (24.13in) long; 4 grooves; right-hand twist
Effective range:	500m (1640ft)
Grenade types:	HE; shaped charge; parachute illuminating

.55in Boys Anti-tank Rifle

Development of this weapon, code-named 'Stanchion', was completed in 1936 and was due to enter production when Captain Boys, one of the designers, died. As a tribute, the Small Arms Committee decided that it should be named in his memory, and so it entered service in November 1937 as the 'Boys Rifle'. It was probably the best of its class at the time. Firing a steel-cored bullet at 990m/sec (3250ft/sec) it could penetrate 15mm (0.59in) tank armour at 229m (250yds). The recoil of the heavy cartridge was considerable, so the gun was fitted with a muzzle brake and allowed to recoil in a cradle mounting against a powerful buffer spring. A monopod acted as front support, and the butt was padded with rubber. It saw action in France, Norway and the Far East, but as tank armour became thicker, it was phased out.

Country of origin:	United Kingdom
Caliber:	13.9mm (0.55in)
Length:	1.612m (63.5in)
Weight:	16.32kg (36lb)
Barrel:	914mm (36in) long; 7 grooves; right hand twist
Feed:	5-round; top-mounted; detachable box magazine
Operation:	bolt action
Muzzle velocity:	990m/sec (3250ft/sec)
Penetration:	20/500/90°

PTRS 1941 Anti-tank Rifle

The PTRS rifle was developed at the same time as the PTRD by the designer Simonov. It was a very advanced weapon, using a top-mounted gas cylinder and piston to operate a bolt carrier. This jammed the bolt down to unlock it, then moved it back to extract and eject in the usual loading cycle. The magazine, front-hinged for cleaning like other Simonov designs, took 5 rounds loaded with a special clip which could only be loaded one way – not the best system for use in battle. Although a more advanced design than the PTRD, the PTRS was much less robust in use as well as being heavier and larger. Although retained in service until the late 1940s, it is believed that few were manufactured, the PTRD having the same performance (since it used the same ammunition) and being easier to use and produce.

Country of origin:	USSR
Caliber:	14.5mm (0.57in)
Length:	2.133m (84in)
Weight:	20.96kg (46lb)
Barrel:	1.219m (48in) long; 8 grooves; right hand twist
Feed:	5-round box magazine
Operation:	gas; semi-automatic; tipping bolt
Muzzle velocity:	1012m/sec (3320ft/sec)
Penetration:	25/500/90°

PTRD 1941 Anti-tank Rifle

This weapon was designed by Dogtyarev in 1932 and a new cartridge of 14.5mm (0.57in) calibre, one of the heaviest developed, was produced. The barrel recoils within a slide so that the recoil carries the bolt handle against a cam and lifts it to unlock the breech; the bolt is then held while the barrel moves back to its firing position, during which the empty case is extracted and ejected. The firer then inserts a fresh cartridge and closes the bolt by hand. The opening action is known as 'long recoil', but completing the operation by hand is unique. The steel-cored streamlined bullet carried a small charge of incendiary composition in the nose which gave a flash on impact to indicate the point of strike. In 1941, a square-based bullet with a tungsten carbide core was introduced. This improved velocity and penetration at short ranges.

Country of origin:	USSR
Caliber:	14.5mm (0.57in)
Length:	2.008m (79in)
Weight:	17.24kg (38lb)
Barrel:	1.227m (48.3in) long; 8 grooves; right hand twist
Feed:	single shot
Operation:	bolt action
Muzzle velocity:	1012m/sec (3320ft/sec)
Penetration:	25/500/90°

Type 97 Anti-tank Rifle

Introduced in 1937, this complicated design was capable of dealing with the lighter tanks which the Japanese anticipated in their Chinese and Manchurian campaigns. It operated on a combination of gas and blowback action; the bolt was unlocked by a gas piston but thereafter was driven by the blowback of the spent cartridge case. The barrel and receiver recoiled in a cradle mounting which carried the bipod, pistol grip, monopod and butt. An oil buffer recoil and recuperator mechanism was fitted, probably to cut the recoil blow down. To transport the weapon, it was provided with attachments beneath the butt and under the cradle to which carrying handles could be fitted to allow it to be carried by four men. It was not a success in the infantry role and was eventually given a wheeled carriage and turned into a light anti-tank gun.

Country of origin:	Japan
Caliber:	20mm (0.787in)
Length:	2.089m (82.25in)
Weight:	52.18kg (115lb)
Barrel:	1.064m (41.875in) long; 8 grooves; right hand twist
Feed:	7-round detachable box magazine
Operation:	gas and blowback; tipping bolt; selective fire
Muzzle velocity:	805m/sec (2640ft/sec)
Penetration:	12/200/90°

Type 2 Anti-tank Grenade Launcher

The Type 2 Anti-tank Grenade Launcher, introduced in 1942, was a copy of the German clip-on rifle grenade launcher for the Gewehr 98 or Kar 98k rifles, but slightly modified so as to fit the muzzle of the standard 6.5mm (0.256in) Arisaka rifles. The launcher was a hollow tube of 30mm (1.18in) calibre, rifled with eight broad grooves. The diameter was reduced at the rear end in order to fit around the rifle muzzle, and a hinged section with a quick-release catch locked the attachment on to the rifle. The grenade had an enlarged warhead and a reduced-diameter tail section with a pre-engraved driving band which fitted the grooves in the launcher. It was fired by a blank cartridge.

Country of origin:	Japan
Calibre:	rifle: 6.5mm (0.256in); launcher: 30mm (1.18in)
Length:	203mm (8in)
Weight:	approx 450g (1lb)
Grenade types:	HE; shaped charge
Muzzle velocity:	about 45m/sec (150ft/sec)
Penetration:	40/100/90°

2.8cm Panzerbuchse 41

In 1903, Carl Puff patented a gun barrel with a gradually tapering bore and a bullet with skirts which reduced in diameter as it went through the barrel. Eventually another German called Gerlich was successful in making the idea work, creating some powerful sporting rifles. He then worked for Rheinmetall designing anti-tank guns, and this gun was the first to appear. The bore tapers from 28mm (1.1in) at the breech to 20mm (0.787in) at the muzzle; this stepped up the pressure and gave the shot a higher velocity than anything achieved before. The shot had a tungsten carbide core and soft metal skirts which were swaged down so that a slender and heavy bullet left the barrel. The increasing thickness of tank armour, and the lack of tungsten for ammunition caused the PzB 41 to go out of service in 1942.

Country of origin:	Germany
Calibre:	28–20mm (1.10–0.787in)
Weight in action:	229kg (505lb)
Barrel length:	1.714m (67.48in)
Elevation:	-5° to +45°
Traverse:	90°
Projectile type:	composite shot; 131g (4.62oz)
Muzzle velocity:	1400m/sec (4593ft/sec)
Max effective range:	500m (547yds)
Armour penetration:	66/500/90°

37mm Anti-Tank Gun 1918

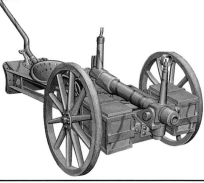

The Allies increasing use of tanks in World War I resulted in the German Army demanding a light anti-tank gun for their infantry, and a number of competing designs were tested at the Kummersdorf Proving Ground during the summer of 1918. Of the various models tested, this 37mm (1.49in) Anti-Tank Gun designed by Rheinmetall appeared to give the best balance between power and handiness. It could be manoeuvred by two men, and the gunner sat on a saddle on the trail and aimed through the elevated ring sights. Performance was poor by today's standards, but quite sufficient to make it a serious threat to the tanks of 1918. Fortunately for the Allies the war ended before production could begin.

Country of origin:	Germany
Calibre:	37mm (1.49in)
Weight in action:	175kg (386lb)
Barrel length:	780mm (30.70in)
Elevation:	-6° to +9°
Traverse:	21°
Projectile type:	AP/HE; 460g (1lb)
Muzzle velocity:	435m/sec (1427ft/sec)
Max effective range:	300m (328yds)
Armour penetration:	15/200/90°

37mm Anti-tank Gun M3

For some years the US Army were confident that their 12.7mm (0.50in) Browning machine gun could deal with any tank, but in the 1930s the tanks armour began to get thicker and the need for a specialist anti-tank gun became apparent. Two German Pak 36 guns were bought from Germany to give the US designers some guidance, and as a result there is a considerable degree of likeness between the German and American weapons. The M3 is distinguished by its shorter and more vertical shield, perforated shoulder guard for the gunlayer, and a different towing connection. Standardised in 1937 and issued in large numbers, it was obsolete by the time of Pearl Harbor, but it remained in wide use in the Pacific Theatre since it could deal with almost any Japanese tank. It was less useful in western Europe.

Country of origin:	USA
Calibre:	37mm (1.49in)
Weight in action:	413.7kg (912lb)
Barrel length:	2.095m (82.5in)
Elevation:	-10° to +15°
Traverse:	60°
Projectile type:	AP/HE; 870g (1.92lb)
Muzzle velocity:	884m/sec (2900ft/sec)
Max effective range:	457m (500yds)
Armour penetration:	36/500/90°

37mm Pak 35/36

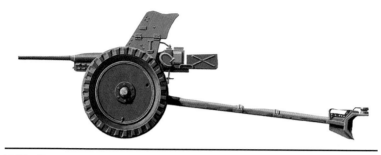

The 37mm (1.49in) Pak 35/36 was the standard German anti-tank gun at the outbreak of World War II in 1939 and a design which was widely copied in many other countries. Developed by Rheinmetall, it was first tested in Spain in 1937–38 and it was also sold to Soviet Russia in large numbers prior to 1940. Its penetrative performance was perhaps not quite so good as some of its contemporaries, but its ease of movement and effective concealment abilities more than compensated for that factor. Eventually defeated by heavier tanks, it had its life extended later in the war by its ability to adopt a heavy shaped charge bomb which could be slipped over the muzzle and fired by a blank cartridge, causing a completely devastating effect at short ranges.

Country of origin:	Germany
Calibre:	37mm (1.49in)
Weight in action:	432kg (962lb)
Barrel length:	1.665m (65.55in)
Elevation:	-5° to +25°
Traverse:	60°
Projectile type:	AP/HE; 1.50lb (680g)
Muzzle velocity:	762m/sec (2500ft/sec)
Max effective range:	600m (656yds)
Armour penetration:	48/500/90°

Anti-armour Weapons

QF 2pdr Mk VII

Developed in the mid-1930s, this gun was used as a towed anti-tank gun and also as a turret gun in British tanks, the reason being that they both had the same targets in mind. What this meant in practice was that the anti-tank gunners were limited because the weapon had to fit into a tank turret. Nevertheless, when issued in 1937 it was the best anti-tank gun in the world, although it was twice the weight of its contemporaries. It performed well in 1940, but after that it was outmatched by the German tanks. However, due to losing over 500 of them in France, Britain continued making them in 1941 in order to build up strength with a known gun, before shifting to a bigger weapon. This was a considerable handicap to the British forces in North Africa when they were confronted with German tanks in 1941–42.

Country of origin:	United Kingdom
Calibre:	40mm (1.57in)
Weight in action:	797kg (1757lb)
Barrel length:	2.082m (81.95in)
Elevation:	-5° to +23°
Traverse:	360°
Projectile type:	AP; 907g (2.0lb)
Muzzle velocity:	808 m/sec (2650ft/sec)
Max effective range:	1000m (1094yds)
Armour penetration:	42/1000/60°

47mm Skoda vz 36

The 47mm (1.85in) Skoda vz 36 was originally made in Czechoslovakia between 1939–1940 and used by the Czech Army; some were also sold to Yugoslavia. The Czech guns passed into the hands of the German Army in 1939 and significant numbers were used by them in the campaigns of 1940. A few were sent to North Africa, but in 1942 they were gradually replaced by more effective weapons, since they had been overtaken by the increasing strength of tanks. The gun was rather unusual for its day because of its ability to swing through 180° in order to place the barrel over the trail for travelling; the trail legs also folded to make a more compact unit. In addition to AP ammunition, it was also provided with an HE shell for infantry support tasks.

Country of origin:	Czech
Calibre:	47mm (1.85in)
Weight in action:	590kg (1300lb)
Barrel length:	2.040m (80/31in)
Elevation:	-8° to +26°
Traverse:	50°
Projectile type:	AP/HE; 1.65kg (3.64lb)
Muzzle velocity:	775m/sec (2543ft/sec)
Max range:	4000m (4375yds)
Armour penetration:	60/1200/90°

47mm Model 01 Anti-tank Gun

The origin of this weapon is not entirely clear, but it appears to have been a copy of the Russian 45mm (1.77in) gun, which in turn was based upon the 37mm (1.49in) German Pak 36 design. It seems that one or two of the Russian guns were captured by the Japanese on one of the many minor border skirmishes which took place along the Manchuria/Mongolia border in 1938–39. The calibre of 47mm (1.85in) was probably chosen because it was already in use by the Japanese Navy and therefore barrel-making and rifling machinery existed. The design was quite modern, with a split trail and pneumatic-tyred wheels, and the muzzle was heavily reinforced. Although designated 'Model 01', indicating approval in 1941, it was mid-1942 before manufacture began and even then it was not built in great numbers.

Country of origin:	Japan
Calibre:	47mm (1.85in)
Weight in action:	753kg (1660lb)
Barrel length:	2.527m (99.48in)
Elevation:	-11° to +19°
Traverse:	60°
Projectile type:	AP; 1.40kg (3.10lb)
Muzzle velocity:	823m/sec (2700ft/sec)
Max effective range:	1000m (1094yds)
Armour penetration:	70/500/90°

QF 6pdr 7cwt Gun Mk 2

Although designed in 1938, the Ordnance QF 6pdr (57mm/2.244in) 7cwt Gun Mk 2 did not go into production until November 1941, after which it remained in use until the 1950s. It was also adopted by the US Army, as the 57mm M1, and used in several British tanks. The name includes the weight of the barrel (7cwt) to distinguish it from other 6-pounders in use as air and coastal defence guns. Originally provided with AP shot, it had a tungsten-cored composite rigid shot for a short time and was then the first gun ever to have a discarding sabot shot as its service round, APDS being issued in June 1944 in time for the Normandy campaign. The gun was also adopted by the Royal Navy for small coastal assault craft, and the RAF fitted it into the Mosquito aircraft for the attack of submarines.

Country of origin:	United Kingdom
Calibre:	57mm (2.244in)
Weight in action:	1144kg (2521lb)
Barrel length:	2.564m (100.95in)
Elevation:	-5° to +15°
Traverse:	90°
Projectile type:	AP: 2.72kg (6.0lb); APDS: 1.47kg (3.25lb)
Muzzle velocity:	AP 821m/sec (2695ft/sec); APDS: 1235m/sec (4050ft/sec)
Max effective range:	1500m (1650yds)
Armour penetration:	AP: 74/1000/60°; APDS: 146/1000/60°

M1A1 2.36in Rocket Launcher

Developed early in 1942, the M1A1 Rocket Launcher became better known as the 'Bazooka', a name taken from a comic musical instrument played by Bob Burns, an American entertainer. A simple, smooth tube with elementary sights, it fired an electrically-ignited rocket which carried a shaped-charge warhead. The M1A1 was a one-piece tube with a wooden shoulder rest; it was replaced by the M9, a two-piece tube joined by a bayonet joint, which made it more convenient for the soldier to carry. In addition to its armour-piercing capability, it had HE and white phosphorus rockets and could be used effectively against field defences, machine gun positions and similar targets. It remained in service until the 1950s, when, during the Korean War, it was replaced by the 3.5in (88.9mm) version, which is still in use in several countries.

Country of origin:	USA
Calibre:	60mm (2.36in)
Weight in action:	5.98kg (13.18lb)
Launcher length:	1.545m (61in)
Elevation:	free
Traverse:	free
Rocket type:	shaped charge; 1.54kg (3.40lb)
Muzzle velocity:	83m/sec (270ft/sec)
Maximum range:	640m (700yds)
Effective range:	137m (150 yds)
Armour penetration:	120mm/all ranges/90°

2.5in Northover Projector

The dark days of 1940 saw some weapons enter British service which would never have been given house-room in more normal times, one of which was the Northover Projector. It was little more than 0.9m (3ft) of smooth-bore steel tube with a screw breech-block at the rear end and a trigger and hammer firing device attached to a short metal butt. The gun pivoted freely on a four-legged (later three-legged) mounting and was aimed by a primitive set of sights. The projectile was either the Hand Grenade No 36, the Anti-tank Rifle Grenade No 68, or the SIP Grenade No 76. These were fired by a small black-powder charge in a celluloid container, ignited by a blank revolver cartridge inserted into the breech-block. It was used by the Home Guard, but a few were issued to Army and RAF units guarding airfields in 1940–41.

Country of origin:	United Kingdom
Calibre:	63.5mm (2.5in)
Weight in action:	61.2kg (135lb)
Barrel length:	914mm (36 in)
Elevation:	free
Traverse:	free
Projectile type:	HE: 795g (1.75lbs); shaped charge: 905g (2.0lb); incendiary: 570g (1.25lb)
Muzzle velocity:	about 60m/sec (200ft/sec)
Max effective range:	251m (275yds)
Armour penetration:	50/100/90°

Anti-armour Weapons

5cm Pak 38

This was the first anti-tank gun to get away from the lightweight 'two men and push it' class of weapon and into the full-scale artillery class, requiring seven men and a tractor. It appeared in 1940, after the campaign in France was over, and, firing a tungsten-cored piercing shot, soon showed that it could defeat any Allied tank then in service. Although the use of tungsten ceased in 1942, it still fired a useful AP/HE shell and remained in use throughout the war, since it was quite capable of dealing with light tanks, and with its high explosive shell could make quite a nuisance of itself to heavier tanks, too. As well as being a towed gun, it was placed on a wide variety of tracked mountings and was even carried by tank-hunting aircraft on the Eastern Front.

Country of origin:	Germany
Calibre:	50mm (1.99in)
Weight in action:	986 kg (2173lb)
Barrel length:	3.187m (125.4in)
Elevation:	-8° to +27°
Traverse:	65°
Projectile type:	APCR: 850g (1.87lb); AP/HE: 2.25kg (4.96lb)
Muzzle velocity:	APCR: 1198m/sec (3930ft/sec); AP/HE: 823m/sec (2700ft/sec)
Max effective range:	2500m (2735yds)
Armour penetration:	APCR: 120/500/90°; AP/HE: 78/500/90°

75mm Pak 40

In 1940, anticipating bigger tanks in the future, the German Army placed contracts with Krupp and Rheinmetall for a heavy anti-tank gun. The 75mm (2.95in) Pak 40 was the Rheinmetall design, and it was little more that the 5cm (1.99in) Pak 39 scaled up, with a similar split-trail carriage and double-skinned shield. It was first issued in 1941 and became the standard anti-tank gun for the remainder of the war, since as long as the crew kept their nerve and let the tank get close, they could destroy any Allied tank. A large number were taken over at the end of the war and put into service by several European armies who were trying to re-equip. The only defect was its weight, which led to several being abandoned in retreats in the Russian winter when they became so bogged in mud that the eight-man crew could not move it.

Country of origin:	Germany
Calibre:	75mm (2.95in)
Weight in action:	1425kg (3141lb)
Barrel length:	3.702m (12.13ft)
Elevation:	-5° to +22°
Traverse:	65°
Projectile type:	APCR: 3.18kg (7lbs); AP/HE: 6.80kg (15lbs)
Muzzle velocity:	APCR: 990m/sec (3248ft/sec); AP/HE: 792m/sec (2598ft/sec)
Max effective range:	AP: 2000m (2190yds); HE shell: 7600m (8310yds)
Armour penetration:	APCR: 154/500/90°; AP/HE: 132/500/90°

Anti-armour Weapons

75mm Pak 41

This was Krupp's revolutionary answer to a 1940 German Army request for a bigger AT gun. The barrel was mounted in a ball mounting inset in the double-skin shield, to which the wheels and trail legs were attached, so making the shield part of the carriage structure. The barrel was a squeeze-bore; it did not taper for all its length but was parallel for 2.95m (3.23yds), then had a 950mm (37.4in) tapered section screwed on. This had two tapered steps and a final short parallel bored length. The shot was thus squeezed down very quickly. This meant more wear on the 'squeeze' section, but being screwed-on it could be rapidly changed in the field when needed. The gun had a superb performance, but the lack of tungsten ammunition rendered it useless in 1943.

Country of origin:	Germany
Calibre:	75 to 55mm (2.95 to 2.16in)
Weight in action:	1356kg (2990lb)
Barrel length:	4.32m (14.17ft)
Elevation:	-12.5° to +16°
Traverse:	60°
Projectile type:	APCR; 2.59kg (5.71lb)
Muzzle velocity:	1125m/sec (3690ft/sec)
Max effective range:	2000m (2185yds)
Armour penetration:	209/500/90°; 177/1000/90°; 124/2000/90°

Ordnance QF 17pdr Gun

Development of the powerful Ordnance QF 17pdr (76mm/3in) Gun began in 1940 and it was issued in the summer of 1942, the first guns being put on 25-pounder carriages and sent to North Africa to counter the Tiger tanks that were proving hard to knock out. These early versions of the gun were soon replaced by the split-trail version, and it became the supreme tank killer on the Allied side. Originally issued with AP shot, it received APDS in August 1944, which helped match the latest German AFVs. Primarily a towed anti-tank gun, it was also adapted to tank and SP guns, notably the M10 Achilles and the Sherman Firefly. Large numbers were also used by the Royal Navy to arm landing craft.

Country of origin:	United Kingdom
Calibre:	76mm (3.0in)
Weight in action:	2097kg (4624lb)
Barrel length:	4.58m (180.35in)
Elevation:	-6° to +16.5°
Traverse:	60°
Projectile type:	AP: 7.26kg (16lb); APDS: 3.45kg (7.62lb); HE: 6.98 kg (15.4lb)
Muzzle velocity:	AP: 884m/sec (2900ft/sec); APDS: 1203m/sec (3950ft/sec); HE: 876m/sec (2875ft/sec)
Max range:	HE: 9145m (10,000yds)
Armour penetration:	AP: 109/1000/60°; APDS: 231/1000/60°

76.2mm Model 1942

The 76.2mm (3in) Model 1942 was originally designed as a field artillery piece; it was first developed in 1935, had the barrel shortened in 1939, was put into the carriage of a 57mm (2in) gun in 1941. When that was found not to work as well as expected, it was finally given a new tubular split-trail carriage of its own in 1942, after which it remained the standard field gun for several years. However, the Soviets, in their wisdom, decreed that all guns capable of direct fire should be provided with anti-tank ammunition and deployed in suitable positions so that they could function as anti-tank guns if necessary. And because of the accuracy and general handiness of the M1942, it was gradually deployed more and more often as a defence against tanks than as a general-purpose artillery piece.

Country of origin:	USSR
Calibre:	76.2mm (3.0in)
Weight in action:	1116kg (2460lb)
Gun length:	3.24m (10.62ft)
Elevation:	-5° to +37°
Traverse:	54°
Shell type:	AP/HE: 7.54kg (16.62lb)
Muzzle velocity:	740m/sec (2427ft/sec)
Max effective range:	2000m (2190yds)
Armour penetration:	108/1000/90°

3in Gun M5

In 1940 the US Army demanded an anti-tank gun capable of dealing with any known or projected tank, and this weapon was the answer. It was put together from a 76.2mm (3in) AA gun barrel and the carriage of the 105mm (4.13in) howitzer and was a very good weapon indeed. Unfortunately the ammunition gave problems during development, and enthusiasm for the gun faded. The problems were solved by early 1944, but by that time the Army was more interested in SP guns and other weapons, so the 3 inch was more or less forgotten. After the invasion of Europe, it was hurriedly re-discovered and put to good use, since it was the only towed anti-tank gun the Americans had that was bigger than their 57mm (2in) weapon. The M10 tank destroyer also used it, but it was eventually replaced by the 90mm (3.54in) gun.

Country of origin:	USA
Calibre:	76.2mm (3in)
Weight in action:	2210kg (4873lb)
Barrel length:	3.81m (150in)
Elevation:	-5° to + 20°
Traverse:	45°
Projectile type:	AP/HE: 6.98kg (15.4lb)
Muzzle velocity:	792m/sec (2600ft/sec)
Maximum range:	14,630m (16,000yds)
Armour penetration:	100/1000/90°

Anti-armour Weapons

8cm
PAW 600

In 1943, the German infantry demanded a lightweight gun which used less propellant than a rocket or recoilless gun, but which would hit a 1m square target at 750m (820yds) range. Devised by Rheinmetall-Borsig, this gun introduced a new ballistic principle, the 'High and Low Pressure System'. A fin-stabilised shaped-charge bomb was attached to a heavy steel plate with small holes in it which closed the mouth of the cartridge case. On firing, the propellant burned efficiently inside the case at very high pressure, and the gas passed through the holes in the plate (locked in place by a step) and filled the space behind the bomb. A shear pin broke when the pressure was high enough and the bomb was released. The low pressure inside the bore meant a lightweight barrel, leading to a lighter recoil system and carriage.

Country of origin:	Germany
Calibre:	81.4mm (3.20in)
Weight in action:	600kg (1322lb)
Barrel length:	2.95m (116.1in)
Elevation:	-6° to +32°
Traverse:	55°
Projectile type:	shaped charge; 2.70kg (5.95lb)
Muzzle velocity:	520m/sec (1706ft/sec)
Max effective range:	750m (820yds)
Armour penetration:	140/750/90°

Raketenpanzerbuchse 43

In 1943, the Americans sent several weapons to the Russians, and among them were a number of 2.36in (60mm) 'Bazooka' rocket launchers. Within a few weeks one or two had been captured by the Germans, and this weapon was their version of the Bazooka. It fired a heavier bomb and had better penetration than the US one, but the principle was exactly the same. Instead of dry batteries, the German weapon used a magnetic coil to generate the electric current to fire the rocket. Another difference was that the rocket was not 'all-burnt' inside the launch tube, so the firer had to wear face protection – a gas mask was the easiest solution – to avoid being burned. A later version had better combustion of the rocket and also had a large square shield in front of the operator to divert the rocket blast.

Country of origin:	Germany
Calibre:	88mm (3.46in)
Weight in action:	9.5kg (20.9lb)
Barrel length:	1.638m (64.48in)
Projectile type:	shaped charge rocket; 3.25kg (7.16lb)
Muzzle velocity:	110m/sec (360ft/sec)
Max effective range:	150m (164yds)
Armour penetration:	100/150/90°

88mm Pak 43/41

Known to its gunners as 'Scheunentor' (Barn-door) because of its weight and awkwardness when being manhandled in the mud, the Pak 43/41 was well-liked, because it did the business. The original Pak 43 gun had a complex four-legged mounting similar to an AA gun, but it was slow and difficult to manufacture, so this cheap and cheerful version was built, using the wheels from the 15cm (5.9in) sFH18 Howitzer and the trail legs from the 105mm (4.13in) leFH18 Field Howitzer. It all went together with some hammering and filing, and proved very effective. One wartime record speaks of firing at a T-34 tank at 500m (546yd) range and blowing the engine clean out and the turret off, both landing some metres away from the hull. Another gun knocked out six T-34 tanks at a range of 3500m (3828yds).

Country of origin:	Germany
Calibre:	88mm (3.46in)
Weight in action:	4380kg (9656lb)
Barrel length:	6.61m (21.68ft)
Elevation:	-5° to +38°
Traverse:	56°
Projectile type:	APCR: 7.30kg (16lb); AP/HE: 10.40kg (22.9lbs)
Muzzle velocity:	APCR: 1130m/sec (3707ft/sec); AP/HE: 1000m/sec (3280ft/sec)
Max effective range:	4000m (4375 yds)
Armour penetration:	APCR: 241/1000/90°; AP/HE: 190/1000/90°

Flak 18

In 1939, the German Army ordered ten 88mm (3.46in) Flak 18 guns to be mounted upon the cargo bed of the Daimler-Benz 18-ton semi-tracked carrier. This was done by simply removing the gun and its pedestal from the four-legged AA mounting and bolting it to the chassis. A three-sided shield was added to protect the gunners, and armour was applied around the engine and the driver's position. The resulting vehicles were issued as anti-aircraft defence for moving columns and were used in the Polish and French campaigns. Their secondary role was as assault guns to attack fortified positions with direct fire, and it was a short step to using them as tank destroyers. Fifteen were built in 1940, but plans to build 112 more in 1941–2 were cancelled as it was clear that a full-tracked, fully-armoured vehicle was a better idea..

Country of origin:	Germany
Calibre:	88mm (3.46in)
Weight in action:	925,300kg (25 tons)
Barrel length:	4.93m (16.17ft)
Elevation:	-3° to +85°
Traverse:	360°
Projectile type:	HE: 9.4kg (20.73lb); AP: 9.5kg (20.95lb)
Muzzle velocity:	820m/sec (2690ft/sec)
Max effective range:	HE: 14,815m (16,200yds)
Effective ceiling:	8000m (26,250ft)
Armour penetration:	105/1000/60°

106mm RCL Rifle M40A1

Amerian development of recoilless guns in World War II resulted in two models, 57mm (2.24in) and 75mm (2.95in) calibre, in service by the end of the war. New designs were developed, resulting in a 105mm (4.13in) weapon in the early 1950s. This proved to be a poor performer and a fresh design was produced. The new design (one of the most successful weapons of its type) was known as the 106mm M40, though it was a 105mm weapon. Like all US RCL guns, the cartridge case is perforated with small holes which allow four-fifths of the propellant gas to exhaust to the rear through vents surrounding the breechblock, so providing the counter-balancing force to cancel out the recoil. Lack of recoil means no need for heavy mountings or recoil systems and the M40 can be placed on a light carriage or clamped to a vehicle.

Country of origin:	USA
Calibre:	105mm (4.13in)
Weight in action:	209.5kg (462lb)
Barrel length:	2.692m (106in)
Elevation:	free
Traverse:	free
Projectile type:	shaped charge, 7.96kg (17,55lb)
Muzzle velocity:	530m/sec (1740ft/sec)
Max effective range:	1350m (1480yds)
Armour penetration:	150mm/all ranges/60°

3.7in RCL Gun

A syndicate known as the Broadway Trust were responsible for the development of several recoilless guns in Britain during World War II, but the war ended before the weapons were ready for service. Some were made for troops trials after the war, but the eventual service RCL gun (the 120mm (4.72in) BAT) bears no relationship to these wartime guns. The 94mm (3.7in) was to be an anti-tank gun, firing a special 'wallbuster' shell which contained plastic explosive and stuck to the armour before detonating. This vibrated the armour and drove off a 'scab' weighing several pounds into the tank, doing enormous damage. The jets at the rear of the breech delivered a blast of high-speed gas to the rear which counter-balanced the recoil of the shell going up the bore, and thus the carriage could be very light.

Country of origin:	United Kingdom
Calibre:	94mm (3.7in)
Weight in action:	170kg (375lb)
Barrel length:	2.86m (112.76in)
Elevation:	-5° to +10°
Traverse:	free
Projectile type:	HESH; 10.2kg (22.5lb)
Muzzle velocity:	1000m/sec (3280ft/sec)
Max effective range:	2185yds (2000m)
Armour defeated:	about 150mm (6in) at any range

12.8cm Pak 44

Britain, the US and Germany all developed their anti-tank gun to the ultimate: Britain with a 94mm (3.7in), the US with a 105mm (4.13in) and Germany with this 128mm (5.03in) weapon. Two designs were developed, by Krupp and Rheinmetall; the ballistics of both were the same but the carriages were different. The Krupp design used a four-wheel, four-legged mounting similar to an AA gun. The Rheinmetall design was a four-legged affair but used six wheels, four in a bogie under the gun and two on a removable limber. The four wheels were lifted from the ground by jacks when the carriage was put into action. Both were effective, but their development was so late that neither went into production. The designs proved that the conventional anti-tank gun was impractical, being too big to be manhandled on the battlefield.

Country of origin:	Germany
Calibre:	128mm (5.03in)
Weight in action:	10,160kg (10 tons)
Barrel length:	7.023m (23.04ft)
Elevation:	-8° to +45°
Traverse:	360°
Projectile type:	AP/HE; 28.30kg (62.38lb)
Muzzle velocity:	1000m/sec (3280ft/sec)
Max effective range:	3500m (3825yds)
Armour penetration:	200/2000/90°

12.8cm K44

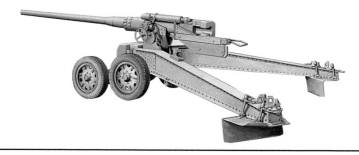

The 12.8cm (5.03in) K44 was the same gun as the 12.8cm Pak 44, but placed on a totally different carriage. It was employed more as a field artillery piece than as an anti-tank weapon, although, of course, it was still a potent threat to any tank that got within two miles of it. The gun was mounted either on the carriage of the French 155mm (6.1in) Mle GPF-T, a split-trail, four-wheel design very similar to the US 155mm Gun M1, or on the carriage of the Russian 152mm (6in) M1937 Howitzer, another split trail design but with the usual two wheels. The results were not entirely satisfactory, but, as with the anti-tank guns, development was not completed before the war ended. The following data is for the gun on the French carriage.

Country of origin:	Germany
Calibre:	128mm (5.03in)
Weight in action:	12,150kg (11.95 tons)
Barrel length:	7.023m (23.04ft)
Elevation:	-4° to +45°
Traverse:	60°
Projectile type:	HE; 28.0kg (61.72lb)
Muzzle velocity:	935m/sec (3068ft/sec)
Max effective range:	24,410m (26,700yds)

Panzerfaust

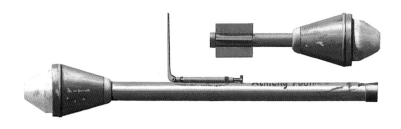

This weapon was actually a recoilless gun, consisting of a steel tube with a trigger mechanism; loaded into this was the bomb and a black-powder cartridge with percussion cap. The bomb was a shaped charge head on a wooden tail boom with four steel fins. The weapon was issued ready-loaded; to fire it, the rearsight was raised, cocking the firing mechanism. The foresight was a pin in the edge of the bomb. The firer tucked the tube under his arm, squeezed the trigger, and the powder charge blew the bomb off to the target; the blast cancelled out the recoil. The tube was then thrown away; it was the first 'expendable' weapon, it being cheaper to make a new one than have a factory re-load it. The Panzerfaust came in a number of sizes, from Pz 30 to Pz150, the number indicating the optimum range.

Country of origin:	Germany
Length of tube:	800mm (31.5in)
Length of bomb:	495mm (19.5in)
Weight of unit:	5.22kg (11.5lb)
Diameter of bomb:	150mm (6in)
Muzzle velocity:	30m/sec (98ft/sec)
Bomb type:	shaped charge; 3.06kg (6.75lb)
Penetration:	200/30/60°

PIAT

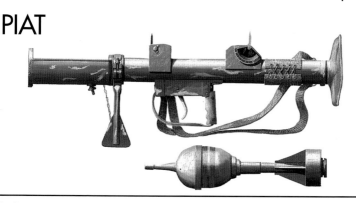

The PIAT (Projector, Infantry, Anti-Tank) is a form of spigot mortar, using a solid metal rod instead of a barrel to give direction and velocity to the projectile. The bomb had a long, hollow tail with drum fins. At the front end of the tail was a cartridge filled with smokeless powder and a percussion cap at the rear end. The projector was a simple tubular casing with a trough at the front end and a shoulder pad at the other. Inside the casing was a powerful spring and the steel rod – a dimple on its face was the firing pin. The weapon was first cocked, pulling the rod back against the spring, the bomb was laid in the trough and the trigger pulled. The rod flew forward, entered the tail of the bomb and struck the cartridge, exploding it. The reaction drove the rod back into the casing, re-cocking it for the next shot.

Country of origin:	United Kingdom
Calibre:	not applicable
Length :	1m (39in)
Weight:	14.52kg (32lb)
Projectile type:	shaped charge; 1.36kg (3lb)
Muzzle velocity:	106m/sec (350ft/sec)
Effective range:	91m (100yds)
Penetration:	75/100/90°

AGS-17 Grenade launcher

The idea of an automatic grenade launcher was explored in the USA in the 1960s, virtually as soon as their 40mm (1.57in) grenade had been perfected, but the idea was turned down. Ten years later this automatic launcher firing 30mm (1.18in) grenades appeared in Russia, whereupon the world's armies all began clamouring for something similar. The AGS-17 is no more than an overgrown blowback-operated machine gun, feeding from a belt and firing small explosive grenades instead of bullets. Although originally intended to be carried by foot troops, it has since been mounted on vehicles and in helicopters, and is now seen on the roof of most Russian armoured infantry vehicles.

Country of origin:	USSR
Calibre:	30mm (1.18in)
Operating system:	blowback, selective single shot or automatic fire
Length overall:	840mm (33in)
Weight, on tripod:	35kg (77.2lb)
Feed systrem:	29-round belt
Muzzle velocity:	185 m/sec (607ft/sec)
Weight of projectile:	350g (77.2lb)
Maxuimum range:	1730m (1891yds)
Rate of fire:	400 rds/min

CIS-40-AFL Grenade launcher

This appeared in the late 1980s. one of several designs which came in the wake of the Russian AGS-17 but firing the American standard 40mm (1.57in) grenade. A special longer-ranged cartridge was developed for these automatic weapons and this gives them a useful range, though like all such launchers it has a relatively flat trajectory and cannot 'search' behind cover to flush out any lurking infantry in the same way that a mortar bomb can with its high trajectory. Nevertheless, as an anti-ambush weapon it has few equals, with its fast rate of fire giving it a lethal punch against unprotected infantry or light vehicles. Like the AGS-17, it is becoming a common armament for light armoured vehicles.

Country of origin:	Singapore
Calibre:	40mm (1.57in)
Operating system:	blowback, selective single shot or automatic fire
Length overall:	966mm (38.03in)
Weight, with tripod:	33kg (72.75lb)
Feed systrem:	disintegrating link belt, any convenient length
Muzzle velocity:	241m/sec (791ft/sec)
Weight of projectile:	190g (6.7oz)
Maxuimum range:	2200m (2405yds)
Rate of fire:	350 rds/min

Light Support Weapons

M203 Grenade launcher

The original US grenade-launching weapon was the M79, a single-shot gun carried by one of the infantry squad. This put him at a disadvantage when he needed a rifle for self-defence, and therefore this M203 launcher was devised, a single-shot weapon which could be attached beneath the M16 rifle, so that the man had both rifle and launcher in one unit. The launcher is breech-loaded by sliding the barrel forward to expose the chamber and loading the round from beneath. The barrel slides back and locks, and behind it is the trigger and self-cocking firing mechanism. There is also a grenade-launching sight, making the M203 a totally separate item from the parent rifle. The grenade uses a low-power cartridge, in order to keep the recoil force down to a manageable level.

Country of origin:	USA
Calibre:	40mm (1.575in)
Operating system:	single-shot, self-cocking
Length overall:	380mm (15in)
Weight:	1.36kg (3lb)
Feed systrem:	Single shot, hand-loaded
Muzzle velocity:	75 m/sec (246ft/sec)
Weight of projectile:	190g (6.7oz)
Maxuimum range:	400m (437yds)
Rate of fire:	8–10 rds/min

45mm Brixia Model 35 Mortar

This was probably one of the most complicated small mortars ever devised, though it was undeniably efficient and remained in Italian service throughout World War II. It was a breech-loading weapon, and was operated by two men. The gunner lay behind the mortar with his chest on a padded rest — or, if conditions allowed, he could sit on it – and operated the lever which opened the breech and loaded a propelling cartridge, while his assistant fed bombs into the breech. The gunner concentrated on firing and aiming, and a well-drilled pair could fire something in the order of 18 rounds per minute, though the official rate was somewhat less than that.

Country of origin:	Italy
Calibre:	45mm (1.77in)
Barrel length:	260mm (10.23in)
Weight as fired:	15.5kg (34.2lb)
Elevation:	+10 to +90°
Traverse:	20°
Weight of bomb:	465g (16.4oz)
Muzzle velocity:	83m/sec (272ft/sec)
Maximum range:	530m (580yds)
Rate of fire:	8–10 rds/min

50mm Type 89 Grenade discharger

This was normally carried strapped to the soldier's leg, and was therefore known to the Japanese as the 'Leg Mortar'. Unfortunately an Allied interpreter got it wrong and called it the 'Knee Mortar', after which several people went to hospital with broken thighs after fitting the curved spade on to their legs and firing the mortar. It was an unusual weapon, in that it used a fixed elevation and the range was varied by screwing a rod up into the barrel so causing the bomb to be fired higher up from the breech. This meant more space for the gas to expand before it started the bomb on its way, and thus gave range control.. As well as a finned bomb, it could also fire the standard hand grenade, though to a much shorter range than the proper bomb.

Country of origin:	Japan
Calibre:	50mm (1.57in)
Barrel length :	254mm (109in)
Weight:	4.53kg (10lb 1oz)
Elevation:	45°
Traverse:	free
Muzzle velocity:	not known
Weight of projectile:	793kg (28oz)
Maxuimum range:	640m (700 yds)
Rate of fire:	25 rds/min

60mm Mortar M1

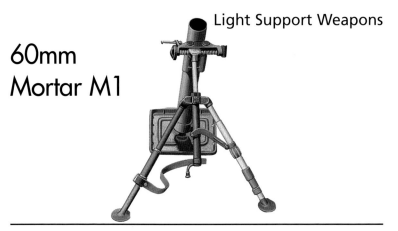

The US Army began examining mortars in the late 1920s and eventually bought this design from Edgar Brandt, the French ordnance engineer, and manufactured it under licence in the USA. It was of the usual pattern, a smooth-bore tube on a baseplate, supported by a simple bipod with elevation and traverse mechanism. The firing pin was fixed in the base cap of the tube, and the bomb fired automatically as it was dropped down the barrel. A simple optical sight was fitted, and the weapon was provided with high explosive, smoke and illuminating bombs. The latter were found to be useful not only for their usual job of battlefield illumination, but also for anti-tank teams, firing the bomb beyond the enemy tank so as to silhouette it at night.

Country of origin:	USA
Calibre:	60mm (2.36in)
Barrel length:	726mm (28.6in)
Weight as fired:	19.05kg (42.0lb)
Elevation :	+40° to +85°
Traverse:	7°
Weight of bomb:	1.33kg (2.94lb)
Muzzle velocity:	158m/sec (518ft/sec)
Maximum range:	1815m (1985yds)
Rate of fire:	18 rds/min

Brandt 60mm LR Gun-mortar

The Brandt Long Range Gun-mortar is an odd weapon – a breech-loading mortar but which is capable of flat-trajectory firing like a gun. It is used solely for the armament of light armoured vehicles such as personnel carriers and gives them a very versatile and quite formidable armament without the weight and complications of a conventional gun. It is smoothbored, and fires the same fin-stabilised bombs as the normal infantry 60mm (2.36in) mortar, and these can be breech-loaded from under armour, or, if preferred, can be drop-loaded in the usual mortar fashion from outside the vehicle. It is also provided with a high-velocity fin-stabilised piercing shot and a fin-stabilised shaped charge bomb, which give the weapon a useful anti-armour performance.

Country of origin:	France
Calibre:	60mm (2.36in)
Barrel length:	1.80m (70in)
Weight as fired:	75kg (165.3lb)
Elevation :	-11° to + 75°
Traverse:	depends upon vehicle mounting; up to 360°
Weight of bomb:	2.20kg (4.85lb)
Muzzle velocity:	250 m/sec (820ft/sec)
Maximum range:	4000m (4375yds)
Rate of fire:	10 rds/min

60mm Mortar M19

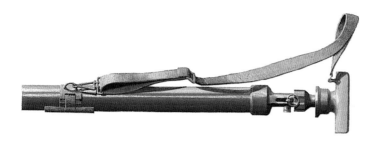

Thís was developed in 1942 from the M1 mortar and was intended to be a simpler and lighter weapon. The original design used a simply spade-like base-plate (shown above), leaving the mortar to be supported by the firer and aim estimated by eye. This was found to be too inaccurate, and the infantry refused the M19 and preferred to keep the M1. A new mount, the M5, was then developed, which used a conventional baseplate and bipod with elevation and traverse adjustment. This gave the desired degree of accuracy but put the weight up beyond that of the M1 and with less range. Relatively few M19 mortars were made; some remained in use into the Vietnam period, but most were given to other armies or scrapped.

Country of origin:	USA
Calibre:	60mm (2.36in)
Barrel length:	819mm (32.2in)
Weight as fired:	20.5kg (45.2lb) (Mount M5); 9.3kg (20.5lb)(with M1 baseplate)
Elevation :	+40° to +85° on M5 mount' Free on M1 mount
Traverse:	14° on M5 mount; free on M1 mount
Weight of bomb:	1.36kg (3lb)
Muzzle velocity:	168m/sec (550ft/sec)
Maximum range:	1790m (1960yd)
Rate of fire:	18 (sustained) to 30 (max) rds/min

70mm Battalion Gun Type 92

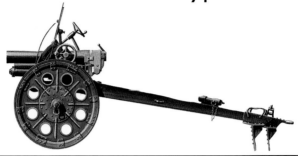

The most common of all Japanese infantry support weapons during World War II, this could function either as a mortar or as a direct-fire assault gun. Light and handy, it could be easily manhandled by a few men, dismantled and moved in pieces or towed by one or two mules or horses. The carriage had a hydro-spring recoil system, and the wheels were on cranked stub-axles so that the gun could be set low for direct firing or high so as to give ample recoil space when used in the mortar role. The standard round was a high explosive shell, though shrapnel and smoke rounds were occasionally encountered. Large numbers of these guns fell into Chinese hands after the Japanese surrender in 1945 and were used by the Chinese Communist army until the mid-1950s.

Country of origin:	Japan
Calibre:	70mm (2.75in)
Weight in action:	212.25kg (468lb)
Gun length:	723mm (28.5in)
Elevation:	-4° to +75°
Traverse:	45°
Shell type & weight:	HE: 3.76kg (8.3lb)
Muzzle velocity:	198m/sec (650ft/sec)
Maximum range:	2788m (650yds)

Bofors 75mm Model 34

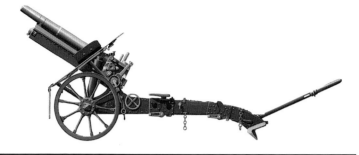

This was developed privately by Bofors in the late 1920s. It was actually designed as a mountain gun, and could be rapidly broken down into eight mule-pack loads, or towed by animals or light motor vehicles. A few were bought by Belgium in 1934 for extended trials; these were still in progress in 1939, whereupon the guns were rapidly put into service, but they saw very little action before being captured by the Germans. A further quantity of guns were sold by Bofors to the Dutch government for outfitting their colonial army in the Dutch East Indies, where their pack-load ability was a useful feature for moving through the jungle. These, too, saw very little combat use before falling into the hands of the Japanese in 1941–42. In neither case did the captors seem to make much use of their new weapon.

Country of origin:	Sweden
Calibre:	75mm (2.95in)
Weight in action:	928kg (2045lb)
Gun length:	1.80m (70.85in)
Elevation:	-10° to +50°
Traverse:	8°
Shell type & weight:	HE: 6.58kg (14.5lb)
Muzzle velocity:	455m/sec (1493ft/sec)
Maximum range:	9300m (10,170yds)

75mm Pack Howitzer M1A1

This was developed in the 1920s as a result of World War I experience and was an ingenious design of howitzer which could be rapidly stripped down into four mule loads. The gun barrel locked into the breech by an interrupted thread, and was retained on the cradle by means of a 'top sleigh' of cast steel and lead. The carriage trail could be removed complete, or split into pieces, or folded and fitted with shafts for animal draught. A notable feature of the design were the lightening holes in the trail sides. In World War II when the US Airborne troops required an artillery piece which could be parachute-dropped, the Carriage M8 was developed, which was simply the standard M1 carriage with pneumatic tyres and steel wheels. The 75mm (2.95in) was used by US and British airborne troops until the mid-1960s.

Country of origin:	USA
Calibre:	75mm (2.95in)
Weight in action:	607.4kg (1339lb)
Gun length:	1.32m (52.0in)
Elevation:	-5° to +45°
Traverse:	6°
Shell type & weight:	HE; 6.35kg (14lb)
Muzzle velocity:	381m/sec (1250ft/sec)
Maximum range:	8787m (9610yds)

SGrW 34
81mm Mortar

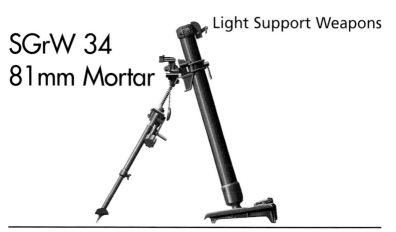

This, the standard German Army mortar, was a conventional Stokes-pattern, with rectangular baseplate, front bipod with elevation, traverse and cross-level controls, a simply collimating sight and a fixed firing pin. The baseplate weighed 19.9kg (44lb), the other two units slightly less, so it could easily be carried by three men in an emergency. The ammunition covered the usual HE, smoke and illuminating bombs, but in addition this mortar had a unique 'bouncing' bomb which, after impact, was blown back up into the air so that it detonated at about five metres above the ground, thus giving a highly lethal spread of fragments. The mortar was largely replaced in the latter part of the war by a shortened version; this had less range but was more convenient since it was almost exactly half the weight.

Country of origin:	Germany
Calibre:	81mm (3.18in)
Barrel length:	1.143m (45in)
Weight as fired:	56kg (125lb)
Elevation :	+40° to +90°
Traverse:	9° to 15° depending upon elevarion
Weight of bomb:	HE 3.4kg (7.5lb)
Muzzle velocity:	175m/sec (574ft/sec)
Maximum range:	2400m (2625yds)

Light Support Weapons

81mm Mortar Mle 27/31

This was designed by Edgar Brandt, who set out to improve the British Stokes mortar of World War I. This particular model was more or less his masterpiece, and in addition to being adopted by the French it was sold worldwide and became the model for the US, Italian, Russian and Yugoslavian service mortars. It was a simple smooth-bore weapon, supported by a baseplate and a bipod with the usual elevating and traversing controls. There was a fixed firing pin in the breech cap, and bombs were simply drop-fired, though some of the mortars sold to other countries were fitted with trip-firing mechanisms which allowed the bombs to be dropped and then fired by lanyard. The design was so good that it differs very little from the modern Thompson-Brandt mortar except for the baseplate shape.

Country of origin:	France
Calibre:	81mm (3.18in)
Barrel length:	1.27m (49.8in)
Weight as fired:	59.7kg (131.6lb)
Elevation:	+45° to +85°
Traverse:	8° to 12° depending upon elevation
Weight of bomb:	3.25kg (7.16lb) or 6.5kg (14.3lb)
Muzzle velocity:	174 m/sec (570m/sec)
Maximum range:	2850/1200m (3115/1312yds)

82mm PM-37 Mortar

In 1936 the Soviets acquired some French 81mm (3.18in) Brandt mortars and, changing the calibre to 82mm (3.22in), they began manufacturing a copy of the French design. After a short period they saw a few points which could be improved and produced the PM-37 in 1937. The principal changes were firstly to put buffer springs between the barrel collar and the bipod, and secondly to adopt a circular baseplate. The design was so successful that significant numbers are still in use to the present day, and later designs are merely minor cosmetic improvements on the original; the basic performance of the weapon has scarcely altered. The mortar saw much use in World War II.

Country of origin:	USSR
Calibre:	82mm (3.22in)
Barrel length:	1.22m (48.23in)
Weight as fired:	11.5kg (123.5lb)
Elevation :	45° or 75°
Traverse:	6° to 15° depending upon elevation
Weight of bomb:	3.05kg (6.72lb)
Muzzle velocity:	211m/sec (692ft/sec)
Maximum range:	3040m (3325yds)
Rate of fire:	25–30rds/min

82mm Vasilek automatic mortar

This is a very complicated weapon which, it was claimed, could function equally well as a high angle mortar or as a flat-trajectory gun. It appeared in the early 1970s and was extensively used in Afghanistan, after which it was removed from general service and replaced by a conventional 120mm (4.7in) mortar. Only the air assault troops of the Russian army have retained the weapon, although it has been seen mounted on some lighter armoured vehicles. The Vasilek ('cornflower') can be loaded at the breech or at the muzzle; in the former case it is automatically reloaded from a four-round clip in a feed unit behind the breech. In the latter case it is hand-loaded with single rounds in the normal manner. The carriage is so complicated to allow stable high angle fire without the breech striking the ground.

Country of origin:	USSR
Calibre:	82mm (3.22in)
Barrel length:	not known
Weight as fired:	632kg (1393lb)
Elevation:	-1° to +85°
Traverse:	60°
Weight of bomb:	HE: 3.23kg (7.12lb)
Muzzle velocity:	270 m/sec (890ft/sec)
Maximum range:	4720m (5162yds)

95mm Infantry Howitzer

In the summer of 1942 the idea of an infantry howitzer was put forward in the British Army. At the time a 95mm (3.7in) howitzer was being designed for close support tanks, and it seemed a good idea to take this and put it on a field carriage for the infantry to have their own artillery for close support. The weapon was put together from a section of 94mm (3.7in) AA gun barrel, grafted to a 25pdr gun breech, carried on a 6pdr recoil system, all placed on a box-trail carriage with shield. Trials in 1943 showed that the recoil system was over-stressed, and re-design was called for. But the problem persisted and eventually (but not before several hundred were built) the weapon was refused approval and declared obsolete in April 1945.

Country of origin:	United Kingdom
Calibre:	95mm (3.7in)
Gun length:	1.88m (74.05in)
Weight in action:	954kg (2105lb)
Elevation:	-5° to +30°
Traverse:	8°
Shell type & weight:	HE: 11.3kg (25lb)
Muzzle velocity:	330m/sec (1083ft/sec)
Maximum range:	7315m (8000yds)

Light Support Weapons

120mm M1938 Mortar

This is the ancestor of every one of the multitude of 120mm (4.72in) mortars in use today; prior to 1939 the only people in the world to have a mortar of this calibre were the Russians, who treated it as an artillery weapon. They soon realised its value as an infantry support weapon, and when, in 1941 the German army captured a large number, they were so impressed they took it into their own service and then developed and built an improved design. It was a conventional mortar which could be drop- or trip-fired, and which had an ingenious design of transporting trailer which could be hooked to the baseplate and lifted the mortar out of the ground and loaded it on to the trailer bed in one swift move. Undoubtedly one of the great designs of World War II.

Country of origin:	USSR
Calibre:	120mm (4.72in)
Barrel length:	1.862m (73.3in)
Weight as fired:	280kg (617lb)
Elevation:	+45° to +80°
Traverse:	6°
Weight of bomb:	16.0kg (35.2lb)
Muzzle velocity:	272m/sec (892ft/sec)
Maximum range:	6000m (6560yds)

Brandt 120mm Mortar

The Thompson-Brandt company make two very similar 120mm (4.72in) mortars, one a normal smoothbore, the other a rather unusual rifled weapon. Both are carried on a two-wheeled trailer designed so that the baseplate remains attached to the mortar barrel, and the whole thing is dropped into action by simply tipping the trailer. The smoothbore weapon fires a conventional finned bomb. The rifled mortar fires a projectile shaped like an artillery shell (shown above with propellant charges wrapped around the tail), but with a cartridge container attached to the base which carries the usual mortar cartridge system. The driving band of the shell is pre-engraved to fit the rifling and has to be carefully inserted into the muzzle to engage band and grooves.

Country of origin:	France
Calibre:	120mm (4.72in)
Barrel length:	2.06m (6ft 9in)
Weight as fired:	682kg (1503lb)
Elevation:	+30° to +85°
Traverse:	14°
Weight of bomb:	15.7kg (34.6lbs)
Muzzle velocity:	not known
Maximum range:	8135m (8900 yds)

Soltam 120mm Mortar

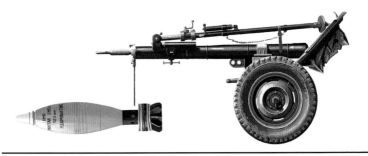

The Soltam120mm (4.72in) is a conventional heavy infantry mortar which is used by the Israeli Defence Force and a number of other armies. It consists of the usual smoothbore barrel, round baseplate and supporting bipod, all carried on a light two-wheeled trailer in the assembled condition. All that is necessary to bring the mortar into action is to tip the trailer so that the baseplate drops to the ground, then lift the tube and bipod clear and erect them, removing the trailer. Conventional finned bombs are used and are drop-loaded; firing is activated by a trip mechanism and lanyard, and the firing pin can be retracted and locked in the safe position. The Israeli Defence Force mortars can be mounted in half-tracks or the M113 'Zelda' APC.

Country of origin:	Israel
Calibre:	120mm (4.72in)
Barrel length:	1.95m (76.8in)
Weight as fired:	231kg (510lb)
Elevation:	+43° to +85°
Traverse:	15°
Weight of bomb:	27.8lbs (12.6kg)
Muzzle velocity:	310m/sec (1017ft/sec)
Maximum range:	6500m (7100yds)

Ordnance ML 3in Mortar

In the late 1920s the British infantry were asking for some sort of light gun for close support, and there were plans to equip special 'light batteries' of artillery for this role. But financial considerations and manpower questions were very powerful arguments, and at the last moment this design of mortar was accepted instead. A conventional Stokes-type mortar, drop-fired, wartime experience showed that it had insufficient range compared to its German equivalent the 81mm (3.18in) Model 34 (2377m (2600 yards)), so a new and stronger barrel was designed to fire the same bomb but with a more powerful propelling charge, which put the range up to 2560metres (2800 yards). This became the Mark 2 mortar, and it was to remain in service until replaced by the 81mm mortar in the 1960s.

Country of origin:	United Kingdom
Calibre:	76.2mm (3.0in)
Barrel length:	1.37m (51.0in)
Weight as fired:	50.8kg (112lb)
Elevation :	+45° to +80°
Traverse:	11°
Weight of bomb:	4.53kg (10lb)
Muzzle velocity:	198m/sec (650ft/sec)
Maximum range:	1463m (1600yds) (Mk 1); 2560m (2800yds) (Mk 2)

15cm sIG 33 infantry gun

One of the oldest weapons used by the German Army in World War II, this had first appeared in 1927 as the armament of the Heavy Gun Company of the infantry regiment. It was also the heaviest weapon ever to be classified as an 'infantry gun' in any army. Conventional in design, it was simple and robust and gave no trouble even in the worst conditions, but customers complained of the weight. A lightweight version was designed and tested in 1938 but it showed little improvement and, with the outbreak of war, it was abandoned. The range of ammunition covered the usual HE, smoke and shaped charge options, plus a remarkable stick bomb with a 27kg (62lb) warhead which was for use against fortifications.

Country of origin:	Germany
Calibre:	150mm (5.9in)
Weight in action:	1688kg (3722lb)
Gun length:	1.75m (68.8in)
Elevation:	0° to +73°
Traverse:	11°
Shell type & weight:	HE: 28.8kg (63.6lb)
Muzzle velocity:	240m/sec (790ft/sec)
Maximum range:	4700m (5140yds)

160mm Mortar M1943

This started out to be simply a larger edition of the 120mm (4.72in) mortar M38, but it was soon apparent that drop-loading a 40kg (90lb) bomb into a 3 metre (9ft 11in) barrel was asking a lot of the gunners, and it was re-designed as a breech-loading weapon. The barrel sits in a cradle which is attached to the usual baseplate and tripod, so that it can be hinged forward, rather like a shotgun, to expose the rear end of the barrel for loading. The bomb is loaded, retained in place by a catch, and the barrel swung back into the cradle, which in effect closes the breech. There is also a substantial recoil system to soak up some of the firing shock and prevent it burying the baseplate too deeply.

Country of origin:	USSR
Calibre:	160mm (6.29in)
Barrel length:	3.03m (9ft 11in)
Weight as fired:	1170kg (2580lb)
Elevation:	+45° to +80°
Traverse:	25°
Weight of bomb:	40.8kg (90lb)
Muzzle velocity:	245 m/sec (804ft/sec)
Maximum range:	5150m (5630yds)

RAW (Rifleman's Assault Weapon)

This remarkable device is actually a rocket-propelled bomb launched off the end of a standard M16-type rifle. The warhead of the rocket contains plastic explosive which plasters itself on to the target before detonating, and so drives a concussion wave through the target, shaking off a large piece of the interior of the armour or concrete and turning it into a very destructive missile. The rocket is spherical but stabilised by offset jets which give it roll stabilisation as well as thrust. An adapted on the rifle taps off some of the propelling gas from an ordinary ball cartridge and directs it down a tube to strike a firing pin and so ignite the rocket motor; this first spins the rocket and then launched it from the bracket on the rifle.

Country of origin:	USA
Rocket diameter:	140mm (5.51in)
Rocket length:	305mm (12in)
Weight:	4.73kg (10lb 4oz)
Rocket payload:	plastic HE, 1.0kg (2lb 2oz)
Velocity at 200m:	73m/sec (240ft/sec)
Time of flight to 200m:	1.9 seconds
Maximum range:	1500m (1640yds)
Effective range:	300m (328yds)

B-300 Light Support Weapon

The B-300 is a man-portable, shoulder-fired rocket weapon with which field defences, armoured vehicles or personnel can be engaged, for which different warheads are provided. The weapon comes in two parts, the launch tube, which carries the sight and firing mechanism, and the pre-packed, sealed rocket tube. This rocket container connects quickly to the rear of the launch tube, making all the necessary electrical and mechanical connections. The complete assembly is then shouldered, the firer takes aim and fires. The empty rocket tube is then removed from the launcher and a fresh one added for the next shot. The standard warhead is a shaped charge for armour, but there is also a follow-through warhead which blows a hole in the target and then launches a secondary missile into the hole.

Country of origin:	Israel
Calibre:	82mm (3.2in)
Weight, as fired:	8kg (17.64lb)
Length, as fired:	1.35m (53.15in)
Rocket weight:	3.10kg (6.61lb)
Launch velocity:	270m/sec (885ft/sec)
Effective range:	400m (437yds)
Armour penetration:	400mm (15.75in) at 65° slope at any range

AP/AV 700 multiple grenade launcher

This weapon was designed to extract the best possible performance out of standard rifle grenades. Firing them off a man's shoulder is not the most stable or accurate method, and using a dedicated launcher which gives a solid resistance to the firing impulse and can be carefully aimed and adjusted, ensured the maximum effect from the grenades. The AP/AV 700 therefore consists of a robust baseplate with three barrels, adjustable for elevation and direction. These are not rifle barrels but are specially made with a central hole which tapers from base to tip. The barrels are chambered for either 7.62mm (0.3in) or 5.56mm (0.2in) cartridges. The cartridge is loaded, the bomb slipped over the barrel, and the firing pin released to fire the cartridge and expel the grenade.

Country of origin:	Italy
Calibre:	22mm (0.866in) exterior, for NATO-standard rifle grenades
Barrel length:	300mm (11.81in)
Weight as fired:	11kg (24.25lb)
Weight of grenade:	0.93kg (2.05lb)
Min range:	100m (109yds)
Max range:	700m (765yds)

SMAW

SMAW (Shoulder-fired Multi-purpose Assault Weapon) is a man-portable rocket launcher with a variety of warhead options to use against different target types. It resembles the Israeli B-300 or the earlier French LRAC in that it consists of two parts, the launch tube with sights and aiming rifle, and the disposable rocket container which locks on to the back of the launch tube and is discarded after the rocket has been fired. The spotting rifle fires a special 9mm (0.35in) explosive bullet which is matched to the rocket. The firer fires the rifle until he gets a hit, then holds the same aim and fires the rocket. The basic warhead is HE Dual Purpose which can be used against light armour or hard fortifications, and there is also a specialised HEAA anti-armour warhead capable of defeating main battle tanks.

Country of origin:	USA
Calibre:	83mm (3.26in)
Weight, empty:	7.5kg (16.5lb)
Length of launcher:	825mm (32.5in)
Length as fired:	1.378m (54.25in)
Weight of HEDP:	5.950kg (13.1lb)
Weight of HEAA:	6.4kg (14.1lb)
Launch velocity:	220m/sec (721ft/sec)
Effective range:	500m (550yds)

Surface-to-surface Missiles

Pluton

Pluton is a French tactical nuclear missile installed on, and fired from, a modified AMX-30 tank chassis. The missile container is used as the launching ramp. The launch vehicle is, of course, accompanied by the usual caravanserai of computers, radars, command vehicles and so forth. Guidance is inertial, and the available warheads are of 15 and 25kT capability so that a choice can be made according to the type of target and its proximity to the front line. The 15kT warhead is an airburst weapon for use in the main battle area; the 25kT warhead is for rear area targets. The missile entered service with the French army in 1974, and 42 launch vehicles were produced.

Country of origin:	France
Length:	7.64m (26ft 1in)
Diameter:	650mm (25.6in)
Launch weight:	2423kg (5342lb)
Guidance:	inertial
Propulsion:	solid fuel, two-stage
Warhead:	nuclear, 15kT or 25kT
Range:	120km (75 miles)

SSBS S-3

The SSBS S-3 is a French medium-range, two-stage, solid propellant missile with nuclear warhead, which is stored in, and launched from, an underground silo. These silos were dispersed throughout France and hardened to survive nuclear attack. Development of the S-3, which was the second-generation system replacing the S-2, began in 1973. This improved on earlier patterns by creating a more powerful second stage motor and an advanced independent re-entry vehicle warhead, hardened against the effect of a nuclear burst from an anti-ballistic missile. Improvements were also made to the inertial guidance system and the ground maintenance system.

Country of origin:	France
Length:	13.7m (44ft 11in)
Diameter:	1.50m (50in)
Launch weight:	25,800kg (25.39 tons)
Guidance:	inertial
Propulsion:	solid fuel, two-stage
Warhead:	thermonuclear, 1.2MT
Range:	3500km (2175 miles)

Surface-to-surface Missiles

CSS-1

The Chinese CSS-1 was a single-stage, liquid-fuelled, medium range ballistic missile generally similar to the Soviet SS-3 'Shyster' and probably built with some Soviet assistance. Called the T1 Tong Feng (East Wind) by the Chinese, it is variously claimed to have been put into service by 1966 or 1970 and was phased out during the late 1980s. Early versions are believed to have carried a simple 15kT warhead, but this was later replaced by a 25kT design and towards the end of their service most are understood to have been refitted with thermonuclear warheads. Latterly they were used to maintain a useful threat against the Soviet Far Eastern territories.

Country of origin:	China
Length:	21m (68.8ft)
Diameter:	1.6m (63in)
Launch weight:	26,000kg (25.58 tons)
Guidance:	inertial
Propulsion:	liquid fuel, single stage
Warhead:	nuclear, 20kT
Range:	1200km (745 miles)

CSS-2

The CSS-2 (or T2) was a single-stage intermediate-range ballistic missile using storable liquid propellant. It is believed that a small number (less than 60) were built and deployed as a stop-gap due to setbacks in the Chinese ICBM programme in the 1970s. Deployment is believed to have been principally oriented towards targets in Central and Eastern Asia, and other sources suggested that the system was capable of being re-deployed if necessary, but that this would have entailed building completely new facilities since it could not be described as mobile or easily portable, being fired from above-ground fixed launch pads. All of these missiles are believed to have been removed from service by 1990.

Country of origin:	China
Length:	20.62m (67.65ft)
Diameter:	2.46m (8.07ft)
Launch weight:	27,000kg (26.57 tons)
Guidance:	inertial
Propulsion:	liquid fuel, single stage
Warhead:	thermonuclear, 1.3MT
Range:	3000km (1865 miles)

CSS-3

The CSS-3 (or T3) is a Chinese long-range, two-stage ballistic missile, a limited number of which were deployed in underground silos in the 1970s and early 1980s. The first Chinese ICBM, with an estimated range of 7000km (4340 miles), deployment is said to have been concentrated in western China, suggesting targets in Central Europe or the USSR but, on the other hand, these may be figments of an intelligence officer's imagination. So far as we know, production of this missile has been relatively small, and no more than about 50 are said to have been built. The warhead carried by the missile is believed to be two megatons. Propulsion is provided by a liquid propellant.

Country of origin:	China
Length:	26.71m (87.63ft)
Diameter:	2.45m (8.03ft)
Launch weight:	not known
Guidance:	inertial
Propulsion:	liquid fuel, two-stage
Warhead:	thermonuclear, 2 MT
Range:	7000km (4340 miles)

CSS-4

The CSS-4 (orT4) was first heard about in May 1980 when the Chinese Army fired two missiles into an impact area in the South Pacific, indicating the presence of an intercontinental ballistic missile of some power. The impact area was large, so no precise estimate of range could be made by outside observers, and the missiles did not carry warheads, which can also confuse the range question. It seems probable that the data given below is a reasonabaly sound estimate, although some of the information cannot even be guessed at. It seems fair to presume that a number of these missiles are aimed at both Russia and America. The missile also forms the basis of one of the Chinese satellite launching platforms, the CSL-2 (or FBI).

Country of origin:	China
Length:	33m (108ft)
Diameter:	not known
Launch weight:	not known
Guidance:	inertial
Propulsion:	liquid fuel, two-stage
Warhead:	thermonuclear, 5 MT
Range:	13,000km (8000 miles)

Rocket, MGR-1B, Honest John

T he design of this simple spin-stabilised rocket began in 1950 and manufacture began in 1953. The motor is a solid propellant with four auxiliary rockets arranged just behind the warhead and slightly canted so that their exhaust causes the rocket to spin. This initial spin is then maintained by the skewed fins, which give the whole affair a slow rotation. Like any finned rocket it is affected by wind, and the accuracy is not as good as a conventional artillery shell, but with a nuclear warhead the difference was of no consequence. With HE and chemical warheads it was more marked, but as an area weapon it served well for several years before it was replaced by guided weapons. As well as serving with the US Army, it was supplied to most NATO armies, plus South Korea and Taiwan.

Country of origin:	USA
Calibre:	762mm (30in)
Launcher weight:	not known
Length of rocket:	7.57m (24ft 10in)
Weight of rocket:	1950kg (4300lb)
Propulsion:	solid fuel, one stage
Warhead:	nuclear, chemical or HE
Range:	36.8km (23 miles)

Pershing

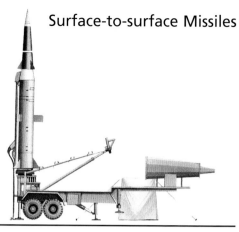

Pershing was a tactical battlefield support system, transportable in various large cargo aircraft. Originally mounted on tracked chassis, the Pershing 1A system moved towards the use of wheeled vehicles. This system also improved the programming of the missile with target information and introduced an automatic count-down system. Pershing 2 appeared in the mid-1980s with an entirely new navigation system and a new re-entry vehicle warhead incorporating a highly accurate terminal guidance system. The range was also increased by about 1800km (1125 miles), bringing Moscow into range for those Pershings based in Germany. The basic missile was a two-stage solid fuel weapon with a nuclear warhead.

Country of origin:	USA
Length:	10.61m (34ft 10in)
Diameter:	1.0m (39.5in)
Launch weight:	4600kg (10,141lb)
Guidance:	inertial
Propulsion:	solid fuel, two-stage
Warhead:	nuclear, 400kT
Range:	740km (460 miles)

MGM-118 Peacekeeper

This intercontinental ballistic missile is a four-stage rocket designed to deliver up to ten independently-targeted re-entry vehicle warheads against targets up to 10,000km (6300 miles) away. Three of the four stages use solid propellant motors, the fourth using liquid propellant. The flight is controlled entirely by self-contained computers and once off the launch pad, the missile is totally independent of any influence from the ground. The missile is placed in a container when built and remains in it until fired; firing involves firing a launch charge inside the container to eject the missile, whereupon the first stage motor ignites as the missile clears the container.

Country of origin:	USA
Length:	21.60m (70.86ft)
Diameter:	2.34m (7.67ft)
Launch weight:	88,450kg (87 tons)
Guidance:	inertial
Propulsion:	solid/liquid, four-stage
Warhead:	ten 500kT MIRV
Range:	8000+km (5000+ miles)

Titan

When Atlas, the first American intercontinental ballistic missile, was created, it was considered wise to start up a second line of development in case Atlas failed; this Atlas 2 was re-named Titan, and eventually became an ICBM in its own right. Titan was created some time after Atlas and therefore was the receptacle for many ideas which had arisen after seeing the result of earlier ideas put into practice on Atlas. But in the same way, some ideas dreamed up for Titan – such as the inertial guidance system – were used for Atlas and Titan ended up with other alternatives. Nevertheless, the result was a sound and serviceable missile, about 50 of which were sunk into silos across the US. Titan 2 was new from tip to tail and was designed to use storable liquid fuel and be permanently ready for immediate launch.

Country of origin:	USA
Length:	29.9m (98ft)
Diameter:	3.05m (10ft)
Launch weight:	99,792kg (98.21 tons)
Guidance:	radio
Propulsion:	liquid, two-stage
Warhead:	thermonuclear, 4MT
Range:	12,875km (8000 miles)

LGM-30F Minuteman 2

Minuteman was an American three-stage intercontinental ballistic missile carrying a single thermonuclear warhead. Minuteman 2 kept the same configuration but with increased range, increased payload, and a superior navigation system. The computer in the missile could now store a large number of alternative targets and the accuracy was greatly improved. Minuteman 3 appeared later and added a fourth stage with the adoption of a warhead containing three independently-targeted re-entry vehicles, each carrying a thermonuclear warhead. This version completely replaced Minuteman 2 in the 1980s. All Minuteman missiles were deployed in underground silos all over the continental United States, many being unmanned and remotely controlled.

Country of origin:	USA
Length:	18.2m (69.72ft)
Diameter:	1.84m (72.4in)
Launch weight:	31,746kg (31.24 tons)
Guidance:	inertial
Propulsion:	solid fuel, three-stage
Warhead:	thermonuclear, 2MT
Range:	12,500km (7770 miles)

BGM-109G Tomahawk

This long range cruise missile was originally provided for the US Navy as a tactical weapon, but over the years the accent has changed and it became the NATO Ground Launched Cruise Missile and was used to good effect in the Gulf War and other engagements. Design began in 1972, the intention being to have a weapon that could be fired out of a torpedo tube from a submerged submarine or from a surface ship. It would use a rocket to gain altitude and then a turbofan sustainer motor would fly it to its designated target. From this development, ground- and air-launched versions were developed, differing in detail from the original but fundamentally adapting to the same formula. It is one of the most versatile weapons ever developed and has demonstrated quite remarkable accuracy.

Country of origin:	USA
Length:	6.40m (21ft)
Diameter:	530mm (20in)
Wing span:	2.60m (8.53ft)
Launch weight:	1443kg (3181lb)
Guidance:	inertial, with terrain comparison
Propulsion:	solid fuel booster, turbofan sustainer engine
Warhead:	nuclear or HE, 454kg (1000lb)
Range:	2500km (1555 miles)

Surface-to-surface Missiles

SS-1 Scud B

The original SS-1 Scud missile was, like the US 'Corporal' of the same era, little more than an improved German V2 missile needing to be fuelled after erection and taking its time about deployment. This did not fit Russian tactical thinking and Scud-B appeared in the mid-1960s. This used a faster and lighter transporter-erector-launcher vehicle based on an 8x8 wheeled chassis, modernised the erecting and positioning mechanisms, and replaced the old radio-controlled fuel-cutoff and ballistic trajectory form of near-guidance with an up-to-date inertial system. All of this technology produced a weapon which could get to its firing site and engage its missile much quicker than the original. The Scud was supplied to Warsaw Pact armies and also to many Middle Eastern countries, where improved versions are still to be found.

Country of origin:	USSR
Length:	11.25m (36ft 11in)
Diameter:	850mm (33.5in)
Launch weight:	6300kg (13,888lb)
Guidance:	inertial
Propulsion:	liquid, single stage
Warhead:	nuclear or HE
Range:	280km (173 miles)

SS-12
Scaleboard

Very few people outside Russia have ever seen a Scaleboard missile because they were always transported and erected inside a missile-shaped cover, which split down the middle and was only opened when the weapon was ready to be fired. Indeed, there are those who think the whole thing was a bluff, to fool the West, but the evidence suggests that they really did exist. The SS-12 was a battlefield support missile carried on an 8x8 transporter-erector-launcher vehicle. It was accompanied by a variety of support vehicles and had to be fuelled immediately before launch, but was far faster into and out of action than the Scud, its predecessor. It was never supplied to other Warsaw Pact armies, nor sold abroad, and by the late 1980s was being replaced by the SS-22 and other more modern designs.

Country of origin:	USSR
Length:	12.0m (39.37ft)
Diameter:	1.0m (39.37in)
Launch weight:	9700kg (9.55 tons)
Guidance:	inertial
Propulsion:	liquid, single stage
Warhead:	nuclear
Range:	900km (555 miles)

SS-4 Sandal

The Soviet SS-4 Sandal, a medium-range ballistic missile, was, in effect, an advanced version of the SS-3 Shyster. It was first issued in 1958 and attained notoriety as being the cause of the Cuban missile crisis of 1962. The complete weapon system consisted of some twelve vehicles towing special trailers, and the weapon had to be laboriously erected and fuelled before firing. Guidance was originally by radio command, but by 1962 this had been changed to a simple form of inertial guidance. Deployed in considerable numbers with field armies, after 1977 it was gradually removed and replaced with SS-20 and other new designs, although the replacement process was not completed until the late 1980s.

Country of origin:	USSR
Length:	22.4m (73ft 6in)
Diameter:	1.65m (5ft 5in)
Launch weight:	27,000kg (59,536lb)
Guidance:	inertial
Propulsion:	liquid, single stage
Warhead:	HE or Nuclear, 1MT
Range:	2000km (1250 miles)

SS-5 Skean

The SS-5 Skean was the first Soviet missile to have near-global capabilities and was little more than a scaled-up version of the SS-4. It was first revealed to the West in 1964 but was apparently brought into service some two or three years earlier. It was one of the first Soviet missiles to do without aerodynamic fins, using vanes in the rocket exhaust for directional control. About 100 are believed to have been deployed in underground silos in various parts of Russia, and they appear to have initiated the use of storable fuel for such rockets. Most were withdrawn in the mid-1970s and replaced with more modern missiles, the final examples being decommissioned in the early 1980s.

Country of origin:	USSR
Length:	25.0m (82ft)
Diameter:	2.44m (8ft)
Launch weight:	60,000kg (59.05 tons)
Guidance:	inertial
Propulsion:	liquid, single stage
Warhead:	nuclear, 1MT
Range:	3500km (2175 miles)

SS-11 Sego

This intercontinental missile formed the backbone of the Soviet nuclear threat for many years, yet it is another of the large number of weapons which have scarcely been seen by anyone outside Russia. Large cylindrical containers have been paraded through Red Square, but the contents have never been displayed. The Models 2 and 3 went operational in 1973, by which time about 1000 silos had been identified by western intelligence. Towards the end of the 1970s the number began to shrink and by the early 1990s they had been replaced. The basic SS-11 was a storable-fuel two-stage rocket carrying a single warhead. The Model 2 had a number of 'penetration aids' – decoys to attract ABM missiles and allow the warhead through. Model 3 changed to multiple re-entry vehicles and penetration aids.

Country of origin:	USSR
Length:	19.0m (62.33ft)
Diameter:	2.40m (7.87ft)
Launch weight:	48,000kg (47.24 tons)
Guidance:	inertial
Propulsion:	liquid, single stage
Warhead:	nuclear, three 300kT MIRV
Range:	10600km (6650 miles)

SS-9 Scarp

This monstrous machine was once described as the largest mass-produced weapon ever made, a description it is difficult to argue with. Deployed in huge underground silos in the mid-1960s, some of its test shots, monitored by radar by the US, displayed such range and accuracy that the West really began to worry about Russian capabilities and intentions. The design continued to advance in complexity, the first models having a warhead of about 20MT, the second 25MT, the third was designed for low-level flight to avoid radars, and the fourth went to multiple warheads. Finally, Model 5 went into orbit with a satellite-destroying capability. By the late 1970s over 300 were deployed, but in the 1980s they were removed, to be replaced by an even bigger weapon, the SS-18.

Country of origin:	USSR
Length:	36.0m (118ft)
Diameter:	3.10m (10.17ft)
Launch weight:	190,000kg (87 tons)
Guidance:	inertial
Propulsion:	liquid, three-stage
Warhead:	nuclear
Range:	12,000km (7455 miles)

SS-13 Savage

A long with the SS-16 this was the first solid-propellant ICBM to be developed by the Soviets, probably by the V N Nadradze missile design bureau. First deployed in 1969, it was actually first seen in public in 1965. By 1972 the maximum operational number of 60 had been achieved. The missile was deployed in the Yoshkar Ola missile field. The three-stage inertially-guided missile is supposed to be comparable with the American Minuteman III missile in terms of performance and capabilities. It is armed with a single 600 kiloton warhead. The two upper stages of the SS-13 were subsequently used to develop the SS-14 Scapegoat mobile IRBM system. The SS-25 missile is apparently an modernised version of the SS-13.

Country of origin:	USSR
Length:	20m (65.6ft)
Diameter:	1.7m (5.57ft)
Launch weight:	34,000kg (33.46 tons)
Guidance:	inertial
Propulsion:	solid, three stage
Warhead:	nuclear; 600kT
Range:	8000km (4970 miles)

SS-17 Spanker

The SS-17 was a two-stage, storable liquid propellant ICBM which, together with the SS-19, would replace the old SS-11. Compared to the older design, this new missile had greater throw-weight, greater warhead capacity, better accuracy, better reliability and greater survivability. It also employed the 'cold launch' in which the missile is blown out of the silo by a gas generator and ignites its first stage as it reaches the open air, thus doing far less damage to the silo. Both the SS-17 and SS-19 introduced the Multiple Independently-targeted Re-entry Vehicle (MIRV) technology in which the warhead consists of a number of autonomous small warheads with rocket motors and guidance systems, which means that after leaving the main missile they can each seek different targets.

Country of origin:	USSR
Length:	24.4m (80ft)
Diameter:	2.5m (8.2ft)
Launch weight:	65,000kg (63.97 tons)
Guidance:	inertial; computer-controlled MIRV
Propulsion:	liquid, two-stage
Warhead:	nuclear; one 3.6MT or four 75-kT MIRV
Range:	11,000km (6835 miles)

SS-19 Stiletto

The SS-19 is a two-stage liquid propellant IRBM with on-board computer and MIRV warhead system. Together with the cold-launch SS-17, the hot-launch SS-19 was intended to replace the earlier SS-11 as a silo-emplaced weapon. It was larger and heavier, and the accuracy was greatly improved because of the on-board computer which compared the programmed trajectory with the actual flight path and made corrections as necessary to bring the missile back on course. It was packed in a transport/launch cylinder in which it was inserted into the silo and from which it was fired by igniting the first stage; the use of this cylinder prevented excessive damage to the silo from the rocket engine and also speeded up re-loading.

Country of origin:	USSR
Length:	27.3m (85.56ft)
Diameter:	2.5m (8.2ft)
Launch weight:	78,000kg (76.78 tons)
Guidance:	inertial; computer-controlled MIRV
Propulsion:	liquid; two-stage
Warhead:	nuclear; one 4.3MT or four or six 200kT MIRV
Range:	10,000km (6200 miles)

SS-18 Satan

The SS-18 was developed as an even bigger successor to the SS-9. A two-stage liquid propellant rocket, it had a very large payload capacity which led to some interesting, if desperate, experiments with 'bus-type' re-entry vehicles which flew around distributing warheads here and there, controlled by an on-board computer. As with most Soviet missiles, the design has been improved at various times and experts recognise four distinct versions with varying payloads (from 1–10 warheads) and ranges (from 12–16,000km/7456–9942 miles). As with other missiles of this period (1974 onwards), the missile is encased in a storage and firing cylinder and loaded into the silo. Huge mobile machinery is necessary to raise the 220,000kg (200 ton) tube to the vertical and then lower it 100 feet down a tight-fitting hole.

Country of origin:	USSR
Length:	37m (121.3ft)
Diameter:	3.2m (10.4ft)
Launch weight:	220,000kg (216.5 tons)
Guidance:	inertial, with computer-controlled MIRV
Propulsion:	liquid fuel, two-stage, cold launch
Warhead:	nuclear; one 25MT; or 8–10 1MT MIRV; or one 20MT; or ten 0.5 MT
Range:	16,000 km (10,000 miles)

SS-20 Saber

If the SS-20 does nothing else, it will be remembered for introducing the 12x12 wheeled vehicle. a massive transporter-erector-launcher which carries the missile in a canister, erects it, and then fires it straight out of the canister. It was the replacement for the old SS-4 and SS-5 systems, which it began ousting in about 1977. It is a two-stage solid propellant mobile IRBM with multiple warhead capacity, using inertial guidance with a claimed probable error of 400m (437yds) at maximum range. By the mid-1980s, it was estimated that there were about 350 of these weapons deployed, of which 240 were in eastern Russia threatening Europe and the West, and the remainder were in Siberia aimed towards China and Japan, and more sites were being built. How many still remain is an open question.

Country of origin:	USSR
Length:	16.4m (53.8ft)
Diameter:	1.40m (55in)
Launch weight:	13,000kg (12.8 tons)
Guidance:	inertial
Propulsion:	solid fuel, two-stage
Warhead:	nuclear: three 150kT MIRV
Range:	5000km (3100 miles)

RSD 58

Their early Swiss design of a SAM was probably the first to be offered on the commercial market. It was developed by Contraves and Oerlikon, two well-known Swiss firms, in 1947. Test firings took place from 1950 and the development was completed in 1952, after which they were adopted by Switzerland, Italy and Japan and evaluated by several other countries. The missiles had rear fins and wings which could slide, thus correcting the trim as the solid-fuel propellant burned away. Control was by a radar beam, the missile being gathered after launch and directed along a very fine beam, which continuously tracked the target. The warhead carried a radio proximity fuse.

Country of origin:	Switzerland
Length:	6.0m (19ft 8in)
Diameter:	40cm (15.75in)
Wingspan:	1.35m (53.0in)
Warhead:	HE; 40kg (88lb)
Launch weight:	400kg (882lb)
Maximum slant range:	30km (19 miles)

Air Defence Missiles

Thunderbird

Development of this British missile began in 1949 with the intention of replacing heavy air defence artillery, and it entered service with the Royal Artillery in 1956. The missile had short wings, four large tail fins, a solid fuel sustainer motor and four boost rockets attached to the exterior. The warhead was a continuous rod casing packed with explosives, so that on detonation a gigantic spinning circle of steel flew at the target and sawed it in half. The warhead could be detonated by command or, more usually, by a radio proximity fuse. An improved version, Thunderbird 2, appeared in the mid-1960s, with greater velocity and more advanced control technology. Thunderbird was eventually taken out of service in the late 1970s.

Country of origin:	United Kingdom
Length:	6.35m (20ft 10in)
Diameter:	527mm (20.75in)
Wingspan:	1.63m (64.0in)
Warhead:	HE; continuous rod
Launch weight:	not disclosed
Maximum slant range:	75km (46 miles)

Seaslug

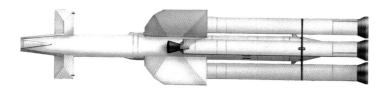

Seaslug was the first British ship defence missile, and although it was an extremely slow development, the result was exceptionally accurate, with a hit probability of 91 per cent. It was of the usual rocket shape, with four forward control surfaces and four wings at the rear, a solid fuel sustainer motor and four solid fuel boost motors attached externally. The boosters gave it a high initial velocity and short time of flight, and it was gathered into a radar beam after launch and then controlled by riding a very fine radar beam to the target. When installed on warships, the system was completely autonomous; the radar would detect a target, track it, and once it was within range, fire the missile and guide it to impact. The warhead was provided with impact and proximity fuses.

Country of origin:	United Kingdom
Length:	6.10m (20ft)
Diameter:	409mm (16.1in)
Wingspan:	1.437m (56.6in)
Warhead:	HE; 135kg (297lb)
Launch weight:	not disclosed
Maximum slant range:	58km (36 miles)

SA-1 Guild

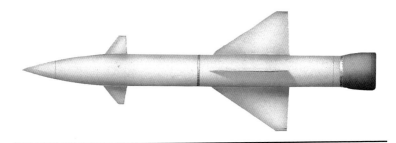

The Soviet SA-1 Guild went into service in the mid-1950s and remained in first-line units until the early 1980s. The design was based upon the German wartime 'Wasserfall' missile, development of which was still in progress when the war ended in 1945. The result was a liquid-fuel rocket motor fed by turbine pumps and controlled in flight by fins and canards. The target is detected by an acquisition radar and passed to a tracking radar which locks on. The missile is steered into the beam and kept there by radio control until its proximity fuse detects the target and detonates the warhead. The missile went through several degrees of modification during its service life, suggesting that the initial design was not particularly good, and it is known that many were fired at US spy planes without success.

Country of origin:	USSR
Length:	12m (39ft 4in)
Diameter:	700mm (27.5in)
Wingspan:	2.70m (8ft 10in)
Warhead:	HE-Frag; 250kg (551lb); impact and proximity fuses
Launch weight:	3500kg (7716lb)
Maximum slant range:	40km (24.8 miles)

Henschel Hs117 Schmetterling

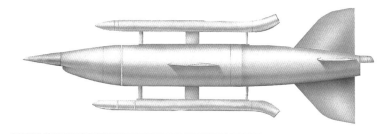

Schmetterling ('butterfly') was the ancestor of all surface-to-air missiles and was very nearly used in World War II. Although development began in 1941, it was a low priority for years until it was revived in late 1943 in the face of increasing Allied air attacks on Germany. The Hs117 was a mid-wing monoplane, propelled by a liquiud-fuel rocket motor and controlled by radio. The controller flew it visually, keeping both missile and target in view from a special tracking station, his radio having 18 channels in order to evade jamming. Two solid-fuel boost rockets assisted at launch and were discarded after a few seconds of flight. However, due to Allied bombing raids on the factories involved in the development, the planned production schedule was never met and the missile was never brought into service.

Country of origin:	Germany
Length:	4.29m (14ft)
Diameter:	350mm (13.77in)
Wingspan:	2.0m (6ft 7in)
Warhead:	HE blast; 25kg; impact and proximity fused
Launch weight:	445 kg (981lb)
Maximum slant range:	32km (20 miles)

SA-3 Goa

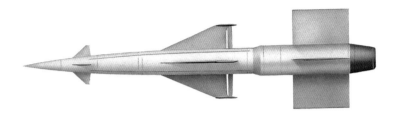

The SA-3 was developed in the mid-1950s by the Soviet Lavochkin design bureau as a low-level defence weapon to accompany the SA-1 and SA-2 high-level missiles. Manufacture began in 1959 and it was issued with a wheeled transporter-launcher carrying two missiles side-by-side for mobile roles, and with a four-missile turntable launcher for fixed positions. It was deployed for airfield and missile site defence, and with field armies as a mobile defence force. The missile itself is slender, with a solid fuel motor, and there is a thicker boost rocket attached at the rear end for launching. Affter launch, the boost motor drops off and the missile is then gathered by the guidance radar and rides the beam to interception with the target. The SA-3 was widely distributed to Communist-oriented countries.

Country of origin:	USSR
Length:	6.7m (22ft)
Diameter:	450mm (17.7in)
Wingspan:	1.22m (4 ft)
Warhead:	HE blast; 60kg (132lb)
Launch weight:	950kg (2094lb)
Maximum slant range:	30km (18.5 miles)

Nike Ajax

Nike Ajax has the distinction of being the first surface-to-air guided missile to enter regular service with a military force when it was deployed to protect Washington DC in December 1953. The missile had wings and canard fins at the forward end and a solid fuel motor. It was launched by a large tandem booster motor attached to the rear of the missile. The entire system was intended as a fixed defensive system and therefore the launchers and emplacements were complex and large structures. Control was by radar which tracked the target and into whose beam the missile was gathered. A target radar also tracked the target and the two were linked to a computer which steered the missile into the future position of the target and then detonated it. Systems were supplied to several Nato and other countries during the 1960s.

Country of origin:	USA
Length:	10.62m (34ft 10in)
Diameter:	305mm (12.0in)
Wingspan:	1.22m (48in)
Warhead:	5.4kg, 55kg and 81kg (12lb, 122lb and 179lb)
Launch weight:	1114kg (2455lb)
Maximum slant range:	40km (25 miles)

Nike Hercules

Nike Hercules was the second generation of Nike and it was an attempt to produce a system which was more efficient, but at the same time simpler to use. It also had to be compatible with Nike Ajax and use as much of that expensive system as possible. The missile itself was vastly improved, with a speed of Mach 3.5 and the ability to intercept a target at altitudes of well over 40,000m (25 miles), and it destroyed the idea, still lingering in the minds of aviators, that missiles could be evaded by flying high and fast. The system was deployed in the US by late 1958 and in subsequent years it was supplied to several countries in order to upgrade their earlier Nike Ajax batteries.

Country of origin:	USA
Length:	12.5m (41ft)
Diameter:	800mm (31.5in)
Wingspan:	1.88m (74in)
Warhead:	HE; 503kg (1108lb) or nuclear
Launch weight:	4720kg (10,405lb)
Maximum slant range:	155km (96 miles)

Talos

Talos was a US Navy missile which introduced the concept of delivering long range by using a ramjet motor for sustained power and which was capable of moving the missile at supersonic speeds. Development of the motor began in March 1945, the missile entered service in 1958 and some remained in service on US warships until the late 1980s. Launched with the aid of two solid fuel booster rockets, the kerosene-fuelled ramjet ignites and takes up the drive after the boosters fall away, setting a constant speed of Mach 2.5. A radar tracks the target and the Talos steers into the radar's beam and then rides it until it can detect the radar reflections off the target. A radar homing system steers the missile towards the target until the proximity fuse detonates the warhead.

Country of origin:	USA
Length:	6.78m (22ft 3in)
Diameter:	762mm (30in)
Wingspan:	2.90m (9ft 6in)
Warhead:	HE; continuous rod or nuclear
Launch weight:	3540 kg (7105lb)
Maximum slant range:	120km (75 miles)

Crotale

Crotale was actually developed in France for South Africa in the 1950s, and was known there as Cactus; the name Crotale applies to the system when used by France or sold to other countries. The system is mobile and the launcher vehicle carries four missile launch tubes on a turntable. In the centre of these four tubes is the dish of the target tracking radar. A second vehicle carries an acquisition radar and can be linked by cable to one or more launch units. The missile is a simple solid-fuel rocket but it reaches Mach 2.3 in just over two seconds from launch. It is gathered into the radar beam and then rides it until the infra-red proximity fuse detects the target and detonates the warhead when it is within lethal distance.

Country of origin:	France
Length:	2.93m (9ft 7in)
Diameter:	156mm (6.14in)
Wingspan:	540mm (21.25in)
Warhead:	HE; 15kg (33lb); infra-red proximity fuse
Launch weight:	85kg (187 3lb)
Maximum slant range:	8.5km (5.3 miles)

Roland

Roland was developed in conjunction by French and German companies in the 1960s. The first missile flew in 1968 but it was 1977 before any were issued to the French Army and 1981 before Germany had its full quota of systems. The long development time paid off in a reliable and efficient system. There were two types in service: Roland 1, a 'fair-weather' system relying upon optical tracking, and Roland 2, an 'all-weather' system using radar tracking. In 1983 an upgrade to a new Roland 3 standard began using improved optical sighting and computer equipment. The two-missile launcher reloads from beneath the armoured protection. The missile is guided by either a radar beam or by automatic guidance signals generated by the optical sight.

Country of origin:	France/Germany
Length:	2.40m (94.5in)
Diameter:	160mm (6.3in)
Wingspan:	500mm (19.7in)
Warhead:	multiple shaped charge; 6.5kg (14.3lb); radio proximity fuse
Launch weight:	63kg (139lb)
Maximum slant range:	6.2km (3.9 miles)

Bloodhound

Bloodhound was the static version of Thunderbird, the mobile air defence equipment. Part of the Air Defence of Great Britain system, it was deployed in some numbers along the east coast of Britain. Firing from static emplacements meant that the missile could be bigger and thus several features of its controls and flight system differed from Thunderbird. The appearance was similar, a winged rocket carrying four booster motors, but instead of an internal solid fuel motor it had two ramjet sustainer motors on the exterior of the missile, the interior being used for fuel storage and supply. Guidance was by semi-active homing, the missile being directed to the vicinity of the target and then homing by detecting the radar signals emitted by a ground Target Illuminating Radar and reflected from the target.

Country of origin:	United Kingdom
Length:	8.46m (27ft 9in)
Diameter:	546mm (27.5in)
Wingspan:	2.83m (9ft 3in)
Warhead:	HE; continuous rod; proximity fused
Launch weight:	not disclosed
Maximum slant range:	In excess of 80km (50 miles)

Blowpipe

Blowpipe was issued to the British Army in 1975, and subsequently adopted by several other countries. It is a man-portable system consisting of a sealed launch tube containing the missile and a sight and firing unit. The two are clipped together, and the operator places the unit on his shoulder and takes aim. Having acquired his target, he presses the trigger; this switches on the missile gyroscope and fires the booster rocket. After launch, the missile is gathered into the line of sight and steered towards the target by the operator using a thumb-joystick, until the proximity fuse detects the target and detonates the warhead. In skilled hands, the Blowpipe was a very effective weapon, but training was long and difficult. The performance of Blowpipe during the 1982 Falklands campaign was disappointing.

Country of origin:	United Kingdom
Length:	1.40m (55.1in)
Diameter:	76.2mm (3.0in)
Wingspan:	274mm (10.8in)
Warhead:	HEAT/blast; 2.2kg (4.85lb); proximity fused
Launch weight:	11.0kg (24.5lb)
Maximum slant range:	3500m (3825yds)

Air Defence Missiles

Rapier

T his British weapon appeared in the mid-1960s and was claimed to be a 'hittile' rather than a missile because it showed remarkable accuracy. A fine-weather system in its first days, it used a simple launcher carrying two or four missiles and was towed by a small 4x4 vehicle. The missile used a two-stage solid-fuel rocket to achieve Mach 2.2 and had a semi-AP warhead with impact fuse. After firing, the missile is tracked optically and automatically guided into the line of sight by an infra-red detector tracking a flare in the missile's tail. This system was then upgraded to an all-weather capability by adding the 'Blindfire' track and guide radar system. Finally, the whole system was put on tracks for greater mobility and became known as 'Tracked Rapier'.

Country of origin:	United Kingdom
Length:	2.24m (88.2in)
Diameter:	133mm (5.25in)
Wingspan:	381mm (15in)
Warhead:	HE/AP; 500g (1.1lb)
Launch weight:	42kg (94lb)
Maximum slant range:	7250m (4.5 miles)

Bofors RBS-70

This shoulder-fired missile has a launch unit incorporates a seat for the operator and a gyro-stabilised sight. It can be wired into a radar or other early-warning network so that the operator has more warning of an approaching target and can at least be facing in the right direction to pick it up. The missile uses a two-stage, solid fuel motor and is supplied in a sealed tube which is dropped into the launcher and connects automatically to the sight and control unit. The sight unit emits a fine laser beam, invisible to the eye, and the missile detects this beam and follows it to the target. A laser proximity fuse detonates the warhead at a lethal distance, or, for engaging very low flying targets where ground reflections might mislead the fuse, it can be switched off, and an impact fuse will function if the missile hits the target.

Country of origin:	Sweden
Length:	1.32m (52in)
Diameter:	106mm (4.17in)
Wingspan:	320mm (12.6in)
Warhead:	HE-pre-fragmented; 1.0kg (2.2lb); impact and proximity fused
Launch weight:	15kg (33lb)
Maximum slant range:	5km (3 miles)

SA-4 Ganef

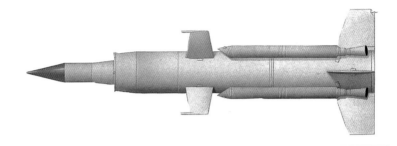

First observed in 1964, this self-propelled system forms the long-range air defence element of Russian field armies. The tracked amphibious carrier mounts a twin launcher on a turntable and has the ability to accompany an armoured division in any sort of terrain. The large missile is a ramjet, fuelled by kerosene, and has four boost rockets attached in order to launch it and reach a speed at which the ramjet can take over. A surveillance radar finds and illuminates the target; the missile is then launched and guided towards the target by radio signals. In the terminal phase of its flight, its own radar detects the radar signals reflected from the target and steers the missile into intercept, the proximity fuse then detonates the warhead. In addition to Russia, Ganef is also in service with the Czech, Hungarian and Bulgarian armies.

Country of origin:	USSR
Length:	9.0m (29ft 6in)
Diameter:	800mm (31.5in)
Wingspan:	2.60m (102in)
Warhead:	HE-Frag; 135kg (298lb); impact and proximity fused
Launch weight:	2500kg (5511lb)
Maximum slant range:	55km (34 miles)

SA-6 Gainful

SA-6 Gainful is probably the most widely-distributed of all the Russian air defence missiles, being used by some 20 countries in Europe, Africa and the Middle East. Developed in the early 1980s, it is a self-propelled system based on a tracked vehicle carrying a triple launcher on the roof. The missile itself is an integral ramjet/rocket unit of great ingenuity. The solid-fuel rocket boosts the missile to Mach 1.5 and burns out; the nozzle is jettisoned, after which the empty tube becomes part of the ramjet motor which accelerates the missile to Mach 2.8 and holds that speed. Little notice was taken of this missile in the West until the 1973 Arab-Israeli war, when SA-6 missiles in Arab hands began downing Israeli aircraft at an astonishing rate.

Country of origin:	USSR
Length:	5.70m (18ft 9in)
Diameter:	335mm (13.2in)
Wingspan:	1.524m (60in)
Warhead:	HE-Frag; 56kg (123.5lb); impact and proximity fused
Launch weight:	600kg (1323lb)
Maximum slant range:	24km (15 miles)

Air Defence Missiles

SA-7 Grail

This shoulder-fired missile must be the premier Russian export line, since it is to be found all over of the world in the hands of legitimate armies , irregular forces, freedom fighters and terrorists of every political shade. It was probably copied from the American Redeye and has similar shortcomings, but as a hand-held weapon it is a reasonable performer. The firer, on seeing a target, merely has to shoulder the weapon, aim and press a firing switch. This turns on the heat-seeking head of the missile which, as soon as it acquires the target, gives a signal, and the firer then presses the trigger and the missile is launched. It steers itself towards the target but can be distracted by anything producing more heat and is easily fooled by pyrotechnic counter-measures.

Country of origin:	USSR
Length:	1.25m (53.25in)
Diameter:	70mm (2.75in)
Launcher weight:	4.17kg (9.20lb)
Warhead:	HE-Frag; 1.15kg (2.53lb); impact fused
Missile weight:	9.2kg (20.3lb)
Maximum slant range:	10km (6 miles)

SA-8 Gecko

T his Soviet self-propelled system, first seen in 1976, consists of a specialised 6x6 wheeled carrier with a multiple launcher unit on the roof. This launch unit sits on the same turntable as a tracking radar and a surveillance radar, so that the whole system is self-contained in one vehicle. The early versions had four exposed missiles set side-by-side on a launching rack, but this was superseded by a version which is loaded by placing three pre-packed missiles in their transit/firing containers, on each side of the surveillance radar unit. This has simplified re-loading; originally they were hand-loaded from within the vehicle (now the last resort), but now loading is completed by a supply vehicle which lifts a pallet of three boxed missiles into place. The missile is radar tracked and command guided.

Country of origin:	USSR
Length:	3.15m (19ft 4lb)
Diameter:	210mm (8.26in)
Wingspan:	640mm (25.1in)
Warhead:	HE-Frag; 19kg (42lb); impact and proximity fused
Launch weight:	130kg (287lb)
Maximum slant range:	12km (7.5 miles)

M48 Chaparral

In the early 1960s, Britain and the US gambled on an American project called 'Mauler', a self-propelled missile system which could do everything. When it failed, they were left needing a medium range missile system. Britain found Rapier; the Americans stitched Chaparral together by taking the air-to-air 'Sidewinder' missile and making a few slight modifications to suit a different launch system. They then built a launcher on a highly-modified M113 APC and fitted an optical sight. A radar could be connected to give early warning, otherwise the missile was simply pointed towards the target, switched on so the infra-red head could lock on, and then fired. In the late 1970s, the design was vastly improved by adding a tracking radar to permit all-weather firing.

Country of origin:	USA
Length:	2.87m (113in)
Diameter:	127mm (5.0in)
Wingspan:	630mm (24.8in)
Warhead:	HE continuous rod; 10.2kg (22.4 lb); proximity fused
Launch weight:	88.5kg (195lbs)
Maximum slant range:	4000m (4375yds)

MIM-104 Patriot

Patriot is the anti-missile missile, and its formidable specification took close to 20 years of study and development before it was allowed into service. It finally got the chance to show its paces during the Gulf War, countering the Iraqi Scuds being fired towards Israel, but argument still rages about whether they were effective or not. The Patriot missile has a high-efficiency 11.5 second solid fuel rocket motor. A surveillance radar detects a target and informs the missile of its general direction, so that it will turn towards the target after launch and thus be gathered by a tracking radar. This guides it to the area of the target where an on-board radar takes charge and homes the missile on to the target. A proximity fuse then detonates the warhead when within lethal distance.

Country of origin:	USA
Length:	5.18m (17ft)
Diameter:	410mm (16.15in)
Wingspan:	920mm (36in)
Warhead:	HE-Frag; 73kg (160lb); proximity fused
Launch weight:	700kg (1545lb)
Maximum slant range:	160km (100 miles)

MIM-23 HAWK

HAWK means 'Homing All-the-Way Killer' and is a surprisingly long-lived US system which began development in 1952 and is still in use worldwide today. It was designed to be a low-level system for deployment with field armies. Although cumbersome and needing large numbers of men and vehicles, it was accepted because nothing else was remotely as good, and with a few modifications it has remained perfectly serviceable. The missile has a two-stage solid fuel motor, giving both an initial high acceleration rate and sustained thrust. The original launcher was a three-missile cluster on a trailer but fixed and mobile launchers with up to nine missiles are now in use. The Hawk is a radar homer which picks up signals from a radar which are reflected by the target, and steers itself to interception.

Country of origin:	USA
Length:	5.12m (16.8ft)
Diameter:	356m (1167.9ft)
Wingspan:	1.206m (3.95ft)
Warhead:	HE; continuous rod; 54.4kg (120lb); impact and proximity fused
Launch weight:	626kg (1380lb)
Maximum slant range:	40km (25 miles)

FIM-92 Stinger

The first shoulder-fired missile in service with the US Army was Redeye which could only work once the attack was over and the enemy was departing and showing a hot tail-pipe. Work began on a replacement in the early 1960s, the aim being an all-aspect system, and it was not until 1979 that production finally commenced. Stinger still uses an infra-red heat-seeking homer, but the principle has been refined and it now has an ultra-violet detector working in conjunction with the IR system to act as a sort of filter and make the system capable of homing on to any target except a head-on attacker (where the aircraft body conceals the exhaust plume). A limited IFF identification system is also incorporated in the latest version, as is the ability to be informed of approaching targets by any local radar network.

Country of origin:	USA
Length:	1.52m (60in)
Diameter:	70mm (2.75in)
Wingspan:	91mm (3.58in)
Warhead:	HE-Frag; 3.0kg (6.6lb); impact fused
Launch weight:	10.1kg (22.25lb)
Maximum slant range:	5000m (3.1 miles)

Type 81 Tan-SAM

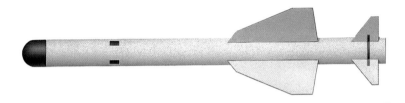

This weapon was developed by Toshiba Electric during the 1970s and was introduced into service with the Japanese Self-Defence Force in 1980. The missile is a single-stage fire-and-forget rocket which uses an automatic pilot for the first part of its flight, and then switches to infra-red homing to acquire the target and intercept it. One advantage of this method is that electronic countermeasures (jamming) cannot affect it, but on the other hand the IR seeker can be fooled by pyrotechnic decoy flares or similar devices. As a result, in the 1980s an improvement programme, known as Tan-SAM Kai, was inaugurated, which resulted in the upgrading of the missile by improving its IR selectivity and range, and also improving the hit probability.

Country of origin:	Japan
Length:	2.70m (8ft 10in)
Diameter:	160mm (6.30in)
Wingspan:	600mm (23.6 in)
Warhead:	HE-Frag; impact and proximity fused
Launch weight:	100kg (220lb)
Maximum slant range:	7km (4.3 miles)

Mistral

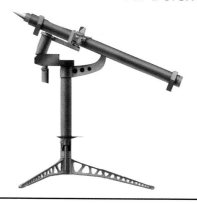

This weapon first appeared in the early 1980s as the SATCP (*Sol-Air Très Court Portée* – ground-air, very short range) which is a fair explanation. It is the French infantry's lightweight shoulder-fired air defence weapon, and was delivered in 1988. The design included a lightweight launcher post on three feet, relieving the operator of the weight of the missile while aiming and firing, which improves the hit probability. The missile is a fire-and-forget infra-red homer, which locks on to the target heat source. Using combined IR-UV detection, this is a true all-aspect missile. It uses a solid-fuel rocket and is pre-packed into a tube which is clipped on to the launcher post and sight. The operator aims, then presses a switch which runs up the gyroscope, switches on the IR detector head, and fires the rocket.

Country of origin:	France
Length:	1.81m (71.25in)
Diameter:	92.5mm (3.64in)
Wingspan:	190mm (7.5in)
Warhead:	HE-Frag; 2.95kg (6.5lb); impact and laser proximity fused
Launch weight:	18.4kg (40.5lb)
Maximum slant range:	6km (3.7 miles)

Starstreak

The British Starstreak fires three warheads at its target to improve hit probability. Shoulder-fired or vehicle mounted, it resembles Blowpipe in its launcher configuration. A two-stage solid-fuel rocket boosts the missile to supersonic speed, between Mach 3–4. The launch unit projects a laser beam at the target, which the missile follows. When the rocket burns out there is a drop in acceleration, which triggers the ejection of three dart-like sub-munitions. These also have laser guidance and adhere to a triangular pattern around the laser beam. The expended missile casing falls behind. On reaching the target the sub-munitions, which are of dense metal and with piercing heads, penetrate the skin; a delay fuse then detonates an explosive charge to fragment the munitions inside the target.

Country of origin:	United Kingdom
Length:	1.40m (55in)
Diameter:	127mm (5in)
Wingspan:	not available
Warhead:	three HE/kinetic darts
Launch weight:	not disclosed
Maximum slant range:	7km (4.4 miles)

ADATS

Developed by the Swiss firm Oerlikon, ADATS is both an Air Defence and Anti-Tank System. It was developed between 1979 and 1985 and adopted by the Canadian Army in 1986. The system consists of a quadruple launcher unit on a modified M113 APC. The unit also carries a surveillance and tracking radar which, having acquired a target, passes it to an electro-optical tracker. This then aims the launcher and fires a missile, which follows a digitally coded laser beam which is held on to the target. The missile warhead is a shaped charge surrounded by a fragmentation sleeve, controlled by a range-gated laser proximity fuse. This ensures optimum fragmentation to destroy aerial targets, and a substantial armour-penetration capability to deal with battlefield armour.

Country of origin:	Switzerland/Canada
Length:	2.08m (6ft 10in)
Diameter:	152mm (6.0in)
Velocity:	mach 3
Warhead:	HEAT/Frag; 12kg (26.5lb); laser proximity fused
Launch weight:	51kg (112.5lb)
Maximum range:	10km (6.2 miles)

235

Canon de 240 Mle 93/96 sur Affuit-truck St-Chamond

This gun was extracted from the coastal defences of various French colonies, returned to France and mounted on this railway carriage by the St Chamond company. The gun is positioned on its coastal pedestal, allowing it to traverse the full circle and fire in any direction. To support the gun when firing across the track, outriggers were provided for the rear side and rail clips for the muzzle side. If firing over the ends of the truck, elevation was restricted to 29°, otherwise the breech would strike the raised ends of the truck. It was issued with an ammunition truck which coupled to the rear and had an overhead rail system which delivered shells to the loading platform behind the breech.

Country of origin:	France
Calibre:	240mm (9.45in)
Barrel length:	10.05m (33ft)
Overall length:	19.50m (64ft)
Weight in action:	140,000kg (137.75 tons)
Elevation:	+15° to +35°
Traverse:	58°
Shell and weight:	HE; 162kg (357lb)
Muzzle velocity:	840m/sec (2755ft/sec)
Maximum range:	23,000m (25,159yds)

Canon de 320 Mle 1870/93 sur Affuit-truck Schneider

The 320mm (12.55in) gun was one of many naval or fortress guns pressed into service on the Western Front due to the French lack of heavy field artillery. To save time, no recoil system was used, the gun trunnions being fitted into reinforced bearings on the carriage sides. To absorb the recoil, six steel crossbeams beneath the carriage were lowered on to the track, and the weight of the mounting taken on them by jacks. On firing, the entire mounting slid backwards along the track, being kept straight by the bogies. There was no traverse; the gun was pushed around a curved track until the barrel pointed in the required direction. After firing a few rounds, it had to be lowered back on to its wheels and pushed back to its original position, jacked down, and only then could begin firing once more.

Country of origin:	France
Calibre:	320mm (12.55in)
Barrel length:	10.442m (34ft 3in)
Overall length:	25.90m (85ft)
Weight in action:	162,000kg (159.3 tons)
Elevation:	+22° to +40°
Traverse:	nil
Shell and weight:	HE; 388kg (854.5lb)
Muzzle velocity:	675m/sec (2215ft/sec)
Maximum range:	24,800m (27,120 yds)

Railway Artillery

21cm K12(E)

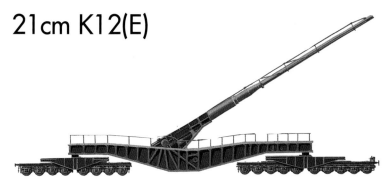

The German Navy's World War I 'Paris Gun' held the long range record, having shelled Paris from 68 miles away. The Army decided to outstrip this with a fresh design in the 1930s, which became the K12(E). This used a shell with curved ribs, matching deep rifling grooves in the barrel, a special sealing ring behind it and a powerful charge. All of this and a very long barrel went on to a railway truck mounting, and in order to allow the gun to recoil at high elevations without striking the track, the carriage was jacked up from the bogies before firing. The gun was fired from a position in France in late 1940 and the shells landed as far as Rainham Marshes, Kent, 88.5km (55 miles) from the nearest point on the French coast. As a weapon it was pointless, but as a technical achievement it was remarkable.

Country of origin:	Germany
Calibre:	21cm (8.31in)
Barrel length:	33.3m (109.25ft)
Length over buffers:	41.3m (139.5ft)
Weight in action:	302,000kg (297.28 tons)
Elevation:	+25° to +55°
Traverse:	1°
Shell and weight:	HE; 107.5kg (237.04lb)
Muzzle velocity:	1500ft/sec (4922m/sec)
Maximum range:	115km (71.46 miles)

28cm K5(E)

Probably the best workaday railway gun ever built, the K5(E) formed the backbone of the German railway artillery force and saw wide use. Designed at the same time as the K12, several features were charted, notably the deep-grooves barrel and ribbed shell. A rocket-boosted shell was developed which increased the maximum range to 86.5km (53.7 miles), although at the expense of accuracy. After this, a barrel was bored out to 31cm (12.2in) smoothbore and a fin-stabilised dart-like shell, the Peenemunde Arrow Shell, was fired with a special propelling charge to give a maximum range of 151km (93.8 miles). Two K5(E) have been preserved, one at Cap Griz Nez in France, and the other at Aberdeen Proving Ground in the US, the only World War II railway guns to have survived.

Country of origin:	Germany
Calibre:	28cm (11.02in)
Barrel length:	21.539m (70.08ft)
Overall length:	41.234m (135.28ft)
Weight in action:	218,000kg (214.59 tons)
Elevation:	0° to 50°
Traverse:	2°
Shell and weight:	HE; 255.5 kg (563.38lb)
Muzzle velocity:	1128m/sec (3700ft/sec)
Maximum range:	62.18km (38.64 miles)

80cm Gustav

The biggest gun the world has ever seen or is ever likely to see, this monster which travelled dismantled into its constituent parts, had a special set of four tracks laid at the firing site, two for the gun and two for the assembly cranes, took weeks to assemble or dismantle and demanded the services of over 1200 men, plus an anti-aircraft gun regiment for protection. Originally designed to defeat the fortifications of the Maginot Line, it took longer to develop and build than expected and was used solely on the Eastern Front against Sebastopol and other hard targets. Two were built, Gustav and Dora, and a third was still being manufactured when the war ended. Sufficient parts to build a complete gun were never found, and the remains of all three were scrapped.

Country of origin:	Germany
Calibre:	80cm (31.4in)
Barrel length:	32.480m (106.56ft)
Length over buffers:	42.976m (141ft)
Weight in action:	1,350,000 kg (1328.9 tons)
Elevation:	+10° to +65°
Traverse:	nil
Shell and weight:	HE: 4800kg (4.73 tons); CP: 7100kg (6.99 tons)
Muzzle velocity:	HE: 820m/sec (2690ft/sec); CP: 710m/sec (2330ft/sec)
Maximum range:	HE: 47km (29.2 miles); CP: 38km (23.61 miles)

Polish Armoured Train

The Polish Army deployed a number of armoured trains in the 1920s, largely as a mobile reserve for their eastern frontier, although the scarcity of railways in that part of Poland barely warranted such equipment. Each train was given a name, usually that of a Polish folk or national hero, such as 'General Sosnkowski', 'Paderewski' and 'Marszalek'. In the 1930s, as the threat moved from east to west, the trains were re-deployed to an area where the lines were more numerous, thus giving the trains a greater chance of influencing the battle.

However, armoured trains of this era suffered from two major defects: firstly, they were constrained to going where the rails went, and unlike railway guns they were not designed to operate over temporary trackage – they had to have properly laid track. And secondly, they had little or no air defence weapons, probably because nobody really understood what a ground attack aircraft was capable of doing to a train. The German invasion in 1939 brought these two defects into sharp focus; the Panzers easily avoided the trains, and the Stukas easily found them and destroyed them. Any surviving trains were taken into German service after the fall of Poland and used for internal security, and later anti-partisan activities in the Soviet Union.

Armament of these trains varied according to what was available at the time they were built; the example shown here is an armoured carriage from the Polish 'Danuta' train, which had two armed wagons, an accomodation and control wagon with a radio, and an armoured locomotive. Two flat-bed waggons could be attached at the front and rear of the train, their only purpose being to absorb any damage from mines laid on the track. The carriage is equipped with a 100mm (3.93in) former Austro-Hungarian howitzer in one turret, a 75mm (2.95in) field gun in the other turret, and a small cupola mounting a 7.92mm (0.31in) machine gun.

German Armoured Trains

Armoured trains are very much a Central European speciality, since their principal utility is firstly as a mobile reserve to move quickly to a threatened spot on a long and empty border, and secondly to protect lines of communication through areas devoid of settlements but probably crawling with guerrillas, partisans and similar irritants. The Russians made good use of armoured trains during their Civil War in the 1917–22 period, and this influenced Poland and Czechoslovakia to build their own. Germany also built them during World War I to cover their supply lines through the long expanses of Poland and eastern Russia, and they, too, continued to use them into the post-1918 period as a method of guarding their eastern frontiers. As a result of their diplomatic manoeuvres and their victorious campaign in 1939, the Germans were able to add Polish, Czech and Austrian trains to their stock, all of which became valuable property when they got involved in the Balkans and then invaded Russia. The only drawback was that the Russians used a different railway gauge to anyone else in Europe and thus the German trains could not cross the borders until some extensive relaying of track

had taken place. In some cases, the German armoured rolling stock was altered to fit the Russian track and captured Russian locomotives were armoured and used as motive power. One way or another, the Germans managed to use trains to patrol the tenuous rail links which joined the Eastern Front with the German manufacturing and supply organisation, thus keeping the depredations of Russian partisans and other dissidents down to a reasonable level.

There was no such thing as a standard armoured train; the design of any train depended entirely upon what was available at the time of manufacture, in rolling stock, locomotives and armament. No neat table of dimensions can therefore be drawn up. However, the train shown here, typical of wartime construction, carried a mixture of 105mm (4.13in) howitzers and 50mm (1.97in) anti-tank guns, plus a quadruple 20mm (0.78in) anti-aircraft mount, showing that the Germans, who used tactical air as an extension of their artillery and used it to wreck Polish and Russian armoured trains, were fully alive to the possibility of having the same weapon used against them.

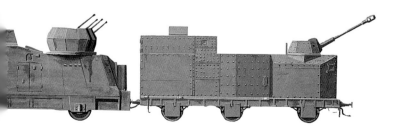

12in Railway Howitzer Mk 5

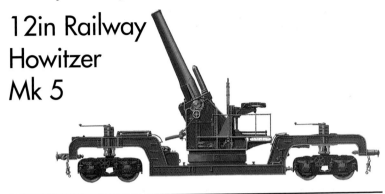

Britain developed three 305mm (12in) Railway Howitzers during World War I. The Mark 1 was 12 calibres long, but the Army demanded something with more range. This led to the 17-calibre Mark 2 which increased the range from 10,177m (11,130yds) to 13,715m (15,000yds) but which could only be fired over the ends of the carriage, within a 40° arc, otherwise it would leap off the track. The Army were glad of the extra range but wanted all-round fire, so Vickers went back for a third try and came up with the Mark 5 Howitzer which had all-round traverse and was stabilised by outriggers and jacks. The Marks 3 and 5 survived the war and were brought out of store in 1939, refurbished, and deployed as anti-invasion guns along the east coast of England.

Country of origin:	United Kingdom
Calibre:	305mm (12in)
Barrel length:	5.715m (225.3in)
Overall length:	12.19m (40ft)
Weight in action:	77,168kg (75.95 tons)
Elevation:	0° to 45 °
Traverse:	240°
Shell and weight:	340kg (750lb)
Muzzle velocity:	447.4m/sec (1468ft/sec)
Maximum range:	13,121m (14,350yds)

13.5in Gun 'Sceneshifter'

During World War I, four 356mm (14in) railway guns were built and deployed in France. During the 1920s, the barrels were scrapped but the mountings were placed in store. In 1940, the Admiralty gave three 343mm (13.5in) guns to the Army, and these were close enough in size to the 14 inch guns to be able to fit them on to the 14 inch mountings. All three were deployed in the Dover area and manned by the Royal Marine Siege Regiment, and all three were used to bombard German gun positions in the Calais area. The three guns had names which had been placed on the mountings during World War I: 'Sceneshifter', 'Piecemaker' and 'Gladiator'. The fourth mounting, 'Boche-Buster', was used to mount a 457mm (18in) howitzer, also deployed close to Dover, but solely for beach defence.

Country of origin:	United Kingdom
Calibre:	343mm (13.5in)
Barrel length:	15.90m (52ft 2in)
Overall length:	26.62m (87ft 4in)
Weight in action:	243,892kg (240 tons)
Elevation:	0° to +40°
Traverse:	4°
Shell and weight:	HE; 567kg (1250lb)
Muzzle velocity:	777m/sec (2550ft/sec)
Maximum range:	36,575m (22.72 miles)

38cm Gun 'Max E'

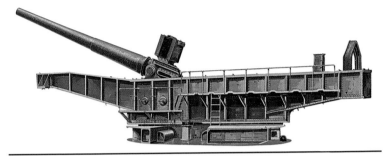

The 38cm (14.96in) Schiffskanone L/35 'Max' Eisenbahn und Bettungs Gerust was a naval gun adaptable to either a railway or fixed barbette mounting, such as those used for coastal defence, and 'Max E' was the Eisenbahn or railway mounted version. It was possible to simply shunt it down a branch line to fire a few shots; but it was preferable to install it properly by digging a pit, installing a concrete and steel pivot, then trundling the massive mounting along on two tracks until it spanned the pit, then lowering it on to the pivot and removing the wheels. At night, this could take some time, and getting it out again was also a slow business, so Max E was usually emplaced well behind the lines. It was used in the 1916 attack on Verdun to bombard the forts, and it was also emplaced near Dunkirk to bombard the British and Belgian lines.

Country of origin:	Germany
Calibre:	38cm (14.96in)
Barrel length:	17.05m (55ft 10in)
Length over buffers:	31.61m (103ft 9in)
Weight in action:	274,333 kg (270 tons) on pivot
Elevation:	-5° to 55° on pivot; -5° to 18.5° on wheels
Traverse:	4°
Shell and weight:	HE; 400kg (882lb)
Muzzle velocity:	800m/sec (2625ft/sec)
Maximum range:	47.5km (29.52 miles)

M163 Vulcan

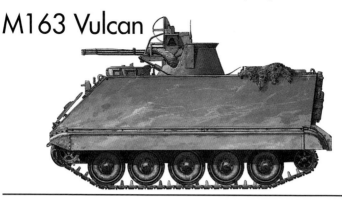

In the early 1960s, Rock Island Arsenal developed a self-propelled air-defence system based on the M113 armoured personnel carrier chassis. GEC began production and the vehicle was soon being deployed to Vietnam, where it was widely used by both US and South Vietnamese troops in a ground-support role. An electrically operated turret was mounted on the M113 chassis and armed with a six-barrelled Gatling-type cannon. This had adjustable rates of fire depending on whether it was being used for ground attack or anti-aircraft defence, and was the same weapon used by F-16 fighter aircraft. In the direct-fire role, the Vulcan has a rate of fire of 1180 rounds per minute. The vehicle was exported to Ecuador, Israel, Morocco, North Yemen, South Korea and Tunisia.

Country of origin:	USA
Crew:	4
Weight:	12,310kg (27,082lb)
Dimensions:	length 4.86m (15ft 11in); width 2.85m (9ft 4in);
	height 2.736m (9ft 11in)
Range:	83km (300 miles)
Armour:	38mm (1.5in)
Armament:	one 20mm (0.78in) six-barrelled M61 series cannon
Powerplant:	one Detroit 6V-53 six-cylinder diesel engine developing 215hp (160kW)
Performance:	maximum road speed 67km/h (42mph); fording amphibious; vertical obstacle 1.61m (2ft); trench 1.68m (5ft 6in)

ZSU-23-490mm M1

The ZSU-23-4 was developed in the 1960s as the replacement for the ZSU-57-2. Although it had a shorter firing range, the radar fire-control and an increased firing rate made the weapon much more effective. The chassis was similar to that of the SA-6 surface-to-air missile (SAM) system and used components of the PT-76 tank. Known to the Soviets as the 'Shilka', the vehicle can create an impassable wall of anti-aircraft fire over an 180° arc. Widely exported, the ZSU-23-4 was particularly effective in Egyptian hands during the Yom Kippur War of 1973, bringing down Israeli aircraft who were forced to fly low by the Egyptian missile defence system. It also saw extensive combat service with the North Vietnamese during the Vietnam War, bringing down numerous American aircraft.

Country of origin:	USSR
Crew:	4
Weight:	19,000kg (41,800lb)
Dimensions:	length 6.54m (21ft 5in); width 2.95m (9ft 8in); height (without radar) 2.25m (7ft 4in)
Range:	260km (162 miles)
Armour:	10-15mm (0.39-0.6in)
Armament:	four AZP-23 23mm (0.9in) anti-aircraft cannon
Powerplant:	one V-6R diesel engine developing 280hp (210kW)
Performance:	maximum road speed 44km/h (27mph); fording 1.4m (4ft 7in); vertical obstacle 1.10m (3ft 7in); trench 2.80m (9ft 2in)

SIDAM-25

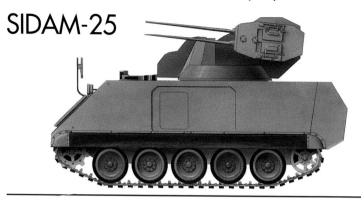

L ike the Otomatic system described elsewhere, the Sidam-25 is a complete turret unit, with four 25mm (0.95in) Oerlikon-Contraves cannon, optical sights, low-light video sights, laser rangefinder and fire control computer. This is fitted into the roof of a standard M113 APC, and has been tested on various other vehicles. The Italian Army has adopted the M113 version which has been modified by Astra, with an uprated Detroit Diesel V6 engine and two new external fuel tanks fitted to the rear of the vehicle. It has also been tested with an add-on SAM missile assembly, firing the French Mistral SAM, and with thermal imaging sights and radar input to the fire control system, all of which appear to have been satisfactory.

Country of origin:	Italy
Crew:	3
Weight:	14,500kg (14.27 tons)
Dimensions:	length 4.86m (20ft); width: 2.69m (8ft 10in); height not known
Range:	500km (310 miles)
Armour#:	44mm (1.73in) maximum
Armament:	four Oerlikon 25mm (0.95in) KBA cannon
Powerplant:	Detroit diesel V-6, 265bhp at 2800 rpm
Performance:	maximum road speed: 65km/h (40mph);fording: n/a; vertical obstacle: 0.7m (2in); trench: n/a

Self-propelled Artillery

AMX-13 DCA

The AMX-13 DCA entered production in the late 1960s to meet French requirements for a self-propelled anti-aircraft gun. It is essentially an AMX-13 main battle tank chassis fitted with a cast-steel turret. The vehicle entered service with the French Army in 1969. A total of 60 were delivered before production ceased and up to the 1980s, the AMX-13 DCA was the only self-propelled anti-aircraft gun in use with French forces. To aid fire control, there is an Oeil Noir 1 radar scanner fitted to the back of the turret, which is retractable while on the move. The DCA turret was fitted to the improved AMX-30 chassis for export to Saudi Arabia in the late 1970s and 1980s. The AMX-13 DCA is an adequate air defence vehicle, although it is now considered to be rather long in the tooth.

Country of origin:	France
Crew:	3
Weight:	17,200kg (37,840lb)
Dimensions:	length 5.40m (17ft 11in); width 2.50m (8ft 2in); height (radar up) 3.80m (12ft 6in); height (radar down) 3m (9ft 10in)
Range:	300km (186 miles)
Armour:	25mm (0.98in)
Armament:	twin 30mm (1.18in) Hispano (now Oerlikon) cannon
Powerplant:	one SOFAM Model 8Gxb eight-cylinder water-cooled petrol engine developing 250hp (186kW)
Performance:	maximum road speed 60km/h (37mph); fording 0.6m (1ft 11in); vertical obstacle 0.65m (2ft 2in); trench 1.70m (5ft 7in)

Wildcat

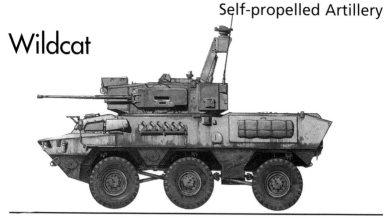

Realising that the self-propelled gun based on the Leopard 1 chassis and the American Sergeant York M247 would be too expensive for many countries, Krauss-Maffei decided to build a new family of anti-aircraft guns for sale abroad to tap into the lucrative market for arms outside of Europe. It was decided to use the automotive components of the 6x6 Transportpanzer already in production for the West German Army. With a laser rangefinder, radar scanner and automatic target-tracking, the fully computerised fire-control system makes the Wildcat an effective weapon, either against aircraft or against ground targets. It is also relatively inexpensive to maintain and spares are easy to come by – two attributes which make it attractive to countries with tight defence budgets.

Country of origin:	West Germany
Crew:	3
Weight:	18,500kg (40,700lb)
Dimensions:	length 6.88m (22ft 7in); width 2.98m (9ft 9in); height (radar down) 2.74m (9ft)
Range:	600km (373 miles)
Armour:	classified
Armament:	twin 30mm (1.18in) Mauser Mk 30-F cannon
Powerplant:	one Mercedes-Benz turbocharged eight-cylinder diesel engine developing 320hp (239kW)
Performance:	maximum road speed 80km/h (50mph); fording amphibious; vertical obstacle 0.6m (1ft 11in); trench 1.1m (3ft 7in)

Self-propelled Artillery

M53/59

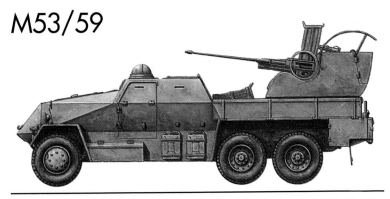

In the 1950s, Czechoslovakia developed and began production of the M53/59 self-propelled anti-aircraft gun. Based on the Praga V3S 6x6 truck chassis with an armoured cab, the vehicle was used instead of the Soviet ZSU-57-2. Essentially a clear-weather system, the vehicle carried neither infra-red night vision equipment nor a nuclear, biological and chemical (NBC) defence system. Both armour-piercing incendiary ammunition for ground targets and high-explosive incendiary for aircraft were carried. Other than its reliance on clear-weather systems, the other main drawback was its poor cross-country mobility, which prevented effective operation with tracked vehicles. In addition to the Czech Army, the M53/59 saw service with both the former Yugoslavia and Libya.

Country of origin:	Czechoslovakia
Crew:	6
Weight:	10,300kg (22,660lb)
Dimensions:	length 6.92m (22ft 8in); width 2.35m (7ft 9in); height 2.585m (8ft 6in)
Range:	500km (311 miles)
Armour:	none (vehicle as a whole)
Armament:	twin 30mm (1.18in) cannon
Powerplant:	one Tatra T912-2 six-cylinder diesel engine developing 110hp (82kW)
Performance:	maximum road speed 60km/h (37mph); vertical obstacle 0.46m (1ft 6in); trench 0.69m (2ft 3in)

Gepard

The Gepard self-propelled anti-aircraft gun system was designed specifically to protect armoured formations. The system uses the hull of the Leopard 1 main battle tank to carry a welded-steel turret capable of powered traverse through 360° and accommodating the weapon system. The two 35mm (1.37in) cannon are located externally to avoid the problem of gun gas in the fighting compartment. Each of the weapons has a cyclic rate of fire of 550 rounds per minute, although it is standard procedure to fire bursts of between 20 and 40 rounds. Ammunition types include high explosive and armour-piercing. The fire-control system is based on a computer supplied with target data by two radars: the acquisition unit and the tracking unit. Other features are optical sights and a land navigation system.

Country of origin:	Germany
Crew:	4
Weight:	47,300kg (104,060lb)
Dimensions:	length: 7.68m (25ft 3in); width: 3.27m (10ft 9in); height: 3.01m (9ft 10in)
Range:	550km (342 miles)
Armour:	40mm (1.57in)
Armament:	two 35mm (1.37in) cannon; eight smoke dischargers
Powerplant:	one MTU MB 838 Ca M500 10-cylinder multi-fuel engine developing 830hp (619kW)
Performance:	maximum road speed 65km/h (40.5mph); fording 2.5m (8ft 2in); vertical obstacle 1.15m (3ft 9in); trench 3m (9ft 10in)

Self-propelled Artillery

GDF-CO3

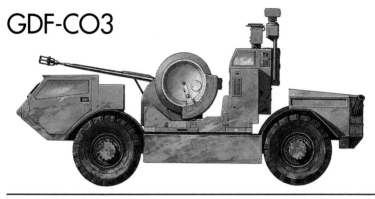

Produced by Oerlikon-Bührle, the GDF series was designed to be a highly mobile anti-aircraft defence system to protect rear-area targets such as factories and air bases. The chassis for the tracked version is derived from the M113 series of armoured vehicles; the wheeled version is based on the 4x4 HYKA cross-country vehicle. The GDF-CO3 has a day/night fire-control system with laser rangefinder, in addition to a Contraves search radar. The vehicle fires a range of ammunition, including armour-piercing discarding sabot-tracer rounds for use against ground targets. Its layout is unusual in that the crew compartment is at the front with the guns behind them. Nevertheless, as a mobile air-defence platform the vehicle is ideally suited to Switzerland's needs.

Country of origin:	Switzerland
Crew:	3
Weight:	18,000kg (39,600lb)
Dimensions:	length 6.70m (22ft); width 2.813m (9ft 3in); height 4m (13ft 2in)
Range:	480km (297 miles)
Armour:	8mm (0.31in)
Armament:	twin 35mm (1.37in) KDF cannon
Powerplant:	one GMC 6V-53T 6-cylinder diesel engine developing 215hp (160kW)
Performance:	maximum road speed 45km/h (28mph); fording 0.6m (1ft 11in); vertical obstacle 0.609m (2ft); trench 1.80m (5ft 11in)

Type 63

To meet their needs for a self-propelled anti-aircraft gun, the Chinese took the chassis of the Soviet T-34 tank (supplied to them in large numbers before relations were broken off between the two countries) and added an open-topped turret with twin anti-aircraft guns. The resulting vehicle, the Type 63, was severely limited in that it had no provision for radar control and had to be sighted and elevated manually, a major drawback when faced with fast, low-flying aircraft, particularly as the gun had to be loaded manually with five-round clips. It was supplied to the Viet Cong during the Vietnam War in the 1960s, but otherwise was only used in small numbers by the People's Liberation Army. Amazingly, given its mediocre qualities, it continued to be used by the Chinese until the late 1980s.

Country of origin:	China
Crew:	6
Weight:	32,000kg (70,400lb)
Dimensions:	length 6.432m (21ft 1in); width 2.99m (9ft 10in); height 2.995m (9ft 10in)
Range:	300km (186 miles)
Armour:	18-45mm (0.7-1.8in)
Armament:	twin 37mm (1.45in) anti-aircraft cannon
Powerplant:	one V-12 water-cooled diesel engine developing 500hp (373kW)
Performance:	maximum road speed 55km/h (34mph); fording 1.32m (4ft 4in); vertical obstacle 0.73m (2ft 5in); trench 2.5m (8ft 2in)

Self-propelled Artillery

M42

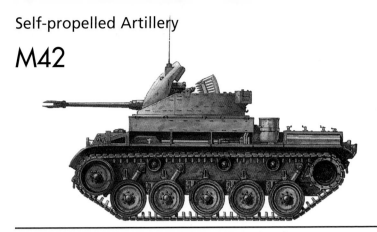

The M42 anti-aircraft system, commonly known as the 'Duster', was based on the M41 Bulldog tank and was one of a family of vehicles developed after the end of World War II. Between 1951 and 1956, around 3700 were built, mainly by Cadillac. The main drawback of the vehicle was its petrol engine, which restricted its operating range, and its lack of a radar fire-control system, the gunner being forced to rely on optic sights. In addition, the open-topped turret afforded the crew little protection. However, it saw extensive service in Vietnam, albeit mainly in a ground-support rather than anti-aircraft role, and it continued to serve with the National Guard into the 1980s. Its power-assisted twin 40mm (1.57in) turret was the same as that used on the M19 self-propelled anti-aircraft gun system used in World War II.

Country of origin:	USA
Crew:	6
Weight:	22,452kg (49,394lb)
Dimensions:	length 6.356m (20ft 10in); width 3.225m (10ft 7in); height 2.847m (9ft 4in)
Range:	161km (100 miles)
Armour:	12-38mm (0.47-1.5in)
Armament:	twin 40mm (1.57in) anti-aircraft guns; one 7.62mm(0.3in) MG
Powerplant:	one Continental AOS-895-3 six-cylinder air-cooled petrol engine developing 500hp (373kW)
Performance:	maximum road speed 72.4km/h (45mph); fording 1.3m (4ft 3in); vertical obstacle 1.711m (2ft 4in); trench 1.829m (6ft)

Sergeant York

The M163 Vulcan was noted for its short range and relative inaccuracy (though not poor rate of fire), so in 1978 the US Army issued a requirement for a self-propelled anti-aircraft gun based on the M48 main battle tank chassis to replace it. The first production M247 arrived in 1983, built by FAC. The vehicle has a comprehensive fire-control system including both surveillance and tracking radar. The M247 is capable of engaging both aircraft and helicopters, as well as tactical missiles (the latter capability being very important on a modern battlefield). The modified M48 chassis gives the vehicle the mobility and protection needed to operate with the M1 Abrams main battle tank and M2 Bradley fighting vehicle, in turn providing viable anti-aircraft defence for both vehicles.

Country of origin:	USA
Crew:	3
Weight:	54,430kg (119,746lb)
Dimensions:	length 7.674m (25ft 2in); width 3.632m (11ft 11in); height 4.611m (15ft 2in)
Range:	500km (311 miles)
Armour:	up to 120mm(4.72in)
Armament:	twin 40mm (1.57in) L/70 Bofors guns
Powerplant:	one Teledyne Continental AVDS-1790-2D diesel engine developing 750bhp (559kW)
Performance:	maximum road speed: 48 km/h (30mph); fording 1.219m (4ft); vertical obstacle 1.914m (3ft); trench 2.591m (8ft 6in)

Self-propelled Artillery

ZSU-57-2

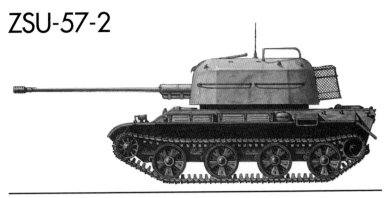

The ZSU-57-2 was the first Soviet self-propelled anti-aircraft gun to see service on a significant scale after World War II. The chassis was a lightened version of the T-54 main battle tank with thinner armour, the distinctive feature of the vehicle being the large, open-topped turret. This created a greater power-to-weight ratio than the T-54 and, coupled with extra fuel tanks, gave the gun good mobility and operating range. Practical firing rate was around 70 rounds per minute, with the empty cartridge cases being transported to a wire basket at the rear by a conveyor belt. The vehicle was exported widely to other Warsaw Pact countries, North Africa and the Middle East, seeing extensive action with Syrian forces during the fighting in Lebanon against the Israelis in 1982.

Country of origin:	USSR
Crew:	6
Weight:	28,100kg (61,820lb)
Dimensions:	length 8.48m (27ft 10in); width 3.27m (10ft 9in); height 2.75m (9ft)
Range:	420km (260 miles)
Armour:	15mm (0.59in)
Armament:	twin 57mm (2.24in) anti-aircraft cannon
Powerplant:	one Model V-54 V-12 diesel engine developing 520hp (388kW)
Performance:	maximum road speed 50km/h (31mph); fording 1.4m (4ft 7in); vertical obstacle 0.80m (2ft 7in); trench 2.70m (8ft 10in)

ASU-57

The ASU-57 was developed in the 1950s specifically for use by Soviet airborne divisions (54 vehicles per division) and was designed to be parachuted with the troops, using pallets fitted with retro-rocket systems to soften impact on landing. The gun was a development of the World War II ZIS-2, while its engine was taken from the Pobeda civilian car. Despite its drawbacks – a hull made of welded aluminium which affords little protection for the crew, a rather underpowered engine and weaponry – the ASU-57 remained in service for around 20 years before being replaced by the ASU-85. For airborne troops such vehicles are invaluable, giving lightly armed soldiers, who are invariably isolated behind enemy lines, mobile artillery support on the battlefield.

Country of origin:	USSR
Crew:	3
Weight:	3300kg (7260lb)
Dimensions:	length 4.995m (16ft 4.7in); width 2.086m (6ft 10in); height 1.18m (3ft 10.5in)
Range:	250km (155 miles)
Armour:	6mm (0.23in)
Armament:	one 57mm (2.24in) CH-51M gun; one 7.62mm (0.3in) anti-aircraft machine gun
Powerplant:	one M-20E four-cylinder petrol engine developing 55hp (41kW)
Performance:	maximum road speed 45km/h (28mph);vertical obstacle 0.5m (20in); trench 1.4m (4ft 7in)

StuG III Ausf F

The StuG III Ausf F was developed in 1941, by personal order of Adolf Hitler himself, to regain superiority over the Soviet KV-1 and T-34 tanks on the Eastern Front. The armour of the Ausf A-E series was upgraded and a new long StuK40 L/48 7.5cm (2.95in) gun was fitted instead of the original short 7.5cm version, which significantly improved the vehicle's anti-tank capability. The basic hull and superstructure remained the same, other than the addition of an exhaust fan to remove gun fumes. The gun mantlet was also redesigned to allow for the recoil mechanism of the larger gun. The Ausf F proved highly effective against the Soviet KV-1s and T-34s and the vehicle remained in service throughout the war – its low silhouette giving it an added advantage in tank-versus-tank combats.

Country of origin:	Germany
Crew:	4
Weight:	21,800kg (47,960lb)
Dimensions:	length 6.31m (19ft 2in); width 2.92m (8ft 11in); height: 2.15m (6ft 7in)
Range:	140km (92 miles)
Armour:	11–50mm (0.4–2in)
Armament:	one 75mm (2.95in) Stuk40 L/48 gun; one 7.92mm (0.3in) machine gun
Powerplant:	one Maybach HL120TRM engine
Performance:	maximum road speed 40km/h (25mph); fording 0.8m (2ft 8in); vertical obstacle 0.6m (2ft); trench 2.59m (8ft 6in)

StuG III Ausf G

The StuG III Ausf G was the last StuG to enter production in World War II. Based predominantly on the chassis of the PzKpfw III, which was being phased out of tank service in favour of the much more lethal Panther, the Ausf G carried thicker armour than its predecessors, which was fortunate, as the Stug III was called upon more and more to fill the role of a tank, being cheaper and easier to build. However, its lack of mobility proved a liability as it was vulnerable to infantry with anti-tank projectiles. The addition of armoured 'skirts' (*Schützen*) went some way towards improving protection, but despite a valiant effort, the StuG IIIs were not really suited for the tank role in which they found themselves. Nevertheless, the Ausf G version was the best of the bunch, and performed well on the battlefield.

Country of origin:	Germany
Crew:	4
Weight:	24,100kg (53,020lb)
Dimensions:	length 6.77m (20ft 7in); width 2.95m (9ft); height 2.16m (6ft 7in)
Range:	155km (97 miles)
Armour:	16–80mm (0.62–3.14in)
Armament:	one 75mm (2.95in) Stuk40 L/48 gun; one 7.92mm (0.3in) machine gun
Powerplant:	one Maybach HL120TRM engine
Performance:	maximum road speed 40km/h (25mph); fording 0.8m (2ft 8in); vertical obstacle 0.6m (2ft); trench 2.59m (8ft 6in)

Self-propelled Artillery

76mm Otomatic
Air Defence Tank

The 76mm (3in) Otomatic Air Defence Tank was developed primarily as a weapon for keeping helicopters and ground attack aircraft off the back of ground troops, and secondarily as a useful weapon against light armoured vehicles should they appear. The Otomatic System consists of a turret assembly with a 76mm gun, surveillance and tracking radars, electro-optical sights, fire control computer and all the sundry equipment that ties these items together. This complete unit can then be dropped into any tank with a large enough turret ring. For the purposes of the Italian Army trials, the Leopard 1 was selected and the whole ensemble fits together well and has performed successfully.

Country of origin:	Italy
Crew:	4
Weight:	47,000kg (46.26 tons)
Dimensions:	length 7.08m (23ft 3in); width 3.25m (10ft 8in); height 3.07m (10ft 1in) (radar stowed)
Range:	500km (310 miles)
Armour:	not disclosed
Armament:	one 76mm (3in) gun
Powerplant:	MTU V-10 multi-fuel, 830bhp at 2200 rpm
Performance:	maximum road speed 60km/h (37mph); fording 1.2m (47in); vertical obstacle 1.15m (45in); trench 3m (9ft 10in)

SU-76

The battles of 1941 showed the Soviet light tanks to be virtually useless. It was thus decided to combine the T-70 already in production with the excellent ZIS-3 and ZIS-76 guns to create a highly mobile anti-tank weapon. A wartime expedient, there were few comforts for the crew and it was known to troops as 'The Bitch'. The first SU-76s appeared in late 1942 and by mid-1943 they were deployed in appreciable numbers. Better German armour had by this time reduced the effectiveness of the ZIS gun and thus the vehicle's role was changed from anti-tank to infantry support. By 1945, many SU-76s were converted into ammunition carriers or recovery vehicles. After the war, many were transferred to China and North Korea, seeing service during the Korean War.

Country of origin:	USSR
Crew:	4
Weight:	10,600kg (23,320lb)
Dimensions:	length 4.88m (16ft 0.1in); width 2.73m (8ft 11.5in); height 2.17m (7ft 1.4in)
Range:	450km (280 miles)
Armour:	up to 25mm (0.98in)
Armament:	one ZIS-3 76mm (3in) gun
Powerplant:	two GAZ six-cylinder petrol engines, each developing 70hp (52.2kW)
Performance:	maximum road speed 45km/h (28mph); fording 0.89m (2ft 11in); vertical obstacle 0.70m (2ft 3.6in); trench 3.12m (10ft 2.8in)

Bishop

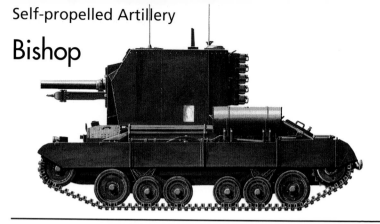

The Bishop was designed to relieve the 25-pounder (87.6mm/3.45in) batteries in North Africa of their role as anti-tank weapons, in which they were taking a pounding from the Germans. A 25-pounder gun was therefore mounted on the chassis of a Valentine tank – it was not a success. The new vehicle had a high, slab-sided turret which made an excellent target for enemy gunners. The gun was mounted in a fixed turret with limited elevation. By the time they were introduced, the 25-pounder was no longer being used in an anti-tank role, so the Bishops were diverted for artillery use. The Bishop was the first British effort at a self-propelled gun and was useful in showing the potential of the type and what to avoid in future designs. When the M7 Priest arrived, the Bishop soon fell out of use.

Country of origin:	United Kingdom
Crew:	4
Weight:	7879kg (17,333lb)
Dimensions:	length 5.64m (18ft 6in); width 2.77m (9ft 1in); height 3.05m (10ft)
Range:	177km (110 miles)
Armour:	8–60mm (0.315–2.36in)
Armament:	one 25-pounder (87.6mm/3.45in) gun
Powerplant:	one AEC six-cylinder diesel engine developing 131hp (97.7kW)
Performance:	maximum road speed 24km/h (15mph); fording 0.91m (3ft); vertical obstacle 0.83m (2ft 9in): trench 2.28m (7ft 6in)

Sexton

In 1941, the British were searching for a suitable armoured vehicle to mount the standard British 25-pounder (87.6mm/3.45in) gun. The Canadians were producing the Ram tank, soon to be replaced by American M3s, and these were altered to accommodate the 25-pounder, becoming known as the Sexton. Used mainly as a field artillery weapon to support armoured divisions, the Sexton saw action in Northwest Europe in 1944 and 1945. By the time production ceased shortly after the war, a total of 2150 had been built. The main variant was a purpose-built command tank with the weapon removed and extra radios added. A reliable, rugged and effective weapon, the Sexton continued in service with the British Army until the 1950s, and until very recently with some other armies.

Country of origin:	Canada
Crew:	6
Weight:	25,300kg (55,660lb)
Dimensions:	length 6.12m (20ft 1in); width 2.72m (8ft 11in); height 2.44m (8ft 0in)
Range:	290km (180 miles)
Armour:	up to 32mm (1.25in)
Armament:	one 25-pounder (87.6mm/3.45in) howitzer; two 7.69mm (0.303in) Bren Guns; one 12.7mm (0.5in) Browning machine gun
Powerplant:	one nine-cylinder radial piston engine developing 400hp (298.3kW)
Performance:	maximum road speed 40.2km/h (25mph); fording 1.01m (3ft 4in); vertical obstacle 0.61m (2ft); trench 1.91m (6ft 3in)

Self-propelled Artillery

M56

After World War II, the US Army issued a requirement for a highly mobile anti-tank gun which could be dropped with the first wave of airborne troops and have a firepower similar to that of a tank. Cadillac began production of the M56 (also known as the Scorpion) in 1953 and ceased production in 1959. The M56 was deployed with the 82nd and 101st Airborne Divisions and saw action in the Vietnam War (although not on a large scale), mainly in a fire-support role. In addition, small numbers were exported to Spain and Morocco. The main drawbacks were a lack of armour and the massive recoil, which often moved the vehicle several feet and obscured the target with dust. In the 1960s, the vehicle was replaced by the M551, another flawed armoured fighting vehicle design.

Country of origin:	USA
Crew:	4
Weight:	7000kg (15,400lb)
Dimensions:	length 5.841m (19ft 2in); width 2.577m (8ft 5.5in); height 2.067m (6ft 9.3in)
Range:	225km (140 miles)
Armour:	classified
Armament:	one 90mm (3.54in) gun
Powerplant:	one Continental six-cylinder petrol engine developing 200hp (149kW)
Performance:	maximum road speed 45km/h (28mph); vertical obstacle 0.762m (2ft 6in); trench 1.524m (5ft)

M7 Priest

Nicknamed the 'Priest' by British crews because of its pulpit-shaped machine-gun turret at the front, the M7 was developed from US experience with howitzers mounted on half-tracked vehicles. A fully tracked carriage was required, and the M3 tank was modified to fill the role. The British received many under the Lend-Lease scheme and first deployed them at the second Battle of El Alamein in 1942. Some measure of their popularity is suggested by the British order for 5500 to be delivered within one year of their first use. The drawback was that the howitzer was not standard British issue, and thus required separate supplies of ammunition. Mobile and reliable, the M7 fought to the end of the war and remained in service in the role of armoured personnel carrier – it was also widely exported.

Country of origin:	USA
Crew:	5
Weight:	22,500kg (49,500lb)
Dimensions:	length 6.02m (19ft 9in); width 2.88m (9ft 5.25in); height 2.54m (8ft 4in)
Range:	201km (125 miles)
Armour:	up to 25.4mm (1in)
Armament:	one 105mm (4.13in) howitzer; one 12.7mm (0.5in) machine gun
Powerplant:	one Continental nine-cylinder radial piston engine developing 375hp (279.6kW)
Performance:	maximum road speed 41.8km/h (26mph); fording 1.219m (4ft); vertical obstacle 0.61m (2ft); trench 1.91m (6ft 3in)

Self-propelled Artillery

Abbot

Post-war British designs for self-propelled guns focused on the excellent Centurion tank chassis with 25-pounder (87.6mm/3.45in) or 140mm (5.5in) guns. However, NATO required a standard 105mm (4.13in) or 155mm (6.10in) gun. As a result, Vickers developed the 105mm Abbot self-propelled gun during the 1950s for deployment with the British Army of the Rhine. Fully armoured, the Abbot served with the Royal Artillery until it was replaced by the American M109 in the 1980s. Like most British post-war armoured fighting vehicle designs, the Abbot was reliable, rugged and a potent force on the battlefield. One variant was the Value Engineered Abbot, produced for the Indian Army without extras such as a flotation screen, night vision and nuclear, biological and chemical (NBC) protection.

Country of origin:	United Kingdom
Crew:	4
Weight:	16,494kg (36,288lb)
Dimensions:	length 5.84m (19ft 2in); width 2.641m (8ft 8in); height 2.489m (8ft 2in)
Range:	390km (240 miles)
Armour:	6–12mm (0.23–0.47in)
Armament:	one 105mm (4.13in) gun; one 7.62mm (0.3in) anti-aircraft machine gun; three smoke dischargers
Powerplant:	one Rolls-Royce six-cylinder diesel engine developing 240hp (179kW)
Performance:	maximum road speed 47.5km/h (30mph); fording 1.2m (3ft 11in); vertical obstacle 0.609m (2ft); trench 2.057m (6ft 9in)

M1974

After World War II the USSR concentrated development on towed artillery pieces, in contrast to NATO's drift towards self-propelled guns. It was not until 1974 that the first Soviet self-propelled howitzer made an appearance in public, hence its Western designation. Known as the Gvozdika in the USSR, the vehicle was deployed in large numbers (36 per tank division, 72 per motorised rifle division). Differing from the M1973 in being fully amphibious, the chassis has been used for a number of armoured command and chemical warfare reconnaissance vehicles, as well as a mine-clearing vehicle. It can also be fitted with wider tracks to allow it to operate in snow or swamp conditions. The M1974 was widely exported to Soviet client states as well as Angola, Algeria and Iraq.

Country of origin:	USSR
Crew:	4
Weight:	15,700kg (34,540lb)
Dimensions:	length 7.30m (23ft 11.5in); width 2.85m (9ft 4in); height 2.40m (7ft 10.5in)
Range:	500km (310 miles)
Armour:	15–20mm (0.59–0.78in)
Armament:	one 122mm (4.8in) gun; one 7.62mm (0.3in) anti-aircraft MG
Powerplant:	one YaMZ-238V V-8 water-cooled diesel engine developing 240hp (179kW)
Performance:	maximum road speed 60km/h (37mph); fording amphibious; vertical obstacle 1.10m (3ft 7in); trench 3.00m (9ft 10in)

Self-propelled Artillery

sIG 33

T he sIG 33 was a self-propelled howitzer used to equip German infantry battalions of World War II. The first version appeared during the French Campaign of May 1940, and was simply the standard sIG 33 heavy infantry gun mounted on a PzKpfw I chassis and fitted with armoured shields to protect the crew. It was developed to provide armoured infantry with close fire support from a self-propelled armoured platform. The centre of gravity was rather high, though, and the chassis was overloaded. In consequence, the PzKpfw II chassis was converted for use in 1942, giving better armour protection, followed by the PzKpfw III. The vehicle served throughout the war and was still in production in 1944, with over 370 vehicles being made.

Country of origin:	Germany
Crew:	4
Weight:	11,505kg (25,300lb)
Dimensions:	length 4.835m (15ft 10.4in); width 2.15m (7ft 0.6in); height 2.40m (7ft 10.5in)
Range:	185km (115 miles)
Armour:	6-13mm (0.23-0.5in)
Armament:	one 15cm (5.9in) sIG 33 howitzer
Powerplant:	one Praga six-cylinder petrol engine developing 150hp (111.9kW)
Performance:	maximum road speed 35km/h (21.75mph); fording 0.914m (3ft); vertical obstacle 0.42m (1ft 5in); trench 1.75m (5ft 9in)

Hummel

The Hummel ('Bumble Bee') was a hybrid of the PzKpfw III and IV hulls, with a lightly armoured open superstructure, which formed the heavy artillery element of German panzer and panzergrenadier divisions from 1942 onwards. The Hummel first saw action at the Battle of Kursk in July 1943. They were useful and popular weapons and were used on all fronts, having plenty of room for the crew of five and the mobility to keep up with the panzer divisions. Well over 600 had been produced by late 1944, and 150 were converted into ammunition carriers as lorries proved inadequate for the task. Other variants included the Oskette, a wider-tracked version produced for winter fighting on the Russian Front. It was usual for 18 rounds of ammunition to be carried in the vehicle.

Country of origin:	Germany
Crew:	5
Weight:	23,927kg (52,640lb)
Dimensions:	length 7.17m (23ft 6.3in); width 2.87m (9ft 5in); height 2.81m (9ft 2.6in)
Range:	215km (134 miles)
Armour:	up to 50mm (1.97in)
Armament:	one 15cm (5.9in) sIG 33 howitzer or one 88mm (3.5in) anti-tank gun
Powerplant:	one Maybach V-12 petrol engine developing 265hp (197.6kW)
Performance:	maximum road speed 42km/h (26.1mph); fording 0.99m (3ft 3in); vertical obstacle 0.6m (2ft); trench 2.20m (7ft 3in)

Self-propelled Artillery

Type 4

The Japanese produced few heavy armoured vehicles, partly because they were deemed unnecessary based on experiences in China and Manchuria, and partly because their industrial capacity was inadequate for the task. The Type 4 was a self-propelled howitzer using the Type 97 medium tank as a base. The howitzer itself dated from 1905 and had been with withdrawn from service in 1942 but continued to be used in the self-propelled version. The Type 4 was poorly armoured and a had a slow rate of fire, mainly because of the breech mechanism employed. The Japanese were unable to produce them on a mass scale, so they were deployed in ones and twos, mainly for island defence. They were hopelessly outnumbered against American artillery in the Pacific battles in World War II.

Country of origin:	Japan
Crew:	4 or 5
Weight:	13,300kg (29,260lb)
Dimensions:	length 5.537m (18ft 2in); width 2.286m (7ft 6in); height to top of shield 1.549m (5ft 1in)
Range:	250km (156miles)
Armour:	25mm (0.98in)
Armament:	one Type 38 150mm (5.9in) howitzer
Powerplant:	one V-12 diesel engine developing 170hp (126.8kW)
Performance:	maximum road speed 38km/h (23.6mph); fording 1.0m (3ft 3in); vertical obstacle 0.812m (2ft 8in); trench 2.0m (6ft 7in)

ISU-152

The ISU-152 was the first of the Soviet heavy self-propelled artillery carriages of World War II, entering service in 1943, just in time to take part in the Battle of Kursk in July. Built on a KV-2 heavy tank chassis, it was intended for a dual role as an anti-tank weapon and heavy assault gun. The vehicle was in the vanguard of the Soviet advances of 1944 and 1945, and the vehicles were amongst the first to enter Berlin at the end of the war. The ISU-152's major drawback was a lack of internal stowage space for ammunition, and each vehicle thus required constant supply by ammunition carriers, which was hazardous and affected tactical mobility. Nevertheless, the ISU-152 remained in service after the war, being used during the crushing of the 1956 Hungarian uprising.

Country of origin:	USSR
Crew:	5
Weight:	45,500kg (100,100lb)
Dimensions:	length overall 9.80m (32ft 1.8in) and hull 6.805m (22ft 3.9in); width 3.56m (11ft 8.2in); height 2.52m (8ft 3.2in)
Range:	180km (112 miles)
Armour:	35–100mm (1.38–3.94in)
Armament:	one 152mm (6in) howitzer; one 12.7mm (0.5in) anti-aircraft machine gun
Powerplant:	one V-12 diesel engine developing 520hp (387.8kW)
Performance:	maximum road speed 37km/h (23mph); fording 1.3m (4ft 3.2in); vertical obstacle 1.20m (3ft 8in); trench 2.59m (8ft 6in)

Self-propelled Artillery

M1973

Known as the 2S3 Akatsiya in the former Soviet Union (the designation M1973 is a US Army term), 18 vehicles were deployed as support for each tank division and motorised rifle division in the Red Army. The chassis was a shortened version of that used for the SA-4 surface-to-air missile system and the GMZ armoured minelayer, both of which were used in the USSR for many years. Fitted with nuclear, biological and chemical (NBC) protection and with a tactical nuclear capability, the vehicle was not equipped for amphibious operations. During operation it was normal for two of the crew to stand at the rear of the vehicle and act as ammunition handlers, feeding projectiles via two hatches in the hull rear. The M1973 proved a popular vehicle amongst Soviet client states and was exported to Iraq and Libya.

Country of origin:	USSR
Crew:	6
Weight:	24,945kg (54,880lb)
Dimensions:	length 8.40m (27ft 6.7in); width 3.20m (10ft 6in); height 2.80m (9ft 2.25in)
Range:	300km (186 miles)
Armour:	15–20mm (0.59–0.78in)
Armament:	one 152mm (6in) gun; one 7.62mm (0.3in) anti-aircraft machine gun
Powerplant:	one V-12 diesel engine developing 520hp (388kW)
Performance:	maximum road speed 55km/h (34mph); fording 1.5m (4ft 11in); vertical obstacle 1.10m (3ft 7in); trench 2.50m (8ft 2.5in)

Self-propelled Artillery

DANA

The DANA was the first wheeled self-propelled howitzer to enter service in modern times. Wheeled vehicles have the advantage of being cheaper to build and easier to maintain, with greater strategic mobility. First seen in 1980, the DANA was built by Skoda and was based on the 8x8 Tatra 815 truck, the best off-road truck in existence at the time. Tyre pressure can be regulated to allow good mobility over rough terrain, and steering is power-assisted on the front four wheels. It carries three hydraulic stabilisers to be lowered into the ground before firing, and carries a crane on the roof to assist with loading the ammunition. Rate of fire is three rounds per minute for a period of 30 minutes, and the vehicle is in service in Libya, Poland, Russia, the Czech Republic and Slovakia.

Country of origin:	Czechoslovakia
Crew:	4 to 5
Weight:	23,000kg (50,600lb)
Dimensions:	length 10.5m (34ft 5in); width 2.8m (9ft 2in); height 2.6m (8ft 6in)
Range:	600km (375 miles)
Armour:	12.7mm (0.5in)
Armament:	one 152mm (6in) gun; one 12.7mm (0.5in) machine gun
Powerplant:	one V-12 diesel engine developing 345hp (257kW)
Performance:	maximum road speed 80km/h (49.71mph); fording 1.4m (4ft 7in); vertical obstacle 1.5m (4ft 11in); trench 1.4m (4ft 7in)

Self-propelled Artillery

M40

The M40 entered development in December 1943 and was based on the M4 tank chassis and used the 155mm (6.1in) 'Long Tom' gun. A heavy spade was attached to the rear which could be dug into the ground to help absorb recoil after firing. The first production vehicles appeared in January 1945, and arrived just as World War II in Europe was ending. It continued in service, with a total of 311 being built, and saw its main action in the Korean War (1950–53), where it proved an excellent weapon, and in Indochina with the French Army. The M40 appeared at a time when nuclear warfare was making its debut, and thus it was used extensively for post-war trials designed to provide protection against fallout for the crew, forming the blueprint for modern self-propelled vehicles.

Country of origin:	USA
Crew:	8
Weight:	36,400kg (80,080lb)
Dimensions:	length 9.04m (29ft 8in); width 3.15m (10ft 4in); height 2.84m (9ft 4in)
Range:	161km (100 miles)
Armour:	up to 12.7mm (0.5in)
Armament:	one 155mm (6.1in) gun
Powerplant:	one Continental nine-cylinder radial piston engine developing 395hp (294.6kW)
Performance:	maximum road speed 38.6km/h (24mph); fording 1.067m (3ft 6in); vertical obstacle 0.61m (2ft); trench 2.26m (7ft 5in)

Mk F3 155mm

In the 1960s, the French Army replaced their American M41 howitzers with an indigenous design, based on the AMX-13 tank chassis and known as the Mk F3. It was equipped with two rear spades which were reversed into the ground to give added stability. The F3 fired a standard 155mm (6.1in) high-explosive projectile, other types of ammunition being rocket-assisted, smoke and illumination. There was no nuclear, chemical and biological (NBC) protection, though. It remained in production until the 1980s, being exported to a number of South American and Middle East countries. One drawback of the vehicle, apart from the lack of protection for the crew, was that it could only carry two people, the rest of the crew having to follow behind in support vehicles.

Country of origin:	France
Crew:	2
Weight:	17,410kg (38,304lb)
Dimensions:	length 6.22m (20ft 5in); width 2.72m (8ft 11in); height 2.085m (6ft 10in)
Range:	300km (185 miles)
Armour:	20mm (0.78in)
Armament:	one 155mm (6.1in) gun
Powerplant:	one SOFAM 8Gxb eight-cylinder petrol engine developing 250hp (186kW)
Performance:	maximum road speed 60km/h (37mph); vertical obstacle 0.6m (2ft); trench 1.5m (4ft 11in)

GCT 155mm

The GCT 155mm (6.1in) was the designated successor to the Mk F3 in the French Army. Production began in 1977. Saudi Arabia received deliveries first, before the French Army, but it finally entered service in the 1980s and was deployed in regiments of 18 guns each. By 1995 some 400 had been built for the home and export markets. The main improvements over the Mk F3 were an automatic loading system, giving a rate of fire of eight rounds a minute, and protection for the increased on-board crew of four, as well as night vision, nuclear, biological and chemical (NBC) protection and the ability to fire a range of projectiles, including a round carrying multiple anti-tank mines. The GCT 155mm saw active service during the Iran–Iraq War, Iraq having received 85 of the vehicles.

Country of origin:	France
Crew:	4
Weight:	41,949kg (92,288lb)
Dimensions:	length 10.25m (33ft 7.5in); width 3.15m (10ft 4in); height 3.25m (10ft 8in)
Range:	450km (280 miles)
Armour:	20mm (0.78in)
Armament:	one 155mm (6.1in) gun; one 7.62mm (0.3in)/12.7mm (0.5in) MG
Powerplant:	one Hispano-Suiza HS 110 12-cylinder water-cooled multi-fuel engine developing 720hp (537kW)
Performance:	maximum road speed 60km/h (37mph); vertical obstacle 0.93m (3ft 0.7in); trench 1.90m (6ft 3in)

M109

The M109 was developed following a 1952 requirement for a self-propelled howitzer to replace the M44. The first production vehicles were completed in 1962 and survived numerous adaptations and upgrades to become the most widely used howitzer in the world, seeing action in Vietnam, in the Arab–Israeli Wars and the Iran–Iraq War, and being exported to nearly 30 countries worldwide. It has an amphibious capability and fires a variety of projectiles including tactical nuclear shells. To date some 4000 are in use around the world, and the M109 has undergone numerous upgrades, including a new gun mount, new turret with longer barrel ordnance, automatic fire control, upgraded armour and improved armour. It will continue to serve well into the next century.

Country of origin:	USA
Crew:	6
Weight:	23,723kg (52,192lb)
Dimensions:	length 6.612m (21ft 8.25in); width 3.295m (10ft 9.75in); height 3.289m (10ft 9.5in)
Range:	390km (240 miles)
Armour:	classified
Armament:	one 155mm (6.1in) howitzer; one 12.7mm (0.5in) anti-aircraft MG
Powerplant:	one Detroit diesel Model 8V-71T diesel engine developing 405hp (302kW)
Performance:	maximum road speed 56km/h (35mph); fording 1.07m (3ft 6in); vertical obstacle 0.533m (1ft 9in); trench 1.828m (6ft)

M109A6 Paladin

The 155mm (6.1in) M109A6 Paladin has the same hull and suspension as the previous M109s, but everything else has been changed. The turret is larger with improved armour, Kevlar ballistic lining and a full-width bustle, the new 39-calibre M284 howitzer has a new chamber contour and several detail improvements to the breech ring and mechanism, a reinforced muzzle and muzzle brake has been added, as well as a new firing mechanism. In addition, there is an entirely new fire control system which is allied to a position-finding system, thus permitting the automatic pointing of the gun when supplied with target data. The modifications have created a weapons system that can react quicker to target opportunities, hit targets that are further away and is far better protected than the original M109.

Country of origin:	USA
Crew:	4
Weight:	28,738kg (28.28 tons)
Dimensions:	length 6.19m (20ft 4in); width 3.149m (10ft 4in); height 3.236m (10ft 7in)
Range:	405km (252 miles)
Armour:	not disclosed
Armament:	one 155mm (6.1in) howitzer M284
Powerplant:	one Detroit Diesel 8V-71T, V-8 turbocharged two-stroke diesel, 405hp (302kW) at 2300 rpm
Performance:	maximum road speed 56km/h (35mph); fording 1.95m (6ft 5in); vertical obstacle 0.53m (21in); trench 1.83m (6ft)

Palmaria

The Palmaria was developed by OTO Melara specifically for the export market and included Libya as its first purchaser. The prototype appeared in 1981, based heavily on the OF-40 main battle tank already in service with Dubai, and the first production vehicles were completed a year later. One unusual feature is the auxiliary power unit for the turret, thus conserving fuel for the main engine. It comes equipped with an automatic loading system and a wide range of munitions, including rocket-assisted projectiles, although these pay the penalty of lower explosive content. The vehicle has an automatic loader, giving it a rate of fire of one round every 15 seconds. There are no variants as such, although its chassis has been fitted with twin 25mm (0.98in) guns in an anti-aircraft configuration.

Country of origin:	Italy
Crew:	5
Weight:	46,632kg (102,590lb)
Dimensions:	length 11.474m (37ft 7.75in); width 2.35m (7ft 8.5in); height 2.874m (9ft 5.25in)
Range:	400km (250 miles)
Armour:	classified
Armament:	one 155mm (6.1in) howitzer; one 7.62mm (0.3in) machine gun
Powerplant:	one eight-cylinder diesel engine developing 750hp (559kW)
Performance:	maximum road speed 60km/h (37mph); fording 1.2m (3ft 11in); vertical obstacle 1m (3ft 3in); trench 3m (9ft 10in)

Self-propelled Artillery

Bandkanon

Bofors produced the prototype of the Bandkanon 1A in 1960, but with extensive trials and modifications being carried out, the first production models did not appear until 1966. It had the distinction of being the first fully automatic self-propelled gun to enter service with any army. Ammunition is kept in a 14-round clip carried externally at the rear of the hull. Once the first round is loaded manually, remaining rounds are loaded automatically. However, it was not produced in quantity (production ceased after only two years) mainly because its size and lack of mobility hindered its performance on the battlefield and made it very difficult to conceal. It has undergone some improvements, such as the addition of a Rolls Royce diesel engine and a new fire-control system.

Country of origin:	Sweden
Crew:	5
Weight:	53,000kg (116,600lb)
Dimensions:	length 11m (36ft 1in); width 3.37m (11ft 0.7in); height 3.85m (12ft 7.5in)
Range:	230km (143 miles)
Armour:	10–20mm (0.4–0.8in)
Armament:	one 155mm (6.1in) gun; one 7.62mm (0.3in) anti-aircraft MG
Powerplant:	one Rolls-Royce diesel engine developing 240hp (179kW) and Boeing gas turbine, developing 300hp (224kW)
Performance:	maximum road speed 28km/h (17.4mph); fording 1m (3ft 3in); vertical obstacle 0.95m (3ft 1.5in); trench 2.00m (6ft 6.75in)

AS-90

Vickers Armstrong, while carrying out sub-contract work on the failed SP70 project, could see the defects in the design and thus set about preparing an improved version of their own. At first it was developed as a turret and gun unit which could be dropped into a suitable tank hull in order to produce an SP gun, but as SP70 became more impractical, a complete vehicle was developed. When SP70 was aborted, the British had the choice between the latest version of the US M109, or the AS-90. The former was , by this time, stretching its design to the limits, whereas the latter was new and had a long upgrade life ahead of it. It was selected and went into service in 1993. It mounts a 39-calibre howitzer, but is capable of mounting 45- and 52-calibre weapons and will probably standardise on the latter in the near future.

Country of origin:	United Kingdom
Crew:	5
Weight:	45,000kg (44.29 tons)
Dimensions:	length 7.20m (23ft 8in); width 3.40m (11ft 2in) height: 3m (9ft 10in)
Range:	240km (150 miles)
Armour:	17mm (0.66in) maximum
Armament:	one 155mm (6.1in) howitzer
Powerplant:	one Cummins V-8 diesel developing 660hp (492kW) at 2800 rpm
Performance:	maximum road speed 55km/h (34 mph); fording 1.50m (5ft); vertical obstacle 0.88m (35in); trench 2.8m (9ft 2in)

Self-propelled Artillery

G-6

The 155mm (6.1in) G-6 was the second wheeled SP to astonish the world in the early 1980s (the other being the Czech Dana), and although the South African Army has used it effectively and speaks well of it, nobody else appears willing to take the plunge and adopt it. It uses a specially-designed 6x6 chassis, well armoured, and has ample working space at the rear carrying a turret mounting the same 155mm gun used in the towed role as the G5. Jacks are provided to support the vehicle and keep it steady while firing, and the large-wheel suspension absorbs the worst cross-country conditions. A massive wedge-shaped prow acts as a magazine containing shells, as well as holding the driver's cab.

Country of origin:	South Africa
Crew:	6
Weight:	47,000kg (46.25 tons)
Dimensions:	length 9.20m (30ft 2in); width 3.40m (11ft 2in); height 3.30m (10ft 10in)
Range:	700km (435 miles)
Armour:	not disclosed
Armament:	one 155mm (6.1in) gun
Powerplant:	one diesel developing 525hp (391.5kW)
Performance:	maximum road speed 90km/h (56mph); fording 1m (3ft 3in); vertical obstacle 0.5m (1ft 7in); trench 1m (3ft 3in)

Panzerhaubitse 2000

As a result of the collapse of the tri-national SP70 project, Germany had to find a new SP howitzer. Designs were solicited from two companies, and after examination, the one offered by Wegmann/MaK was accepted and contracts were issued. Development is still continuing and production will commence in 2000, about 250 equipments being envisaged. The hull and running gear are based on those of the Leopard II tank, but with the engine and transmission at the front of the hull. The rear is surmounted by a large turret containing the 52-calibre length gun which has a sliding block breech and a large multi-baffle muzzle-brake. The gun and turret are entirely power-operated and there is an automatic mechanical loading system which permits the firing of three rounds in ten seconds.

Country of origin:	Germany
Crew:	5
Weight:	55,000kg (54.13 tons)
Dimensions:	length 7.87m (25ft 10in); width 3.37m (11ft); height 3.40m (11ft 2in)
Range:	420km (260 miles)
Armour:	not disclosed
Armament:	one 155mm (6.1in) howitzer
Powerplant:	one MTU 881 V-12 diesel developing 1000hp (745.7kW)
Performance:	maximum road speed 60km/h (27mph); fording 2.25m (7ft 5in); vertical obstacle 1m (3ft 3in); trench 3m (9ft 10in)

Rascal Light 155mm SP Howitzer

The 'Rascal' was a private venture by Soltam, the Israel manufacturers, and represents an entirely new design of SP gun. The object was to produce a gun that was light enough not to be restricted by the carrying capacity of rural bridges, and to be air-lifted. The vehicle is not based upon any existing tank; the hull has a raised driver's compartment at the left front, with the engine behind the driver, and a central compartment for the commander and two gunners. The 155mm (6.1in) howitzer is installed on a platform at the rear of the vehicle and is power-operated; the gun may be either 39- or 52-calibres in length. A total of 40 rounds of ammunition are carried, the shells in racks alongside the gun and the cartridges in an armour-protected compartment in the hull.

Country of origin:	Israel
Crew:	4
Weight:	19,500kg (10.19 tons)
Dimensions:	length 7.50m (24ft 7lb); width 2.46m (8ft 1in); height: 2.30m (7ft 6in)
Range:	350km (218 miles)
Armour:	not disclosed
Armament:	one 155mm (6.1in) howitzer
Powerplant:	one diesel developing 350hp (260.9kW)
Performance:	maximum road speed 48km/h (30mph)

155/45 Norinco SP Gun

The Chinese 155/45 Norinco SP Gun is of conventional form – a tracked chassis with the driver and engine forward, leaving space at the rear of the hull for a fighting compartment surmounted by a large turret carrying a 45-calibre 155mm (6.1in) gun. The gun has a muzzle brake and fume extractor, and is provided with mechanical assistance for loading and ramming at any angle of elevation. Since 155mm is not a Chinese service calibre and the system is capable of firing NATO standard ammunition, it is assumed that this weapon was produced for export, but there is no information available about possible purchasers. There are rumours that some were sold to a country in the Middle East in 1996.

Country of origin:	China
Crew:	5
Weight:	32,000kg (31.50 tons)
Dimensions:	length 6.10m (20ft); width 3.20m (10ft 6in); height 2.59m (8ft 6in)
Range:	450km (20 miles)
Armour:	not disclosed
Armament:	one 155mm (6.1in) gun WAC-21
Powerplant:	one diesel developing 525hp (391.4kW)
Performance:	maximum road speed 56 km/h (35mph); fording 1.20m (4ft); vertical obstacle 0.70m (28in); trench 2.70m (8ft 10in)

Self-propelled Artillery

M110A2

The 203mm (8in) howitzer is commonly used as a 'partner piece' to the 155mm (6.1in) gun, using the same carriage, but for some reason the US Army did not produce a partner for the M109, but put the 8 inch on the same tracked carriage as the M107 175mm (6.88in) gun. The latter did not live up to expectations and was withdrawn from service. This left a gap in the US artillery armoury as there was no heavy SP gun capable of reaching deep into enemy territory or firing a nuclear shell. A new, longer 8 inch howitzer barrel was developed which replaced the earlier M110, turning it into the M110A1. Produced in 1978, the M110A2 had the addition of a muzzle brake, allowing the use of a more powerful propelling charge and increasing the maximum range of the gun to 22.9km (14.22 miles).

Country of origin:	USA
Crew:	5
Weight:	28,350kg (27.91 tons)
Dimensions:	length 5.72m (18ft 9in); width 3.14m (1ft 4in); height 2.93m (9ft 8in)
Range:	520km (325 miles)
Armour:	not disclosed
Armament:	one 203mm (8in) howitzer
Powerplant:	one Detroit Diesel V-8, turbocharged, developing 405hp (335.5kW) at 2300 rpm
Performance:	maximum road speed 56km/h (34mph); fording 1.06m (3ft 6in); vertical obstacle 1.01m (3ft 4in); trench 2.32m (7ft 9in)

Panzerwerfer 42

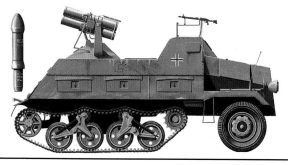

The German Nebelwerfer rocket, described on page 300, had only two real defects, and that was the cloud of dirt and debris kicked up behind the launcher when the rockets were fired, and the trail of smoke left in the air during its flight. The victims of the weapon soon realised that these two 'signatures' could give the location of the launcher, whereupon artillery retaliation could soon follow. To counter this, the Germans mounted a ten-barrel version on the back of an armoured weapons carrier so that the launcher could be moved rapidly after firing. The Opel company built about 300 of these in the latter part of 1942 and they were in use for the rest of the war, particularly on the Eastern Front.

Country of origin:	Germany
Calibre:	150mm (5.9in)
Launcher weight:	800kg (1764lb)
Length of rocket:	979mm (28.55in)
Weight of rocket:	31.80kg (70lb)
Warhead:	HE; 2.5kg (5.5lb)
Maximum velocity:	342m/sec (1120ft/sec)
Maximum range:	7060m (7725yds)

Free-flight Rockets

Army 20cm Rocket

The Japanese Army and Navy, in a classic example of non-cooperation, both designed 20cm (7.95in) bombardment rockets during World War II. The end results looked much the same, although they had various minor differences. The Army rocket, pictured here, resembled an artillery shell in shape but the forward section was filled with high explosive and the rear portion carried the smokeless powder rocket motor. The burning propellant was exhausted through canted jets in the rear end of the rocket, so that the rocket was spun as well as being propelled forward. The Type 4 launcher resembled a large mortar, but the barrel opened up and the rocket could then be dropped into the tube and the barrel closed again for firing.

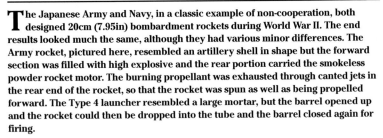

Country of origin:	Japan
Calibre:	202mm (7.95in)
Launcher weight:	227kg (500lb)
Length of rocket:	983mm (38.75in)
Weight of rocket:	92.60kg (204lb)
Warhead:	HE; 16.2kg (35.7 lb)
Maximum velocity:	not known
Maximum range:	2930m (3200yds)

Wurfgranate 42

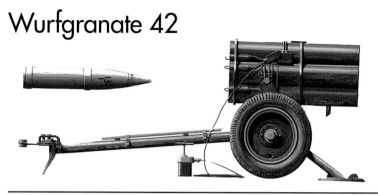

The German 21cm (8.27in) Wurfgranate 42 was a spin-stabilised HE rocket which resembled an artillery shell in shape. The forward part held a filling of 10.16kg (22.4lb) of Amatol, while the rear section carried the rocket motor, seven thick sticks of smokeless powder with an electrical igniter. This was exhausted through 22 canted vents in the base to spin and propel the rocket. The nose was covered by a ballistic cap which concealed an impact fuse. The launcher was the 21cm Nebelwerfer 42, a cluster of five barrels mounted on the same two-wheeled, split trail carriage as the 15cm Nebelwerfer. The rockets were fired by depressing a plunger from a safe distance away.

Country of origin:	Germany
Calibre:	210mm (8.27in)
Launcher weight:	1100kg (,425lb)
Length of rocket:	1.249m (49.21in)
Weight of rocket:	109.55kg (241.3lb)
Warhead:	HE; 10.17kg (22.4lb)
Maximum velocity:	320m/sec (1050ft/sec)
Maximum range:	7850m (8585yds)

Free-flight Rockets

M-13

The Russian M-13 system comprised of a 132mm (5.2in) rocket with an open-rail launcher which was usually seen on the back of a 6x6 truck, although they were also fitted on to redundant light tanks, tractors, and anything else which was close at hand. Development of this system began in the early 1930s but was kept a very close secret, not only from the rest of the world but even from the rest of the Soviet Army, since the launchers were operated by NKVD troops. Indeed, it was not until July 1941 that they were finally revealed. They were immediately countered by the German 15cm (5.9in) Nebelwerfer, and for the remainder of the war there was more or less a permanent duel between the German and Russian rocket troops.

Country of origin:	USSR
Calibre:	132mm (5.2in)
Launcher weight:	not known
Length of rocket:	1.42m (53.9in)
Weight of rocket:	42.5kg (93.7lb)
Warhead:	HE
Maximum velocity:	355m/sec (1165ft/sec)
Maximum range:	8500m (9300yds)

M-30

L ittle is known about this 300mm (11.81in) Soviet rocket system, since it did not survive after the war, and was kept secret during its service. Few photographs survived, and even they were uninformative. The rocket itself was a simple design with solid fuel motor and an impact fuse on the HE-Fragmentation warhead. The launcher was no more than a rectangular frame with four launch rails, with the rear resting on the ground and the front propped up at the desired angle on two legs. These launchers were brought to the launch site on trucks and erected in rows. This weapon appears to have been used solely for preliminary bombardments prior to mass attacks. It was never used on any form of mobile mounting.

Country of origin:	USSR
Calibre:	300mm (11.81in)
Launcher weight:	not known
Length of rocket:	not known
Weight of rocket:	72kg (158.75lb)
Warhead:	HE
Maximum velocity:	not known
Maximum range:	2800m (3060yds)

Free-flight Rockets

M8 4.5in

The 114mm (4.5in) M8 was perhaps the most widely used American rocket of World War II, since it was originally provided as an aircraft rocket for ground attack. It was then adapted as a ground artillery rocket. The design was well thought-out: the warhead formed the forward part of the rocket, and had a long tail tube which, when assembled, lay in the centre of the rear portion, surrounded by smokeless powder sticks. These formed the motor and were exhausted through a central venturi. The rocket was stabilised in flight by jack-knife fins which flipped out into the airstream as the rocket left the launcher tube. Numerous modifications were made to the design as a result of experience, leading to the M8A1, A2 and A3, but they were all more or less the same.

Country of origin:	USA
Calibre:	114mm (4.5in)
Launcher weight:	23.6 kg (52lb)
Length of rocket:	838mm (33in)
Weight of rocket:	17.5kg (38.5lb)
Warhead:	HE; 1.95kg (4.30lb)
Maximum velocity:	259m/sec (850ft/sec)
Maximum range:	4200m (4600yds)

2in Rocket

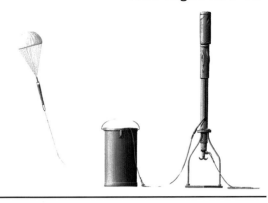

The British 57mm (2in) rocket acted as the test-bed for the development of the better-known 76mm (3in) AA rocket and then became an air defence weapon in its own right. The smaller size meant a less destructive blast when the rocket was fired, and this was acceptable to the Royal and Merchant Navies, who fitted these launchers into most of their ships. As well as a simple HE rocket, the 2in system was provided with a variety of PAC (Parachute and Cable) rockets which went up to about 3048m (10,000ft) and then released a few hundred feet of steel cable attached to a parachute. A number of these fired in the face of a dive-bomber soon persuaded the pilot to go somewhere else. These PAC rockets were deployed around most RAF fighter airfields in the south of England in 1940 to protect them against low-flying German attacks.

Country of origin:	United Kingdom
Calibre:	57mm (2.244in)
Launcher weight:	not known
Length of rocket:	914mm (36in)
Weight of rocket:	4.88kg (10.75lb)
Warhead:	HE: 0.25kg (9oz)
Maximum velocity:	457m/sec (1500ft/sec)
Maximum ceiling:	3048m (10,000ft)

Free-flight Rockets

SBAT-70

The SBAT-70 was designed in Brazil as an aircraft rocket, but was then adopted for ground firing. It is a single-stage solid fuel rocket with folding fins which spring out into the air stream after launch. The launcher is mounted on a light two-wheeled trailer and consists of a bank of 36 tubes set in a frame which is capable of being elevated and traversed as necessary. A crew of four is needed to operate the SBAT-70. A variety of warheads are available, including standard HE-Fragmentation, a shaped charge anti-tank/anti-personnel head, a flechette head containing several thousand small darts, a white phosphorus smoke head and a practice head. The system is available for export but has not as yet been bought by any country.

Country of origin:	Brazil
Calibre:	70mm (2.75in)
Launcher weight:	1000kg (2204lb)
Length of rocket:	1.41m (55.5in)
Weight of rocket:	11.7kg (29.80lb)
Warhead:	HE; 3.2kg (7.05lb)
Maximum velocity:	700m/sec (2296ft/sec)
Maximum range:	8500m (9295yds)

3in Rocket

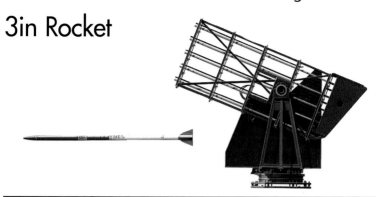

The British 76.2mm (3in) rocket was developed in the mid-1930s as a cheap alternative to the 3in AA gun, and was designed to propel a shell of similar weight to a similar ceiling in a similar time. It was a very successful design and was installed at many seaports and naval bases around Britain and overseas. A seaside location was preferred because these rockets were fired in salvoes of 64 rockets, and shortly afterwards 64 spent motors fell from the sky. As with the 57mm (2in) rocket, some exotic projectiles were developed, notably the 'K' rocket which went up to about 6770m (22,000ft) and released a large parachute with several hundred feet of steel cable hanging beneath it, and an explosive mine. Any aircraft flying into the cable caused the parachute to drag until the mine struck the aircaft and blew it up.

Country of origin:	United Kingdom
Calibre:	76.2mm (3in)
Launcher weight:	2-barrel No.2: 566kg (1247lb)
Length of rocket:	1.93m (76in)
Weight of rocket:	24.5kg (53.97lb)
Warhead:	HE; 1.94kg (4.28lb)
Maximum velocity:	457m/sec (1500ft/sec)
Maximum ceiling:	6770m (22,200ft)

Free-flight Rockets

D-3000 Walid

The D-3000 system comprises a 12-barrel launcher mounted in the open-topped crew compartment of a Walid armoured personnel carrier. The rockets are of 80mm (3.15in) calibre and are fitted with warheads containing a smoke-producing mixture as the sole purpose of this equipment is to generate smoke screens. Since the terrain of the Egyptian desert does not offer very much natural cover for troop movements or assemblies, it becomes necessary to rely on smoke screens, and the Walid unit can, with one volley, generate a screen about 915m (1000yds) long, which can then be built up and maintained by a slow rate of fire. A similar weapon, the D-6000, using a 6-barrel unit firing a 122mm (4.8in) rocket, is used when it is necessary to deliver smoke screens at longer ranges, up to 6000m (6561yds).

Country of origin:	Egypt
Calibre:	80mm (3.15in)
Launcher weight:	5400kg (5.31 tons)
Length of rocket:	26.5kg (58.42lb)
Weight of rocket:	1.51m (59.44in)
Warhead:	7.8kg (17.2lb)
Maximum velocity:	not known
Maximum range:	2500m (2735yds)

Land Mattress

Land Mattress was a meaningless cover name for a 32-barrel rocket launcher for artillery use that was developed in 1944. The launcher was a fairly simple cluster of 'barrels' on a two-wheeled trailer, and the rocket was constructed from the motor of the 76mm (3in) AA rocket and the warhead of a naval 127mm (5in) bombardment rocket, to which a grossly unsafe impact fuse was attached. The Ordnance Board were horrified, but the Canadian Army took a battery of these to Walcheren and gave the defenders of that island a terrible surprise. One launcher could deliver as much high explosive as a battery of medium guns in a single salvo. A version was developed that could be towed by a Jeep, but the war finished before it reached service.

Country of origin:	United Kingdom
Calibre:	76.2mm (3in)
Launcher weight:	1118kg (2464lb)
Length of rocket:	1.770m (69.70in)
Weight of rocket:	30.53m (67.25lb)
Warhead:	HE: 3.18kg (7lb)
Maximum velocity:	353m/sec (1100ft/sec)
Maximum range:	7230m (7900yds)

Free-flight Rockets

Nebelwerfer 41

Under the terms of the Versailles Treaty, Germany could not develop heavy artillery. However, the Treaty said nothing about rockets. Therefore, rockets were developed as a substitute for artillery from 1931 onwards and the Nebelwerfer was one of the products of this programme. The launcher was a six-barrelled device on a split trail two-wheeled mounting, and the rocket was an ingenious design which had the motor in the front section, exhausting through a ring of vents halfway down the body, and the explosive 'warhead' was actually the sail section of the round. This gave good accuracy, since the rocket was pulling instead of pushing, and also gave better terminal effect because the bursting charge was above the ground when it detonated.

Country of origin:	Germany
Calibre:	158mm (6.22in)
Launcher weight:	770kg (1697.9lb), loaded
Length of rocket:	979mm (38.55in)
Weight of rocket:	31.8kg (70lb)
Warhead:	HE; 2.83kg (5.70lb)
Maximum velocity:	342m/sec (1120ft/sec)
Maximum range:	7060m (7725yds)

Type 70

Type 70 is the designation of the Chinese 130mm (5.11in) rocket system when mounted on the Type YW 531 armoured personnel carrier. The vehicle is fitted with a 19-barrel launcher on a rotating and elevating mount above the crew compartment. The mount can be aimed and fired from under armour, but it is not clear whether it can be reloaded through the crew hatches from below, or whether the crew have to come out from the vehicle in order to reload the tubes. The rocket is a simple single-stage solid fuel weapon with an HE -Fragmentation warhead. In standard form, it is capable of reaching to a maximum range of 10,115m (11,061yds), but there is a special long-range version with a more powerful and slightly longer motor which gives a range of 15,000m (16,404yds).

Country of origin:	China
Calibre:	130mm (5.11in)
Launcher weight:	14,000kg (13.77 tons)
Length of rocket:	1.063m (41.85in)
Weight of rocket:	32.80kg (72.30lb)
Warhead:	HE-Fragmentation; 14.73kg (32.47 lb
Maximum velocity:	436m/sec (1430ft/sec)
Maximum range:	10,1115m (11,060yds)

Free-flight Rockets

Type 63

T he 107mm (4.21in) Type 63 is a 12-round rocket launcher in widespread use with the People's Liberation Army. It was developed in the late 1950s as a replacement for the 102mm (4.02in) six-round Type 50. Each Chinese infantry division is equipped with 18 Type 63 equipments. The launcher has three rows of four barrels mounted on a rubber-tyred split-pole trailer carriage that can be towed by a number of vehicles. The wheels are removed for firing, the launcher resting on two legs at the front and the trails. A lighter model is used by the Chinese airborne and mountain infantry units, which can be broken down easily into loads for carriage by men or horses. The launcher can also be fitted on a 4x4 truck with an enlarged cab to accomodate the four man crew and 12 reload rounds.

Country of origin:	China
Calibre:	107mm (4.21in)
Launcher weight:	602kg (1327lb)
Length of rocket:	0.84m (2.76ft)
Weight of rocket:	18.8kg (41.45lb)
Warhead:	HE-Fragmentation, incendiary; 8.33kg (18.36lb)
Maximum velocity:	not known
Maximum range:	8500m (5.28 miles)

BM-21

The Soviet 122mm (4.8in) BM-21 system was developed in the early 1950s and might be considered to be the successor to the various wartime 'Katyusha' rocket systems, since it uses the same principle of firing a solid-fuel rocket from a bank of launchers mounted on the cargo bed of a 6x6 truck. Instead of the old open rails, however, this uses closed tubes in a cluster of 40 barrels, on a frame capable of 55° of elevation and 120° of traverse to either side. There are also 12- and 36-round variants of the basic launcher mounted on different vehicles. The rocket can be used with HE-Fragmentation, incendiary or bomblet warheads, and the rocket has four spring-put fins set at a slight angle in order to give the rocket a slow roll to stabilise it.

Country of origin:	USSR
Calibre:	122mm (4.80in)
Launcher weight:	13,700kg (13.48 tons), loaded
Length of rocket:	3.226m (10.58ft)
Weight of rocket:	77.5kg (170.85lb)
Warhead:	HE-Fragmentation, incendiary, bomblet; 19.4kg (42.76lb)
Maximum velocity:	690m/sec (2264ft/sec)
Maximum range:	20.380m (12.66 miles)

ASTROS 2

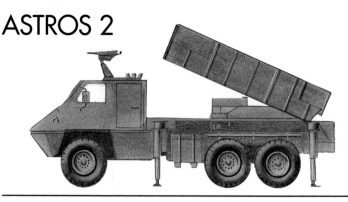

ASTROS stands for Artillery Saturation Rocket System, which was developed in Brazil, primarily for export, in the early 1980s. The whole system incorporates three different calibres of rocket (127mm (5in), 180mm (7.08in) and 300mm (11.8in)) and three corresponding launchers (32, 16 and 4 tubes respectively), controlled by a Contraves 'Fieldguard' radar and computing system. The system has been adopted by the Brazilian Army and has also been exported. All launchers are mounted on 6x6 armoured trucks of various sizes, and there are also armoured resupply vehicles. The rockets are solid fuelled, with HE-Fragmentation warheads, and the SS-60 300mm rocket also has a bomblet warhead carrying 65 dual-purpose anti-tank/anti-personnel sub-munitions. The details below are for the SS-40 system.

Country of origin:	Brazil
Calibre:	180mm (7.08in)
Launcher weight:	not known
Length of rocket:	4.20m (13.77ft)
Weight of rocket:	152kg (335lb)
Warhead:	HE-Fragmentation
Maximum velocity:	not known
Maximum range:	16,000m (17,500yds)

BM-27

This Soviet 16-tube launcher appeared in the early 1970s and has collected a confusing series of names and numbers, from the M1977 to the most recent BM-9P140. It consists of an 8x8 truck carrying a launch unit with two layers of four tubes and two layers of six tubes. This can be elevated to 55° and traversed 120° to either side of the vehicle. Four stabiliser jacks are lowered to provide support for the launcher while firing. The rocket is a solid-fuel type with a variety of warheads: HE-Fragmentation, chemical and sub-munition, the latter carrying either anti-tank/anti-personnel bomblets, incendiary bomblets, 24 anti-tank mines or 312 anti-personnel mines.

Country of origin:	USSR
Calibre:	220mm (8.66in)
Launcher weight:	20,000kg (19,88 tons)
Length of rocket:	4.832m (15.85ft)
Weight of rocket:	260kg (573lb)
Warhead:	HE-Fragmentation; 100kg (220lb)
Maximum velocity:	not known
Maximum range:	25,000m (15.5 miles)

Free-flight Rockets

MLRS

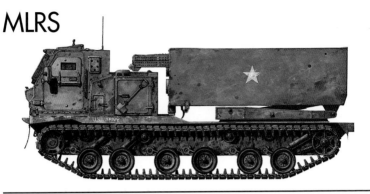

The Vought Multiple Launch Rocket System (MLRS) had its origins in a 1976 feasibility study into what was known as a General Support Rocket System. Following trials, the Vought system was chosen and entered service with the US Army in 1982. These Self-Propelled Launcher Loaders on the chassis of the M2 Infantry Fighting Vehicle carry two pods of six rounds each. These rounds might consist of fragmentation bomblets, anti-tank mines, chemical warheads or mine-dispensing munitions. The Vought MLRS was licensed to the UK, France, Italy, West Germany and the Netherlands for production. It saw action during the 1991 Gulf War, when Allied MLRS batteries tore large holes in Iraqi defence lines prior to the ground offensive to free Kuwait.

Country of origin:	USA
Calibre:	227mm (8.94in)
Launcher weight:	25,191kg (55,420lb)
Length of rocket:	3.94m (12.93ft)
Weight of rocket:	308kg (679lb)
Warhead:	submunition; chemical; weights not known
Maximum velocity:	not known
Maximum range:	42km (26.1 miles)

BM-24

The 240mm (9.45in) BM-24 entered Soviet Army service in the early 1950s and, like the BM-21, was simply a modern version of the wartime 'Stalin Organ' rockets, a collection of launching racks mounted on the back of a 6x6 cargo truck. This appears to have been the last of the wartime open-frame launcher types, with curved rails to give the ginned rocket a degree of roll stabilisation. The BM-24 was issued to motorised divisions in the Soviet Army but was later replaced by the BM21, after which it was sold widely to Middle and Far Eastern countries. Numbers are still in use in Africa. The rockets are solid fuel with conventional HE-Fragmentation warheads.

Country of origin:	USSR
Calibre:	240mm (9.45in)
Launcher weight:	9,200kg (9.05 tons), loaded
Length of rocket:	1.18m (46.45in)
Weight of rocket:	112.5kg (248lb)
Warhead:	HE-Fragmentation; 46.9kg (103.35lb)
Maximum velocity:	363m/sec (1190ft/sec)
Maximum range:	10,300m (11,265yds)

Avibras X-40

The Avibras X-40 was the largest rocket employed by the Brazilian Army. It was developed by the Military Engineering Institute and manufactured by Avibras, the Brazilian aviation consortium. It was a single-stage solid propellant rocket with an exceptionally powerful motor, as can be seen by the maximum velocity and range. The three-rail launcher was mounted into the turret ring of an X1A1 light tank, which allowed for traverse and elevation, and the tank was fitted with three hydraulic jacks to level and stabilise it for firing. Avibras later developed this into the Astros system, and the X-40 was replaced in the early 1990s after extensive use in armament research trials.

Country of origin:	Brazil
Calibre:	300mm (11.8in)
Launcher weight:	17,000kg (16.80 tons)
Length of rocket:	4.85m (191in)
Weight of rocket:	654kg (1442lb)
Warhead:	HE; 147kg (324lb)
Maximum velocity:	1285m/sec (1405ft/sec)
Maximum range:	68,000m (42.2 miles)

FROG-7

FROG stands for 'Free Rocket Over Ground' and the Soviet FROG-1 rocket was first seen in 1957. FROG-7 appeared in 1969 after a series of improved models were developed as experience was gained. The system has been widely exported to several countries and the earlier -3, -4, -5 and -6 versions are probably still in use. FROG is a large single-stage solid fuel rocket provided with a variety of warheads and carried on an 8x8 transporter-erector-launcher vehicle. It is unusual in that it uses air-brakes in flight in order to alter the trajectory and thus achieve the desired range. The launch rail is elevated and the brake setting done before launch, according to the range desired. Like all fin-stabilised free rockets, crosswinds affect it and its accuracy is no better than a 500m (546yd) circle around the aiming point.

Country of origin:	USSR
Calibre:	550mm (21.65in)
Launcher weight:	23,000kg (22.63 tons)
Length of rocket:	9.11m (29.88ft)
Weight of rocket:	2500kg (5512lb)
Warhead:	nuclear, 5 or 25kT, chemical, HE; 450kg (992lb)
Maximum velocity:	not known
Maximum range:	70km (43.5 miles)

Light Artillery Rocket System (LARS)

This system entered service with the German Army in 1970, but has now been almost entirely phased out and the equipments have been given to Greece, Portugal and Turkey, where they will doubtless serve for several more years. The rocket has a solid fuel motor, and the standard warhead is a high explosive-fragmentation type with pre-formed fragments. There are also training and smoke warheads, and a cargo warhead which carries eight anti-tank mines and releases them over the target area. The launcher is an 18-barrel unit carried on the back of a standard MAN 6x6 military truck. The unit can be elevated and traversed by a gunlayer seated on the mount, but before firing, he dismounts, two stabilising jacks are lowered to the ground, and the crew enter the vehicle cab to fire the rockets.

Country of origin:	Germany
Calibre:	110mm (4.33in)
Launcher weight:	17,480kg (17.2 tons), loaded
Length of rocket:	2.263m (7.42ft)
Weight of rocket:	35kg (77.16lb)
Warhead:	HE; 17.3kg (38.14lb)
Maximum velocity:	640m/sec (2100ft/sec)
Maximum range:	14,000m (15,310yds)

Valkyr

The 127mm (5in) Valkyr was developed in South Africa in the 1970s to counter the many Russian rocket launchers being used by their adversaries. It was first deployed in 1982 and soon made its presence felt on the Angolan border. The launcher consists of 24 tubes (three rows of eight) carried in the back of a standard 4x4 light truck. The truck is provided with a normal canopy which completely conceals the rocket launcher when not in use, making its detection by reconnaissance aircraft almost impossible. The rockets are solid fuel types, fin stabilised, and the warhead is lined with a layer of epoxy resin in which some 8599 steel balls are embedded which give a lethal area of about 1500 square metres when detonated. The warhead may be fitted with either an impact or a proximity fuse.

Country of origin:	South Africa
Calibre:	127mm (5in)
Launcher weight:	6400 kg (14,110lb)
Length of rocket:	2.68m (8.79ft)
Weight of rocket:	53.5kg (118lb)
Warhead:	HE; 18kg (39.7lb)
Maximum velocity:	250m/sec (820ft/sec)
Maximum range:	22,700m (14.1 miles)

Glossary

AA: anti-aircraft

AFV: armoured fighting vehicle

AP: armour piercing

APC: armoured personnel carrier

APCR: armour piercing cored round, ammunition with a hard core (usually tungsten)

APDS: armour piercing discarding sabot

BREECH: the closed end of the barrel at the rear of the gun, where most guns are loaded

CALIBRE: the inside diameter of the barrel (also used to measure its length)

EFFECTIVE CEILING: the highest altitude (of an approaching aircraft) to which a AA gun can fire for 30 seconds before it reaches maximum elevation

EFFECTIVE RANGE: the furthest distance a weapon can be accurately aimed

ELEVATION: the amount a gun can be moved vertically

FLASH SUPPRESSOR: a device that minimises the visible flash from the gun when fired

HE: high explosive

HESH: high explosive shaped head, ammunition with a shaped charge warhead

MG: machine gun

MUZZLE: the front, open end of the barrel

MUZZLE BRAKE: a device that directs exhaust gases backwards to help counteract recoil

PENETRATION (OF ARMOUR): given in the form AA/BBB/C, where AA is the thickness of armour penetrated in millimetres; BBB is the range at which it occurred; and C is the slope of the armour. Thus, 75/1000/30° means that the shot penetrates 75mm (2.95in) of armour at 1000 metres range, striking at an angle of 30° to the target face

RECOIL: the force that drives a gun backwards when fired

RIFLED (BARREL): a barrel with spiral grooves that make the shell spin, for greater accuracy

SABOT: a protective sleeve that fits round a (usually finned) shell fired from a smoothbore gun

SHAPED (CHARGE): explosive that is shaped or becomes shaped on impact in a way that gives it maximum destructive value when it burns

SHRAPNEL: ammunition that, when it explodes, spreads small pieces of hot metal in all directions, most effective against infantry

SMOOTHBORE: a barrel that does not have rifled grooves

TRAVERSE: the amount a barrel can be moved horizontally

Index

Note: Page numbers in **bold** refer to main entries.

2.8cm (1.1in) Panzerbuchse 41 **134**
5cm (1.98in) Flak 41 **112**
5cm (1.98in) Pak 38 **144**
7.5cm (2.95in) Infantry Gun IG18 **22**
8cm (3.20in) PAW 600 **150**
10cm (4.14in) M1917 Gun **36**
10cm Škoda Light Howitzer vz 14/19 **24**
12.8cm (5.03in) Flak 40 **126**
12.8cm (5.03in) K44 **157**
12.8cm (5.03in) Pak 44 **156**
13.5cm (5.31in) FK 1909 **49**
15cm (5.87in) Field Howitzer FH17 **52**
15cm (5.87in) Howitzer M1915 **69**
15cm (5.87in) L/40 Feldkanone i.R. **51**
15cm (5.87in) Gun M1877 **54**
15cm (5.87in) sIG 33 infantry gun **180**
21cm (8.31in) Haubitze 520(i) *see* Obice da 210/22
21cm (8.31in) Howitzer **80**
21cm (8.31in) K12(E) **238**
21cm (8.31in) Mrs 18 **82**
22.5cm (8.86in) Heavy Trench Mortar **74**
24.5cm (9.64in) Heavy Trench Mortar **86**
28cm (11.02in) K12(E) **239**
28cm (11.02in) Kustenhaubitze **88**
38cm (14.96in) Gun `MaxE' **246**
42cm (16.5in) Howitzer **9**
80cm (31.4in) Gustav **240**
155/45 Norinco SP Gun **287**
0.55in (13.9mm) Boys Anti-tank rifle **129**
2in (57mm) Rocket **295**
2.5in (63.5mm) Northover Projector **143**
2.75in (70mm) Mountain Gun **15**
3in (76.2mm) M3 **117**
3in (76.2mm) Gun M5 **149**
3in (76.2mm) Rocket **297**
3.7in (94mm) QF Gun Mk1 **123**
3.7in (94mm) RCL Gun **155**
4.7in (120mm) Field Gun M1906 **47**
7.2in (182.9mm) Howitzers Marks 1 to 4 **75**
8in (203mm) Howitzer M1 **78**
8in (203mm) Mark V Howitzer **7**
12in (305mm) Railway Howitzer Mk 5 **244**
13.5in (343mm) Gun `Sceneshifter' **245**
16in (406.4mm) M1919 Coast Gun **91**
7.92mm (0.311in) Panzerbuchse 39 **127**
20mm (0.78in) Breda Model 35 **101**
20mm (0.78in) Flak 30 **99**
20mm (0.78in) Flakvierling 38 **100**
20mm (0.78in) Tarasque **95**
23mm (0.90in) ZU-23 **104**
37mm (1.45in) Flak 37 **107**
37mm (1.45in) Flak 43 **108**
37mm (1.45in) M1A2 **106**
37mm (1.49in) Anti-Tank Gun 1918 **135**
37mm (1.49in) Anti-tank Gun M3 **136**

37mm (1.49in) Pak 35/36 **137**
40mm (1.57in) Bofors l/60 **109**
40mm (1.57in) Bofors L/70 **110**
40mm (1.57in) Breda 40/L/70 **111**
45mm (1.77in) Brixia Model 35 mortar **163**
47mm (1.85in) Model 01 Anti-tank Gun **140**
47mm (1.85in) Skoda vz 36 **139**
50mm (1.57in) Type 89 Grenade discharger **164**
60mm (2.36in) Mortar M1 **165**
60mm (2.36in) Mortar M19 **167**
65mm (2.55in) Mountain Gun **14**
70mm (2.75in) Battalion Gun Type 92 **168**
75mm (2.95in) Mountain Gun Geb G.36 **23**
75mm (2.95in) Pack Howitzer M1A1 **170**
75mm (2.95in) Pak 40 **145**
75mm (2.96in) Bofors Model 29 **113**
75mm (2.96in) Type 88 **114**
75mm (2.96in) Gun Mle 97 7
75mm (2.96in) Pak 41 **146**
76mm (2.99in) Otomatic Air Defence Tank **262**
76.2mm (3in) Field Gun M1939 **29**
76.2mm (3in) Field Gun M1942 **28**
76.2mm (3in) Model 1942 **148**
77mm (3.03in) Field Gun M96nA **31**
77mm (3.03in) FK16 **30**
77mm (3.03in) German 1914 **118**
81mm (3.18in) Mortar Mle 27/31 **172**
82mm (3.22in) PM-37 mortar **173**
82mm (3.22in) Vasilek automatic mortar **174**
85mm (3.34in) M39 **119**
88mm (3.46in) Flak 18 **120**
88mm (3.46in) Flak 41 **121**
88mm (3.46in) Pak 43/41 **152**
90mm (3.54in) M1 **122**
95mm (3.7in) Infantry Howitzer **175**
105mm (4.13in) Flak 38 **124**
105mm (4.13in) Howitzer M2A1 **40**
105mm (4.13in) Howitzer M3 **43**
105mm (4.13in) leFH18 **41**
105mm (4.13in) leFH18(M) **42**
105mm (4.13in) Light Gun L118 **39**
106mm (4.13in) RCL Rifle M40A1 **154**
120mm (4.72in) Krupp Howitzer M1905 **44**
120mm (4.72in) M1938 Mortar **176**
122mm (4.80in) D-30 **45**
149mm (5.86in) Skoda Model 14 Howitzer **35**
149mm (5.87in) Siege Gun, Model of 1877 **58**
152mm (6.0in) Gun-Howitzer M1937 (ML-20) **55**
152mm (6.0in) Howitzer M09/30 **58**
152mm (6.0in) Howitzer M1943 (D-1) **56**
155mm (6.10in) Gun G-5 **65**
155mm (6.10in) Gun M2 **59**
155mm (6.10in) Gun Model TR **68**
155mm (6.10in) Howitzer FH-70 12, **64**
155mm (6.10in) Howitzer FH-77A **66**
155mm (6.10in) Howitzer M198 **67**
155mm (6.10in) Howitzer Mle 1950 **73**
155mm (6.10in) Model 77 Howitzer **62**

155mm (6.10in) ODE FH-88 Gun-howitzer **70**
155mm (6.10in) Rimailho Howitzer Model
   1904TR **60**
155mm (6.10in) Royal Ordnance Light Towed
   Howitzer **72**
155mm (6.10in) Santa Barbara SB-155/39
   Howitzer **71**
160mm (6.29in) Mortar M1943 **181**
194mm (7.63in) Gun GPF **76**
203mm (8.0in) Howitzer M1931 (L/25) **79**
240mm (9.45in) Howitzer M1 **84**
305mm (12in) Howitzer 305/17 Mod 17 **90**
914mm (36.0in) Mortar 'Little David' **93**
13pdr 9cwt AA Gun **116**
15pdr BLC Field Gun **26**
2S3 Akatsiya (M1973) 274
Abbot **268**
ADATS **235**
AGS-17 Grenande launcher **160**
air defence artillery
   5cm (1.98in) Flak 41 112
   12.8cm (5.03in) Flak 40 126
   3in (76mm) M3 117
   3.7in (94mm) QF Gun Mk1 **123**
   20mm (0.78in) Breda Model 35 101
   20mm (0.78in) Flak 30 99
   20mm (0.78in) Flakvierling 38 **100**
   20mm (0.78in) Tarasque 95
   23mm (0.90in) ZU-23 **104**
   37mm (1.45in) Flak 37 107
   37mm (1.45in) Flak 43 108
   37mm (1.45in) M1A2 106
   40mm (1.57in) Bofors l/60 109
   40mm (1.57in) Bofors L/70 110
   40mm (1.57in) Breda 40/L/70 111
   75mm (2.96in) Bofors Model 29 113
   75mm (2.96in) Type 88 114
   77mm (3.03in) German 1914 **118**
   85mm (3.34in) M39 119
   88mm (3.46in) Flak 18 120
   88mm (3.46in) Flak 41 121
   90mm (3.54in) M1 122
   105mm (4.13in) Flak 38 **124**
   13pdr 9cwt AA Gun **116**
   M167 Vulcan 96
   Oerlikon 20mm (0.78in) 102
   Oerlikon GAI-BO1 98
   Oerlikon GDF-001 35mm (1.37in) 105
   Ordnance QF 3in (76mm) 20cwt 115
   Ordnance QF 4.5in (114mm) Gun 125
   Polsten 20mm (0.78in) 103
   Rh202 97
   TCM-20 94
air defence missiles
   ADATS 235
   Bloodhound 220
   Blowpipe 221
   Bofors RBS-70 223
   Crotale 218
   FIM-92 Stinger 231
   Henschel Hs 117 Schmetterling 213
   M48 Chaparral 228
   MIM-23 HAWK 230

   MIM-104 Patriot 229
   Mistral 233
   Nike Ajax 215
   Nike Hercules 216
   Rapier 222
   Roland 219
   RSD 58 209
   SA-3 Goa 214
   SA-4 Ganef 224
   SA-6 Gainful 225
   SA-7 Grail 226
   SA-8 Gecko 227
   Seaslug 211
   Starstreak 234
   Talos 217
   Thunderbird 210
   Type 81 Tan-SAM 232
air defence tank, 76mm (3in) Otomatic Air
   Defence Tank 262
AMX-13 DCA **250**
anti-aircraft guns 10
   see also air defence artillery
anti-armour weapons
   2.8cm (1.1in) Panzerbuchse 41 134
   5cm (1.98in) Pak 38 144
   8cm (3.20in) PAW 600 150
   12.8cm (5.03in) K44 157
   12.8cm (5.03in) Pak 44 156
   0.55in (13.9mm) Boys Anti-tank rifle 129
   2.5in (63.5mm) Northover Projector 143
   3in (76.2mm) Gun M5 149
   3.7in (94mm) RCL Gun 155
   7.92mm (0.311in) Panzerbuchse 39 127
   37mm (1.49in) Anti-Tank Gun 1918 135
   37mm (1.49in) Anti-tank Gun M3 146
   37mm (1.49in) Pak 35/36 137
   47mm (1.85in) Model 01 Anti-tank Gun 140
   47mm (1.85in) Skoda vz 36 139
   75mm (2.95in) Pak 40 145
   75mm (2.95in) Pak 41 146
   76.2mm (3.0in) Model 1942 148
   88mm (3.46) Pak 43/41 152
   106mm (4.13in) RCL Rifle M40A1 154
   Flak 18 153
   Granatbuchse 39 128
   M1A1 2.36in 60mm) Rocker Launcher 142
   Ordnance QF 17pdr Gun 147
   Panzerfaust 158
   PIAT 159
   PTRD 1941 Anti-tank rifle 131
   PTRS 1941 Anti-tank rifle 130
   QF 2pdr Mk VII 138
   QF 6pdr 7cwt Gun Mk 2 141
   Raketenpanzerbuchse 43 151
   Type 2 Anti-tank Grenade Launcher 133
   Type 97 Anti-tank Rifle 132
anti-balloon guns 9
anti-missile missile, MIM-104 Patriot 229
anti-tank guns 10
   5cm (1.98in) Pak 38 144
   12.8cm (5.03in) Pak 44 156
   3in (76.2mm) Gun M5 149
   37mm (1.49in) Anti-tank Gun 1918 135

37mm (1.49in) Anti-tank Gun M3 146
37mm (1.49in) Pak 35/36 137
47mm (1.85in) Model 01 Anti-tank Gun 140
75mm (2.95in) Pak 40 145
75mm (2.95in) Pak 41 146
Ordnance QF 17pdr Gun 147
QF 2pdr Mk VII 138
anti-tank rifles
    0.55in (13.9mm) Boys Anti-tank rifle 129
    7.92mm (0.311in) Panzerbuchse 39 127
    PTRD 1941 Anti-tank rifle 131
    PTRS 1941 Anti-tank rifle 130
    Type 97 Anti-tank Rifle 132
anti-tank weapon, SU-76 263
AP/AV 700 multiple grenade launcher **184**
Army 20cm (7.95in) Rocket **290**
assault guns 11
ASTROS 2 (Artillery Saturation Rocket System)
    304
ASU-57 **259**
Atlas 195
automatic guns 13
Avibras X-40 **308**

B-300 Light Support Weapon **183**
ballistic calculations, and computers 12
Battalion Gun Type 92 168
Battle of Albert 7
Battle of Kursk 273
Bazooka (M1A1) 2.36in (60mm) Rocket
    Launcher 142, 151
Becker cannon 102
BGM-109G Tomahawk **197**
Big Bertha 9, **92**
Bishop **264**
'The Bitch' (SU-76) 263
BL 6in (152mm) 26-cwt Howitzer Mk 1 **57**
BL 6in (152mm) 30-cwt Howitzer **61**
BL 8in (203mm) Howitzer Mark 7 **77**
Bloodhound **220**
Blowpipe **221**
BM-9P140 *see* BM27
BM-21 **303**
BM-24 **307**
BM-27 **305**
Bofors 109, 110, 113
    40mm (1.57in) L/60 109
    40mm (1.57in) L/70 110
    75mm (2.95in) Model 29 113
    75mm (2.95in) Model 34 **169**
    RBS-70 **223**
Boys, Captain 129
Brandt
    60mm (2.36in) LR Gun-mortar **166**
    120mm (4.72in) Mortar **177**
Brandt, Edgar 172
Breda 40/L/70 111
Breda Model 35 101
breech-loading field howitzer, Ordnance BL 5in
    (127mm) Howitzer Mk I 46
Broadway Trust 155
Browning, John M. 106

Bull, Dr. Gerald 65
'Bumble Bee' (Hummel) 8, 271

Cactus 218
Canon de 105mm (4.13in) Schneider Mle 1913
    37
Canon de 240 L Model 1884 **85**
canon de 240 Mle 93/96 sur Affuit-truck St-
    Chamond **236**
Canon de 320 Mle 1870/93 sur Affuit-truck
    Schneider **237**
Canone de 75 Mle 1897 7, **16**
Canonne da 75/27 **17**
Chaparral 228
CIS-40-AFL Grenade launcher **161**
coast gun, 16in (406.4mm) M1919 Coast Gun
    91
Colt company 106
computers, and ballistic calculations 12
Contraves 209
'Corporal' 198
Crotale **218**
CSS-1 (T1) **188**
CSS-2 (T2) **189**
CSS-3 (T3) **190**
CSS-4 (T4) **191**

D-30 45
D-3000 Walid **298**
DANA **275**
Deport, Colonel 17
Dogtyarev 131
Dora 240
dual-function weapon, 20mm (0.78in) Breda
    Model 35 101
'Duster' 256

Empresa Nacional Santa Barbara 71

Famous French 75 *see* Canone de 75 Mle 1897
field guns
    4.7in (120mm) Field Gun M1906 47
    76.2mm (3in) Field Gun M1939 29
    76.2mm (3in) Field Gun M1942 28
    77mm (3.03in) Field Gun M96nA 31
    77mm (3.03in) FK16 30
    105mm (4.13in) LeFH 18 41
    149mm (5.86in) Skoda Model 14 Howitzer
        35
    305mm (12in) Howitzer 305/17 Mod 17 90
    15pdr BLC Field Gun 26
    Krupp 75mm (2.95in) Field Gun M1903 18
    Ordnance QF 4.5in (114mm) Howitzer 33
field and heavy artillery
    7.5cm (2.95in) Infantry Gun IG18 22
    10cm (4.14in) M1917 Gun 36
    10cm (4.14in) Skoda Light Howitzer vz
        14/19 24
    13.5cm (5.31in) FK 1909 49

15cm (5.87in) Field Howitzer FH17 52
15cm (5.87in) Howitzer M1915 69
15cm (5.87in) l/40 Feldkanone i.R. 51
15cm (6.0in) Gun M1877 54
21cm (8.31in) Howitzer 80
21cm (8.31in) Mrs 18 82
22.5cm (8.86in) Heavy Trench Mortar 74
24.5cm (9.64in) Heavy Trench Mortar 86
28cm (11.02in) Kustenhaubitze 88
2.75in (70mm) Mountain Gun 15
4.7in (120mm) Field Gun M1906 47
7.2in (182.9mm) Howitzers Marks 1 to 4 75
8in (203mm) Howitzer M1 78
16in (406.4mm) M1919 Coast Gun 91
65mm (2.55in) Mountain Gun 14
75mm (2.95in) Mountain Gun Geb G.36 23
76.2mm (3in) Field Gun M1939 29
76.2mm (3in) Field Gun M1942 28
77mm (3.03in) FK16 30
105mm (4.13in) Howitzer M2A1 40
105mm (4.13in) Howitzer M3 43
105mm (4.13in) leFH18(M) 42
105mm (4.13in) LeFH 18 41
105mm (4.14in) Light Gun L118 39
120mm (4.72in) Krupp Howitzer M1905 44
122mm (4.80in) D-30 45
149mm (5.86in) Skoda Model 14 Howitzer 35
149mm (5.87in) Siege Gun, Model of 1877 50
152mm (6.0in) Gun-Howitzer M1937 (ML-20) 55
152mm (6.0in) Howitzer M09/30 58
152mm (6.0in) Howitzer M1943 (D-1) 56
155mm (6.10in) Gun G-5 65
155mm (6.10in) Gun M259
155mm (6.10in) Gun Model TR 68
155mm (6.10in) Howitzer FH-70 64
155mm (6.10in) Howitzer FH-77A 66
155mm (6.10in) Howitzer M198 67
155mm (6.10in) Howitzer Mle 1950 73
155mm (6.10in) Model 77 Howitzer 62
155mm (6.10in) ODE FH-88 Gun-howitzer 70
155mm (6.10in) Rimailho Howitzer Model 1904TR 60
155mm (6.10in) Royal Ordnance Light Towed Howitzer 72
155mm (6.10in) Santa Barbara SB-155/39 Howitzer 71
194mm (7.63in) Gun GPF 76
203mm (8.0in) Howitzer M1931 (L/25) 79
240mm (9.45in) Howitzer M1 84
305mm (12in) Howitzer 305/17 mod 17 90
914mm (36.0in) Mortar `Little David' 93
15pdr BLC Field Gun 26
Big Bertha 92
BL 6in (152mm) 26-cwt Howitzer Mk 1 57
BL 6in (152mm) 30-cwt Howitzer 61
BL 8in (203mm) Howitzer `Mark 7 77
Canon de 105mm (4.13in) Schneider Mle 1913 37
Canon de 240 L Model 1884 85
Canone de 75 Mle 1897 16

Canonne da 75/27 17
Krupp 75mm (2.95in) Field Gun M1903 18
Obice da 210/22 81
Obice de 75/18 Mod 35 20
Ordnance BL 5in (127mm) Howitzer MkI 46
Ordnance BL 5.5in (140mm) Gun Mk2 48
Ordnance BL 60pdr (127mm/5in) Mk1 34
Ordnance QF 4.5in (114mm) Howitzer 33
Ordnance QF 13pdr 25
Ordnance QF 18pdr Gun 32
OTO-Melara 105mm (4.13in) Mod 56 38
Paris Gun 83
QF 15pdr Gun Mk 1 27
St Chamond Mortier de 280 sur Chenilles 87
sFH18 53
Skoda 75mm Mountain Gun M1915 19
Skoda 305mm (12.0in) Howitzer 89
Soltam M68 Gun 63
Type 35/75mm (2.95in) Gun 21
Filloux, Colonel 76
FIM-92 Stinger **231**
FK16 30
FK 1909 49
Flak 18 **153**
Flak guns
    5cm (1.98in) Flak 41 112
    12.8cm (5.03in) Flak 40 126
    20mm (0.78in) Flak 30 99
    37mm (1.45in) Flak 37 107
    37mm (1.45in) Flak 43 108
    88mm (3.46in) Flak 18 120
    88mm (3.46in) Flak 41 121
    105mm (4.13in) Flak 38 124
    Flak 18 153
Flakvierling 38 100
'Free Rocket Over Ground' see FROG
free-flight rockets
    2in (57mm) Rocket 295
    3in (76.2mm) Rocket 297
    Army 20cm (7.95in) Rocket 290
    ASTROS 2 (Artillery Saturation Rocket System) 304
    Avibras X-40 308
    BM-21 303
    BM-24 307
    BM-27 305
    D-3000 Walid 298
    FROG-7 309
    Land Mattress 299
    Light Artillery Rocket System (LARS) 310
    M8 4.5in 294
    M-13 292
    M-30 293
    MLRS (Vought Multiple Launch Rocket System) 306
    Nebelwerfer 41 300
    Panzerwerfer 42 289
    SBAT-70 296
    Type 63 302
    Type 70 301
    Valkyr 311
    Wurfgranate 42 291

FROG-7 **309**

G-6 **284**
Gainful 225
Ganef 224
GCT 155mm (6.1in) **278**
GDF-CO3 **254**
Gecko 227
Gepard **253**
German 1914 118
German Armoured Trains **242-3**
'Gladiator' 245
Goa 214
Grail 226
Granatbuchse 39 **128**
grenade discharger, 50mm (1.57in) Type 89
    Grenade discharger 164
grenade launchers
    AGS-17 Grenade launcher 160
    AP/AV 700 multiple grenade launcher 184
    CIS-40-AFL Grenade launcher 161
    Granatbuchse 39 128
    M203 Grenade launcher 162
    Type 2 Anti-tank Grenade Launcher 133
'Gretel' (28cm (11in) Howtizer) 89
guided missiles 11
Guild 212
Gulf War 11
gun-howitzers
    152mm (6.0in) Gun-Howitzer M1937
        (ML-20) 55
    155mm (6.10in) ODE FH-88 Gun-Howitzer
        70
    Soltam M68 Gun 63
gun-mortars, Brandt 60mm (2.36in) LR Gun-
    mortar 166
Gustav 240
Gvozdika (M1974) 269

heavy trench mortars
    22.5cm (8.86in) Heavy Trench Mortar 74
    24.5cm (9.64in) Heavy Trench Mortar **86**
Henschel Hs 117 Schmetterling **213**
Hitler, Adolf 260
Honest John 192
Hummel ('Bumble Bee') 8, **271**

infantry guns
    7.5cm (2.95in) Infantry Gun IG18 22
    15cm (5.9in) sIG 33 Infantry Gun 180
infantry howitzer, 95mm (3.7in) Infantry
    Howitzer 175
infrared 12
intercontinental ballistic missiles 13
ISU-152 **273**

K5(E) 239
K12(E) 238
'Kaiser Wilhelm Geschutz' *see* Paris Gun
Kanone 564 (f) 85

Krauss-Maffei 251
Krupp 9, 49, 53, 80, 82, 83, 92, 145, 146
    75mm (2.95in) Field Gun M1903 **18**
Kustenhaubitze 88

L/40 Feldkanone i.R. 51
Land Mattress **299**
LARS (Light Artillery Rocket System) 310
Lebel rifle 8
leFH18(M) 42
leFH 18 41
'Leg Mortar' 164
LGM-30F Minuteman 2 **196**
Light Artillery Rocket System (LARS) **310**
light support weapons
    15cm (5.9in) sIG 33 infantry gun 180
    45mm (1.77in) Brixia Model 35 Mortar 163
    50mm (1.57in) Type 89 Grenade discharger
        164
    60mm (2.36in) Mortar M1 165
    60mm (2.36in) Mortar M19 167
    70mm (2.75in) Battalion Gun Type 92 168
    75mm (2.95in) Pack Howitzer M1A1 170
    81mm (3.18in) Mortar Mle 27/31 172
    82mm (3.22in) PM-37 mortar 173
    82mm (3.22in) Vasilek automatic mortar
        174
    95mm (3.7in) Infantry Howitzer 175
    120mm (4.72in) M1938 Mortar 176
    160mm (6.29in) Mortar M1943 181
    AGS-17 Grenande launcher 160
    AP/AV 700 multiple grenade launcher 184
    B-300 Light Support Weapon 183
    Bofors 75mm (2.95in) Model 34 169
    Brandt 60mm (2.36in) LR Gun-mortar 166
    Brandt 120mm (4.72in) Mortar 177
    CIS-40-AFL Grenade launcher 161
    M203 Grenade launcher 162
    Ordnance ML 3in (76.2mm) Mortar 179
    RAW (Rifleman's Assault Weapon) 182
    SGrW 34 81mm (3.8in) Mortar 171
    SMAW (Shoulder-fired Multi-purpose
        Assault Weapon) 185
    Soltram 120mm (4.72in) Mortar 178
'Little David', 914mm (36.0in) Mortar 93
'Long Tom' (155mm (6.1in) Gun M2) 59

M1 122
M1A1 2.36in (60mm) Rocker Launcher
    (Bazooka) **142**, 151
M1A2 106
M2A1 40
M3 117
M5 149
M7 Priest **267**
M8 4.5in (114mm) **294**
M39 119
M40 **276**
M42 **256**
M48 Chaparral **228**
M53/59 **252**

M56 (Scorpion) **266**
M101 *see* 105mm (4.13in) Howitzer M2A1
M109 **279**
M109A6 Paladin **280**
M110A2 **288**
M163 Vulcan **247**
M167 Vulcan **96**
M203 Grenade launcher **162**
M1877 54
M1917 Gun 36
M1919 Coast Gun 91
M1973 **274**
M1974 **269**
M1977 *see* BM27
M-13 **292**
M-30 **293**
'Machine Fuse Setting No 11' 123
Mauler 228
Mauser 100
'Max E' 246
MGM-118 Peacekeeper **194**
MIM-23 HAWK **230**
MIM-104 Patriot **229**
Minuteman 196
Mistral **233**
Mk F3 155mm (6.1in) **277**
MLRS (Vought Multiple Launch Rocket
    System) 11, **306**
mortars
    45mm (1.77in) Brixia Model 35 Mortar 163
    60mm (2.36in) Mortar M1 165
    60mm (2.36in) Mortar M19 167
    81mm (3.18in) Mortar Mle 27/31 172
    82mm (3.22in) PM-37 Mortar 173
    82mm (3.22in) Vasilek automatic mortar
        174
    120mm (4.72in) M1938 Mortar 176
    160mm (6.29in) Mortar M1943 181
    914mm (36.0in) Mortar `Little David' 93
    Brandt 120mm (4.72in) Mortar 177
    Ordnance ML 3in (76.2mm) Mortar 179
    SGrW 34 81mm (3.8in) Mortar 171
    Soltram 120mm (4.72in) Mortar 178
    see also heavy trench mortars
mountain guns
    2.75in (70mm) 15
    65mm (2.55in) 14
    75mm (2.95in) Mountain Gun Geb G.36 23
    Skoda 75mm Mountain Gun M1915 19
Mrs 18 82

Nebelwerfer 41 **300**
Nike Ajax **215**
Nike Hercules **216**
Norinco SP Gun 287
Northover Projector 143

Obice da 210/22 **81**
Obice de 75/18 Mod 35 **20**
Oerlikon 209, 235
    20mm (0.78in) **102**

GAI-BO1 **98**
    GDF-001 35mm (1.37in) **105**
Oerlikon-Bührle 254
Ordnance
    BL 5in (127mm) Howitzer MkI **46**
    BL 5.5in (140mm) Gun Mk2 **48**
    BL 60pdr (127mm/5in) Mk1 **34**
    ML 3in (76.2mm) Mortar **179**
    QF 3in (76mm) 20cwt **115**
    QF 4.5in (114mm) Gun **125**
    QF 4.5in (114mm) Howitzer **33**
    QF 13pdr **25**
    QF 17pdr Gun **147**
    QF 18pdr Gun **32**
Ordnance Development & Engineering (ODE)
    of Singapore 70
OTO-Melara 105mm (4.13in) Mod 56 **38**
Otomatic Air Defence Tank 262

pack howitzer, OTO-Melara 105mm (4.13in)
    Mod 56 38
Pak 38 144
Pak 40 145
Pak 41 146
Pak 43/41 152
Pak 44 156
Paladin 280
Palmaria **281**
Panzerbuchse 39 127
Panzerbuchse 41 134
Panzerfaust **158**
Panzerhaubitse 2000 **285**
Panzerwerfer 42 **289**
Paris Gun 10, **83**, 238
Patriot 229
PAW 600 150
Peacekeeper 194
Pershing **193**
PIAT (Projector, Infantry, Anti-Tank) **159**
'Piecemaker' 245
Pluton **186**
Polish Armoured Train **241**
Polsten 20mm (0.78in) **103**
Priest (M7) 267
PTRD 1941 Anti-tank rifle **131**
PTRS 1941 Anti-tank rifle **130**
Puff, Carl 134

QF 2pdr Mk VII **138**
QF 6pdr 7cwt Gun Mk 2 **141**
QF 15pdr Gun Mk 1 **27**
QF ('quick-firing') guns 7, 8
    Canone de 75 Mle 1897 16

railway artillery 10
    21cm (8.31in) K12(E) 238
    28cm (11.02in) K12(E) 239
    38cm (14.96in) Gun `Max E' 246
    80cm (31.4in) Gustav 240
    12in (305mm) Railway Howitzer Mk 5 244

13.5in Gun `Sceneshifter' 245
Canon de 240 Mle 93/96 sur Affuit-truck St-Chamond 236
Canon de 320 Mle 1870/93 sur Affuit-truck Schneider 237
German Armoured Trains 242-3
Polish Armoured Train 241
Raketenpanzerbuchse 43 **151**
Rapier **222**
Rascal Light 155mm (6.1in) SP Howitzer **286**
RAW (Rifleman's Assault Weapon) **182**
recoil system 7–8
recoilless guns 10
    3.7in (94mm) RCL Gun 155
    106mm (4.13in) RCL Rifle M40A1 154
Rheinmetall 41, 53, 99, 124, 135, 137, 145
    Rh202 **97**
Rheinmetall-Borsig 150
Rimailho, Colonel 60
rocket launchers
    BM-27 305
    M1A1 2.36in (60mm) Rocker Launcher 142
    SMAW (Shoulder-fired Multi-purpose Assault Weapon) 185
    Type 63 302
rockets 11
    MGM-118 Peacekeeper 194
    MGR-1B, Honest John 192
Roland **219**
Royal Horse Artillery gun *see* Ordnance QF 13pdr
RSD 58 **209**

SA-1 Guild **212**
SA-3 Goa **214**
SA-4 Ganef **224**
SA-6 Gainful **225**
SA-7 Grail **226**
SA-8 Gecko **227**
Saber 208
St Chamond company 85, 236
St Chamond Mortier de 280 sur Chenilles **87**
Sandal 200
Satan 207
SATCP 233
Savage 204
SBAT-70 **296**
Scaleboard 199
Scarp 203
Sceneshifter 245
'Scheunentor' (Barn-door) 152
'Schlanke (slender) Emma' *see* Skoda 305mm (12.0in) Howitzer
Scorpion (M56) 266
'Screw-Gun' 15
Scud 198
Seaslug **211**
Sego 202
seige guns, 15cm (6.0in) Gun M1877 **54**
self-propelled artillery 11, 13
    155/45 Norinco SP Gun 287
    76mm (3in) Otomatic Air Defence Tank 262

Abbot 268
AMX-13 DCA 250
ASU-57 259
Bishop 264
DANA 275
G-6 284
GCT 155mm (6.1in) 278
GDF-CO3 254
Gepard 253
Hummel ('Bumble Bee') 271
ISU-152 273
M7 Priest 267
M40 276
M42 256
M53/59 252
M56 (Scorpion) 266
M109 279
M109A6 Paladin 280
M110A2 **288**
M163 Vulcan 247
M1973 274
M1974 **269**
Mk F3 155mm (6.1in) 277
Palmaria 281
Panzerhaubitse 2000 285
Rascal Light 155mm (6.1in) SP Howitzer 286
Sergeant York 257
Sexton 265
SIDAM-25 249
sIG 33 270
StuG III Ausf F 260
StuG III Ausf G 261
SU-76 263
Type 4 272
Type 63 255
Wildcat 251
ZSU-23-4 248
ZSU-57-2 258
Sergeant York **257**
Sexton **265**
sFH18 **53**
SGrW 34 81mm (3.8in) Mortar **171**
ship defence missiles
    SA-1 Guild 212
    Seaslug 211
'shotgun' breech mechanism 22
SIDAM-25 **249**
Sidewinder 228
siege gun, 149mm (5.87in) Siege Gun, Model of 1877 50
sIG 33 **270**
Simonov 130
Skean 201
Skoda
    47mm (1.85in) Skoda vz 36 139
    75mm (2.95in) Mountain Gun M1915 **19**
    149mm (5.87in) Model 14 Howitzer 35
    305mm (12in) Howitzer **89**
    10cm (4.14in) Light Howitzer vz 14/19 24
'Skyguard' air defence system 105
SMAW (Shoulder-fired Multi-purpose Assault Weapon) **185**

Soltam 286
   120mm (4.72in) Mortar **178**
   M68 Gun **63**
Spanker 205
'Spider Mount' 117
spigot mortar, PIAT 159
split trail guns
   Obice de 75/18 Mod 35 20
   Type 35/75mm (2.95in) Gun 21
squash head (or HE Plastic) shell 11
SS-1 Scud B **198**
SS-4 Sandal **200**
SS-5 Skean **201**
SS-9 Scarp **203**
SS-11 Sego **202**
SS-12 Scaleboard **199**
SS-13 Savage **204**
SS-17 Spanker **205**
SS-18 Satan **207**
SS-19 Stiletto **206**
SS-20 Saber **209**
SSBS S-3 **187**
'Stanchion' 129
Starstreak **234**
Stiletto 206
Stinger 231
Stormovik 79
StuG III Ausf F **260**
StuG III Ausf G **261**
SU-76 **263**
surface-to-surface missiles
   BGM-109G Tomahawk 197
   CSS-1 (T1) 188
   CSS-2 (T2) 189
   CSS-3 (T3) 190
   CSS-4 (T4) 191
   LGM-30F Minuteman 2 196
   MGM-118 Peacekeeper 194
   Pershing 193
   Pluton 186
   Rocket, MGR-1B, Honest John 192
   SS-1 Scud B 198
   SS-4 Sandal 200
   SS-5 Skean 201
   SS-9 Scarp 203
   SS-11 Sego 202
   SS-12 Scaleboard 199
   SS-13 Savage 204
   SS-17 Spanker 205
   SS-18 Satan 207
   SS-19 Stiletto 206
   SS-20 Saber 209
   SSBS S-3 187
   Titan 195

tactical battlefield support system, Pershing
   193
Talos **217**
Tarasque 95
TCM-20 **94**
Thunderbird **210**, 220
Titan **195**

Tomahawk 197
Toshiba Electric 232
traverse howitzer, 122mm (4.80in) D-30 **45**
Type 2 Anti-tank Grenande Launcher **133**
Type 4 **272**
Type 35/75mm (2.95in) Gun **21**
Type 63 **255**, **302**
Type 70 **301**
Type 81 Tan-SAM **232**
Type 88 114
Type 97 Anti-tank Rifle **132**

Valkyr **311**
Versailles Treaty 300
Vought Multiple Launch Rocket System
   (MLRS) 306
Vulcan (M163) 247
Vulcan (M167) 96

Walid 298
weight of guns 9
Wildcat **251**
World War II 10, 11, 294
Wurfgranate 42 **291**

ZSU-23-4 **248**
ZSU-57-2 **258**
ZU-23 104